AROUND THE WORLD IN 80 DAYS

MICHAEL·PALIN

WEIDENFELD & NICOLSON

A W&N PAPERBACK

First published in Great Britain in 1989
by BBC Books
Revised edition published in 2008 by Weidenfeld & Nicolson,
This paperback edition published in 2009
by Weidenfeld & Nicolson
an imprint of Orion Books Ltd,
Carmelite House, 50 Victoria Embankment,
London EC4Y 0DZ

An Hachette UK company

9 10 8

A CIP catalogue record for this book
is available from the British Library.

ISBN 978-0-7538-2324-8

Contents

CONTENTS

CONTENTS

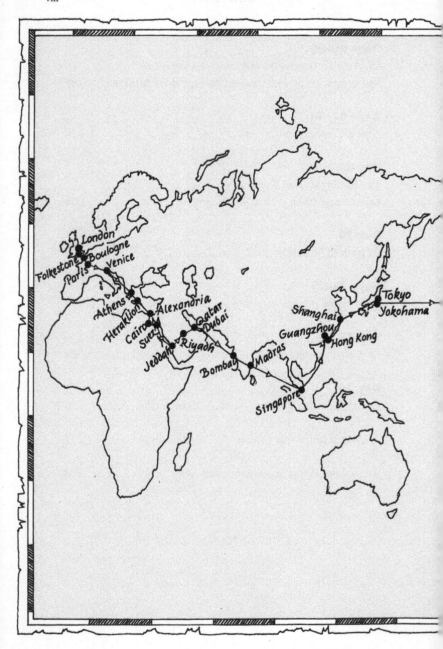

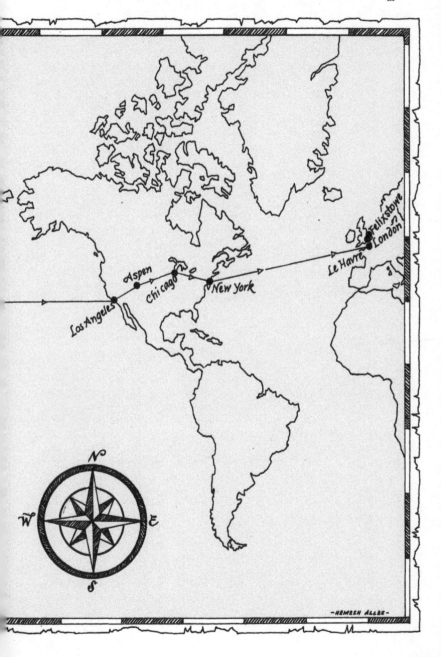

Felixstowe
London
Le Havre
New York
Chicago
Aspen
Los Angeles

N
W E
S

-HEMESH ALLES-

Preface to the new edition

Little did I imagine, as I was turned away from the doors of the Reform Club in London after completing my circumnavigation of the globe back in December 1988, that far from being an end to my travelling career, this was just the beginning. *Around The World In Eighty Days* was to become around the world in twenty years.

I had intended to stop once we reached the unyielding doors of the Reform Club and return to a normal life – slapping people with fish, running over Kevin Kline in a steamroller and singing the Lumberjack Song in German to selected audiences. The attempt to circle the world in less than three months without ever leaving its surface had, I felt, offered me enough adventure to last a lifetime.

But something had happened on all those long sea trips, on battered cargo boats and creaking container ships, on heaving Indian trains and racing dog sleds in the Rockies. Though I had travelled with a course of painful injections and bag full of pills and potions, nothing had protected me against the overpowering, aching desire to do the whole thing again. It was as if a door had been opened through which I could see a big beckoning world. I could see North Poles and South Poles and Equators and Tropics and rapids and volcanoes and it was all much more exciting than slapping people with fish. The success of *Around The World In Eighty Days*, and a very tolerant wife and family, made it possible for me to walk through this door and discover new people, new places, and experience sights and sounds beyond my wildest expectations.

Twenty years on, I and my crew, many of whom had accompanied me on that first journey, have been to every continent in the world, travelled hundreds and thousands of miles across every terrain from ice and snow to burning desert, and regurgitated it all in seven books and television series.

So I must thank my lucky stars, and Clem Vallance and the BBC in particular, for creating for me a role I never expected, that of a sort of tour guide to the world. I also have to thank those who so selflessly agreed to let our camera peer into their lives, for, as I've learnt in all my series, it's the people you meet who make the programmes work.

Bearing that in mind we decided that the best way to celebrate twenty years of travelling would be some sort of a reunion. The choice was easier than I'd expected. Looking back over the years no single experience has remained more powerfully in my memory than our dhow journey from Dubai to Bombay. It was the first time I realised quite how much the success or failure of our series depended on those with whom we were travelling, in this case a crew of eighteen Indian fishermen from a small village north of Bombay. Despite their assurances of getting us to Bombay in six days, we shared the boat with them for a week. We slept on deck, sacks of pistachio nuts beneath us, we learnt to use a toilet which was nothing more than a box suspended over the stern of the ship, we gratefully ate the curries they produced from nowhere and we tried not to think about the lack of life-jackets, or the fate of the captain's brother whose dhow and entire crew had perished in a storm the year before.

It was only when the time came to say goodbye in Bombay that I sensed just how close we'd all become. The combination of my gratitude and their affection made leave-taking difficult and surprisingly emotional. As I said in my commentary, 'It's almost impossible to accept that I shall never see them again.'

So, after twenty years, I took myself at my word and we went in search of the crew of the *Al Shama*. The result of this extraordinary trip is contained in a new chapter at the end of this book.

The way we made *Around The World in Eighty Days* can never be repeated. Now we have mobile phones and global positioning satellites and digital tapes instead of cans of celluloid. But how much the people and their lives have changed is less easy to tell.

There was only one way to find out, and the reissue of the book and our return to India and the Gulf is more than just a celebration of all twenty years on the road, it's an affirmation that, for this traveller at least, there is still no end in sight.

MICHAEL PALIN *London, September 2008*

Note on names

As this is a 20-year-old text, names are sometimes out of date. Bombay has become Mumbai and Madras, Chennai since then. To keep the flavour of the time, we've kept the old names.

Introduction

The compulsive urge to travel is a recognised physical condition. It has its own word, dromomania, and I'm glad to say I suffer from it. The ambition of every dromomaniac is a circumnavigation of the planet, but it's a less fashionable journey now than in Jules Verne's day. Part of the reason is that you can do it by air in 36 hours (a technological feat that Verne would have greatly appreciated). But air travel shrink-wraps the world leaving it small, odourless, tidy and usually out of sight.

There are container vessels which will take you round in 63 days, but you will see only water on 58 of those. The reason why Phileas Fogg's 80-day journey retains its appeal is that it is still the minimum time needed to go round the world and notice it. To see it, smell it and touch it at the same time.

Each time I look at the map and retrace my progress I become painfully aware of the countries I didn't visit, and I'm sure there would be a case for a zig-zag circumnavigation which would take in Australia and Thailand and Russia and Africa and South America and Canada. Nevertheless my route, following Fogg's as closely as possible, still took me through an extraordinary sequence of countries: from the European empires of Britain and Venice and Greece, to Egypt, one of the oldest civilisations on earth, through the heart of the Muslim world, across India into China and the awesomely energetic economies of the Pacific Rim countries – Singapore, Hong Kong and Japan – and finally to America, still the most influential nation in the world.

The pace of this kind of travel has not much changed since Fogg set out in 1872. Trains may be a little faster, but there are certainly no high-speed rail links yet across India, China or the USA. Passenger services have practically disappeared from the world's shipping lanes, whilst at the same time the armoury of bureaucratic obstacles – visas, permits, passports and carnets –

has proliferated. Recourse to air travel, even as a convenient means of escape, was not allowed.

But these were challenges and challenges help to make an adventure, and an adventure was what I was after when I signed up. This diary is a record of success and failure, of euphoria and deep gloom, of friends made and advice and help generously given on what must still be the ultimate terrestrial journey.

There was never time to dig very deep and those expecting profound international insights will be disappointed. I'm particularly aware of how traumatically China suffered only a few months after my visit. But my journey around the world gave me a sense of global scale, of the size and variety of this extraordinary planet, of the relation of one country and one culture to another which few people experience and many ought to.

For this I am eternally grateful to a lot of people. Not least to Clem Vallance of the BBC who dreamt up the whole crazy idea, and thought of me; to Will Wyatt who first asked me and made sure I didn't say no; to my wife Helen and the family who let me go; to my attentive, patient, incredibly hard-working, almost uncomplaining Passepartout* – Nigel Meakin, Ron Brown, Julian Charrington, Nigel Walters, Dave Jewitt and Simon Maggs, who between them shot and recorded film on 77 out of 80 days; to Angela Elbourne and Ann Holland without whose level-headed, panic-free presence I would probably still be at Cairo station; to Basil Pao, without whom none of us might have survived Hong Kong and China, and to Roger Mills who, along with Clem Vallance, directed, guided, encouraged, cajoled and tolerated me for many months.

MICHAEL PALIN *London, 1989*

*Note about my Passepartout

Clem Vallance and Roger Mills (with production assistants Angela Elbourne and Ann Holland) travelled all the way with me. Nigel Meakin, Ron Brown and Julian Charrington filmed me to Hong Kong, then Nigel Walters, Dave Jewitt and Simon Maggs brought me home.

Day 1 25 September

ILEAVE THE REFORM CLUB, Pall Mall, London one hundred and fifteen years, three hundred and fifty-six days, ten and three-quarter hours after Phileas Fogg. It's a wet, stuffy morning, I've had three and a half hours sleep and the only thing I envy Phileas is that he's fictional.

Few buildings could be more fitted to a Great Departure. With its 60-foot-high main hall, marble columns, galleried arcades and the grand scale of a Renaissance palace the Reform Club is a place of consequence, grand and grave enough to add weight to any venture.

This morning it smells of old fish, and glasses and bottles from the night before stand around. I can see no one sampling the sort of breakfast Fogg had taken the day he left: '... a side dish, a boiled fish with Reading sauce of first quality, a scarlet slice of roast beef garnished with mushrooms, a rhubarb and gooseberry tart, and a bit of Chester cheese, the whole washed down with a few cups of that excellent tea, specially gathered for the stores of the Reform Club.'

I have tried to follow Fogg's example and travel light. 'Only a carpetbag,' he had instructed his servant Passepartout, 'in it two woollen shirts and three pairs of stockings ... my mackintosh and travelling cloak, also stout shoes, although we shall walk but little or not at all.' I've managed to find a passable equivalent of a carpet bag and in it packed six shirts, six pairs of socks, six pairs of underpants, three T-shirts, a towel, a pair of swimming trunks, a short-sleeved sweater, three pairs of light trousers (long), two pairs ex-R.A.F. trousers (short), a pair of sports shorts, a sponge bag, various pharmaceuticals, a change of shoes, a jacket and tie, a Sony Walkman, six cassettes, a small short-wave radio, a Panama hat and one or two heavy and serious books with which to improve my mind on long sea journeys. In a shoulder bag I carry my diary, a small Dictaphone recorder for on-the-spot notes, a camera, the BBC's *Get By In Arabic*, a Kingsley Amis novel, some extra-strong mints, a packet of 'Family Wipes', an address book and an inflatable globe to enable me to check on our progress. Phileas Fogg would doubtless have regarded all this as clutter, but it's still less than I would take on a two-week holiday.

These bags I heave up onto my shoulders as the clock shows ten o'clock. I carry them down the stairs, out of the tall doorway and into Pall Mall. I've eighty days left to get back in again.

Fogg went from the Reform Club to Charing Cross station, I leave from Victoria.

Here I find Passepartout, who will travel everywhere with me. Unlike Fogg's Passepartout, mine is five people, has fifty pieces of baggage and works for the BBC. Roger Mills is the director of this first leg of the journey and is already bemoaning the fact that we've just missed some foul weather in the English Channel. 'If only this had been yesterday.' He draws on his pipe despondently. Ann Holland is his Production Assistant. She will keep full details of all the shots we take, and keep in touch with our base camp in London. Nigel Meakin and Julian Charrington are the camera team and Ron Brown is recording sound. The film equipment is in containers of many shapes and sizes and mostly very heavy. As I help them down the platform with a muscle-tearing case of film stock I think of Phileas – 'one of those mathematically exact people ... never hurried ... calm, phlegmatic, with a clear eye' – and how desperately unlike him I am.

However, I am leaving London in a manner of which he would doubtless have approved had it been available in 1872, aboard the Venice–Simplon Orient Express. Last farewells and a check on the exact time of departure by two friends acting as judges. Fogg's friends were bankers. Mine, Messrs Jones and Gilliam, are Pythons. Terry Jones eyes Passepartout, already about his business with the camera. 'You're going to have to look happy for eighty days.' 'No,' I reassure him. 'There'll be no cheating.' Then the whistle sounds, the last door slams and we're off.

I am installed in a sumptuous refurbished Pullman coach called 'Zena'. Behind me are 'Ibis', 'Lucille', 'Cygnus' and 'Ione'. Antimacassars, marble washbasins, upholstered armchairs and inlaid walnut panelling come as a bit of a shock to one used to the Gatwick Express, but I try hard to forget about guilt and silly things like that and sit back and sniff the fresh orchids and sip a little champagne. The leader of a crack force of waiters approaches, issuing brisk directives.

'We *do* advise you to be seated. We're coming through the train with hot soup.'

We are dealt a three-course meal and coffee in 55 minutes flat. It's delicious, but such is the precision with which it has to be served that you feel that any lingering over the menu might result in the aforementioned hot soup being lightly but firmly applied upon some tender area.

A huge scar slices into the landscape on the eastern side of the train. It's the site for the Channel Tunnel terminal, 16 acres of devastation. Jules Verne would surely have approved, being a man fascinated by transport technology. He'd probably have sent his hero to have a look at it. Or rather, he'd have sent Passepartout to do it for him, as Fogg hated sightseeing.

We're in Folkestone now, the last few hundred yards of England, and rumbling down a steep gradient past back gardens close up to the railway line; a world of sheds and extensions, corrugated iron and chicken wire, unself-conscious, domestic and reassuring. The sun breaks momentarily through the leaden cloud causing the mountain of cut-glass on my table to sparkle, but the word is that the Channel is 'rough' to 'very rough', and I'm glad I passed on the ginger profiteroles.

No longer do the ferries carry trains and at Folkestone Harbour I part company with 'Zena' and take up with the *Horsa*, a 6,000-tonne vessel which has been plying the 22-mile crossing to France for 16 years.

'It's that Monty Python bloke!' shouts one of the crew as I mount the first of many gangplanks of the world. He turns confidingly to me: 'If you want a farce, you've got one here.' The passageways of the *Horsa* smell of day-old school food, but we Oriental Expressers are ushered to our own private lounge.

It's a dispiriting place, decorated in International Cowboy Saloon Style. The walls are ringed with reverentially lit alcoves which look as if they might contain international art treasures or religious icons, but which, on closer inspection, are found to be full of duty-free goods.

Seeking refuge from the world of 'Antaeus, Pour Homme' and 'Superkings', I walk out on deck. It's mid-afternoon and the white cliffs of home are now little more than a blur. A huge black cloud seems to be sealing England off behind us. A sharp, squally wind that would test the stoutest toupee rips across from the West. With friends and familiar surroundings disappearing over the horizon, I catch my breath for a moment at the scale of what is just beginning.

The Channel crossing is bumpy, but to the director's chagrin nothing more. A Force 5. 'I've had her out in a Force 12,' says the captain, eyes skinned for stray fishing boats, tankers, ferries, yachts, channel-swimmer's support vessels and every floating thing that makes this one of the busiest waterways in the world.

4.30: On the bridge. From a mile out at sea Boulogne, France, looks to consist of one huge steelworks, but as we get nearer a hard skyline of soot-flecked concrete apartment blocks looms.

Down below, the Orient Express passengers are impatient to party. They so want to have a good time, and the expensive hours are ticking away and the luxury they were promised is not to be found on the *Horsa* or in the passageways of Boulogne's dockside. But spirits rise once they reach the platform of Boulogne station at which stand a dozen coaches sporting the navy-blue livery and solid brass letters of the Compagnie Internationale des Wagons-Lits et des Grands Express Européens. I am billeted in sleeping car 3544, built in 1929, decorated in 'Sapelli Pearl' inlay by René Prou and having been, in the course of a long and distinguished career, a brothel for German officers and part of the Dutch royal train. My cabin is small but perfectly formed, sheathed in veneered mahogany inlaid with Art-Deco panels. From this luxury cocoon I watch grey, seagull-ridden Boulogne slipping away and when its drab suburbs have gone, I turn once more to make-believe, and begin unpacking my dinner jacket.

I dine next to a couple from Southend who are celebrating their twenty-fifth wedding anniversary with an Orient Express trip to Paris. Nice people but, looking round, I'm rather disappointed at the lack of princesses, murderers and deposed heads of Europe. Most of the 188 passengers are either going to a pipeline conference in Venice or are Mid-Westerners on a tour. Instead of falling into risqué conversation with a Mata Hari of the 1980s, I end up in the piano bar with the pipeliners. They seem very interested to hear that, in 70 days from now, I hope to cross the Atlantic from Halifax, Nova Scotia. 'We've got a big pipe there, we could flush you through.'

My cabin has been prepared for the night by Jeff, a down-to-earth, well-informed Englishman who has responsibility for Coach 3544. The bed is soft but short. 'Yes, we do have a bit of trouble with our Americans,' he concedes. 'There's one tonight who's 6 foot 8.' He looks apprehensively down the corridor, listening no doubt for the giant's tread. Feeling for the first time in my life rather smug about being 5 foot 10 and a half, I turn in.

The train is heading for the Belfort Gap, my head is buzzing with an evening's champagne, and so far circumnavigation is a doddle.

Day 2 26 September

Slept as badly as I ever have in a really comfortable bed. Passepartout complains as well so it can't just be me. The ride of these old coaches is not as smooth as their interior design.

8.30: Jeff arrives carrying a tray of croissants, brioches, jams, hot, dark, intensely tasty coffee and the *International Herald Tribune*. More record-breaking from Ben Johnson in the Olympics. Pull back the curtain and there is Switzerland. The murky gloom of Northern Europe has been replaced by clear and cloudless skies, and the *banlieues* of Boulogne by neat meadows grazed by neat cows interspersed with neat factories. All this orderliness is contained within violently twisted cliffs of rock rising thousands of feet to left and right. As we slow through a small town people gaze at us, curiously but not censoriously. The conspicuous luxury of the Orient Express seems not so remarkable here in Switzerland. Perhaps it goes with numbered bank accounts and private nuclear shelters.

A little trouble shaving. There seems to be no hot water to fill my exquisite marble wash basin. Jeff is philosophical.

'Try the cold tap, sir.' Sure enough a steamy, near-boiling torrent pours out.

There's never a dull moment on the Orient Express and flakes of brioche are still fresh on my fingers when the first call comes for brunch. Before I embarked on this journey I sought advice from many experienced travellers, and it was John Hemming, the Director of the Royal Geographical Society, who advised me that a true explorer never turns down a meal. It might be the last he'll be offered for days. I decide to approach brunch in this spirit, tucking into Eggs Benedict but avoiding a 'light breakfast wine' at £24 a bottle.

We cross Liechtenstein between the second and third courses, and are entering our fifth country in less than twenty-four hours, when things begin to go wrong. We are diverted through the town of Buchs because of derailment (which I just can't imagine happening on such an immaculately run system) and worse than this, we are to terminate at Innsbruck as there is a rail strike in Italy. So the Venice–Simplon Orient Express will not, today, visit either Venice or Simplon.

A bus is to be provided at Innsbruck but they are unable to guarantee the arrival time. Nervous now because of our tight ship connection onward from Venice, there's nothing I can do but sit back and enjoy the view. We're winding up to the Ahlberg Pass, through sweeping panoramas of lush green slopes and mountainsides of acid-rain-crippled trees. The villages with their onion-dome steeples lie calm and drowsy in the valleys. From each one there fans out a network of grey pylons carrying the cars, cables and chair-lifts on which their livelihood depends, and in the winter here you'll hardly be able to move.

Twenty-four hours after leaving Victoria the Orient Express pulls into Innsbruck, Austria and from its seventeen coaches in orderly confusion come the pipeliners and the Mid-Westerners and the porters and the apologetic couriers and even the chefs bearing food on silver plates, all of which is carried across the station car park to a fleet of anonymous modern coaches. Everyone tries desperately to pretend that they're still having just as good a time, but the magic's gone.

At the Brenner Pass we are delayed interminably while Austrian customs search for the correct stamp for our film equipment clearance. As the sun sinks behind the mountains I make a quick calculation based on the time it's taking to leave Austria. At a rough estimate I could be spending eight of the next eighty days waiting at customs. Not a problem Fogg had to deal with. Nor was he ever faced with what the Austrians call, rather dramatically, a *streik*. His train would be rattling through the Alps by now.

At the Italian border, a bottle of Orient Express champagne is passed over and this seems to speed up the customs process. Soon, amid smiles, shrugs and assorted gesticulations we are off and running into the land where a *streik* is only a *sciopero*.

Crossing the lagoon which divides Venice from the mainland a dreadful smell assails us. It's sulphur from the massive chemical works at Mestre, sending up a malodorous halo around the Serenissima, and firmly deflating romantic anticipations.

Twenty minutes later: On the canals. Stuck firmly under a bridge. We are in a fully laden 40-foot barge trying to negotiate a 90-degree corner. Sandro, our boatman, skips elegantly but ineffectually about the vessel and blames the tides. A small crowd of Japanese tourists has gathered on the bridge above us. They seem to have eight cameras each. It's all rather embarrassing. When Sandro eventually pushes us, and a fair-sized chunk of sixteenth-century stonework, away from the bridge, we find ourselves backing into a funeral procession. Somebody popular by the looks of things, as fresh gondolafuls of mourners keep appearing round the corner.

Much later: Hot, tired and missing the Orient Express and the antimacassars and the ever-solicitous Jeff to guide me through life, I find myself at the Hotel Atlantide with my bag weighing heavy.

The Italians take being on film very seriously, but not quite as seriously as what they're wearing when they're being filmed, and this costs André, one of the hotel receptionists, the part of Man Who Shows The Presenter To His Room. He goes off to do his hair and put on a suit, leaving the way clear for his colleague Massimo, who is not so worried about his personal appearance, to turn in a splendidly moody performance. There's no lift. My room is at rooftop level with a small balcony which does not enjoy any of the classic views of Venice. As I clean my teeth the first cockroach of the trip scuttles across cracked bathroom tiles.

Day 3 27 September

A few hours to kill in Venice before leaving by boat for Greece, Crete and Egypt. The director thinks it would be nice for me to see the city from the back of a rubbish barge, and very soon, perhaps a little too soon, after breakfast I find myself hosing down the Riva degli Schiavoni and tossing plastic bagfuls of Venetian unmentionables into the garbage barge. Mario, 48 years old, with a 13-year-old son and a daughter of 20, is in charge of our squad. 'Even the rubbish in Venice isn't cheap any more,' he replies to my routine suggestion that this must be one of the most beautiful cities to grow up in. 'The young can't afford to live here now.' The other two members of our crew are Fabbio, who turns out to have weightlifted for his country, and is profoundly embarrassed by the whole filming, and Sandro, curly-headed, beautiful, pre-Raphaelite, and unreachable on most levels.

We move at a stately pace up the canals, hurrying for nobody. Refuse collecting gives one a smug sense of superiority. The veneered-wood and polished brass launches may huff and puff as they try to get past us with their expensive cargoes, but we know they know how much they need us. We've seen what they like to keep out of sight.

I enjoy my refuse-eye view of Venice and suggest to Roger that we make it the first of a Great Dustmen Of The World series, to be followed, if successful, by Great Sewers Of The World.

Ron Passepartout baulks at this. 'I've just spent five weeks in the sewers, thank you!' He is referring not to conditions at TV Centre, but to a programme he's just made about a man who had taken refuge in the war in the sewers of Lvov. Ron has been everywhere and met everyone. On the very first day of filming the phone rang on location and a P.A., covering the mouthpiece, shouted, 'Ron! Can you do the Pope, Friday?'

By boat to the Venice Post Office to send my dinner jacket back to London, the smartest part of the journey being already over. This is one of The Great Post Offices Of The World, located in the Fondaco dei Tedeschi, built between 1505 and 1508 as a base for German merchants in Venice. There's a wide brick-tiled courtyard with a stone fountain in the middle surrounded by three levels of pillared galleries. The walls were once decorated with the works of the great Venetians, like Titian – but of these only, as the guidebook has it, 'one much-impaired nude' by Giorgione remains. I notice a lot of young, beautiful women heaving mailbags out onto the quayside beneath the Rialto Bridge. They also work for the Post Office. The Grand Canal, at this point, is like Piccadilly Circus, and the driving is terrible, with motoscafi cutting up vaporettos and cement barges cutting up taxis and gondolas gliding serenely and suicidally between the lot of them.

I seek refuge at the Hostaria del Milion – good unpretentious food and wine in a tiny, intimate little courtyard. Two doors down there still stands the house where Marco Polo lived and from which he departed on his great journeys to the East. I stand and look up at the modest stone walls, as if there might be something I can learn from them. A photographer takes pictures of me doing this. He's an Italian. His real name's Renato but I've taken to calling him Posso which is the only word I've heard from him today.

'Posso?' Snap. I feel sorry for these still photographers. They're only doing their job, but they keep getting in the way of Passepartout and making him very cross.

Early evening: Our departure for the Levant is not, sadly, from some photogenic quayside flanked by the Lions of St Mark, but from the tourist-neglected backside of Venice, the docks of the

Stazione Marittima. The soft warmth of the day has given way to a chilly evening as our baggage barge chugs past the soaring hulls of a rough assortment of freighters – a Russian boat from Starnov, the *River Tyne* from Limassol (a poignant reminder of where the British shipping industry has gone) and finally the elegant wave-moulded bow and milk chocolate hull of my home for the next four days, the *Espresso Egitto, Venezia.* Maybe because we're all tired, or maybe because we can only count eleven portholes on her side, Passepartout and I are not as responsive as we might be to the promise of the *Egyptian Express.* A shout causes me to turn, lose my footing and almost disembowel myself on the camera tripod.

'Posso?' Snap.

Aboard ship after two hours in bureaucratic limbo on the quayside. 'People Who Need People' echoes from the PA system. 'People Who Need Portholes' would be more appropriate. Ron is in deep decline. His cabin not only lacks portholes but also lights. I keep trying to remember not to tell him what I can see out of my window.

What I *can* see is the delicate skyline of Venice at night, as we pass through the lagoon. A soft, almost insubstantial image, I feel that if I rub my eyes and look again it will be gone.

'The end of civilisation,' someone mutters darkly, as the stone quaysides and lamplit arcades recede into the distance. A bit of an exaggeration, especially if you're a Greek, but it is the end of temperate climates, seasons, and western ways for a month or two, and I allow myself a little homesickness.

Day 4 28 September

The *Espresso Egitto* is a vessel of 4,686 tonnes, built in Livorno 14 years ago. She's owned by the nationalised Adriatic Navigation Company and provides the only regular passenger service between Venice and Egypt. (Fogg travelled from Brindisi to Bombay, a service long since defunct.) The appeal of a two-hour air flight over four days at sea is illustrated by the fact that there are only eighty passengers aboard.

This morning, fortified by a good night's sleep and a lie-in, I set out to explore the boat. From a warren of identical passageways I eventually find my way to an open central area. Here there is a notice board on which, I'm told, will be displayed the day's entertainments. It's blank. Opposite, behind a curving glass panel sits the substantial form of Mr Lalli, the ship's purser. He's coughing.

'I should stop the smoking,' he growls gloomily, 'but I get nervous.' The thought of this massive primate-like figure being nervous is rather like hearing that Arnold Schwarzenegger cries when he can't get to sleep, and is not the only surprise about Mr Lalli. He's a Slovene who wants the Italians to give back Trieste and he sympathises with the separatists in the south of his country, who are currently embroiled in strife with their central Yugoslav government. 'That's why I can understand the Welsh, who also want their own country.'

He'd wanted to be an actor at one time, and remembers being dressed down for chewing a piece of gum during a Shakespearian death scene. Then he wanted to be a film director. He's seen *Battleship Potemkin* seven times. He reaches for a piece of paper and the microphone, and with a bleak smile of apology returns to the job he ended up with. Adjusting an incongruous pair of half-moon spectacles he sets to the laborious business of announcing, in five languages, that the clocks will go forward an hour tonight.

A handful of passengers are sitting in the main lounge watching Popeye dubbed in Italian. Ron is reading *Great Air Disasters* and a small elderly Scotsman is protesting at the bar: 'That's the smallest Coca Cola I've ever seen!' His wife nods in agreement. The barman shrugs and examines something his little finger has just fetched out of his ear.

Up on deck there is sunshine and an extended Egyptian family returning from a holiday in Nice. The womenfolk remain covered despite the heat, but the children chase one another round the empty sun-deck. Their father, Mahmout, grins throughout the voyage, like the cat that's eaten the cream. Maybe he's just done a pipeline deal with my friends from the Orient Express.

The out-of-season feel persists. The small swimming pool is dry and a safety net is slung across it. I ask a crew member if it will be filled. He looks at me in surprise and shakes his head: 'It is for crazies.' The whole of the lower sun-deck is full of Mercedes cars – an overflow from the hold, I suppose.

Passepartout has lost all the Sunday papers he bought at Victoria three days ago with the exception of *Sunday Sport*. As we cut through the deep blue waters of the Adriatic, on our way from one cradle of civilisation to another, I settle down beside the Mercedes and read of 'Lesley's Agony As Her Man Turns Into A Frog'.

Midnight: A last turn on deck. Cool enough to make me grateful for including a sweater in my minimal luggage. After the mad rush of the first 48 hours, the pace of the journey has completely changed. For the first time I'm beginning to sense the immensity of the distance ahead. We're making 18 knots, which is respectable for any ship, but it still means that I'm currently going round the world at less than 30 miles an hour. Trains now seem unimaginably fast, aircraft incomprehensible. We have been moving steadily now for 29 hours and have seen nothing but hazy pale-grey sea. Away to our right (I'm sorry, starboard) is Brindisi, from where my illustrious fictional predecessor set sail.

Back to my cabin, which I can now find with only one wrong turning. In the middle of the Adriatic I put my watch on an hour – the first of 24 time changes before I get back home.

Day 5 29 September

The haze has cleared and the sea is a terrific turquoise. Overnight we've changed course and are now heading due East (which is always welcome news for this circumnavigator) and I can see dry straw-coloured coastline on either side.

No one is lingering over breakfast today, for we are now only a few miles away from one of the most spectacular experiences of the journey – the passage of the Corinth Canal. Its construction began just nine years after Phileas Fogg set out and was completed in 1893. It saves 200 miles sailing and the *Espresso Egitto* is the largest boat it will take.

Our engines slow for the first time since we left Venice. Two small boats are now approaching us, one the tugboat that guides us through, the other the boat containing the pilots – not one, but three – who will assist the captain. They grab the rope ladder and scramble aboard. They're dressed in well-pressed chinos. The senior of them is elderly, bald with grey hair, then there's a younger man with a wild, Gaddafi hairstyle and another, rather distinguished, like a statesman. There's a considerable and quite exciting air of expectation about this operation which, as Roger says, is rather like threading something through the eye of a needle. Gradually everybody on the boat, even the most laid-back sun worshipper, even the catatonic lad on the till in the bar who hasn't taken his eyes off the television for 36 hours, gathers on the rails to watch our progress. The narrow cut ahead of us looks unreal, like a Cecil B. De Mille special effect.

A soldier with a machine gun patrols outside a tiny concrete guard hut as we pass. The trees on either side bend rather wearily: we're in the land of parched grass.

Suddenly we're inside the canal and in the middle of a picture from the *Boy's Book of Wonders*. Walls rise at 90 degrees with only 2 metres leeway on either side of us. The three pilots, one on each side of the bridge, and the chief pilot in the middle, now have their trickiest work to do. If the stern of the ship swings at all, it will strike the dry sandstone walls. The negotiation of the Corinth Canal must be one of the top maritime stunts, a display of navigational skills, not just by this boat but by the tug, which is guiding us and keeping us on course, our own steering being ineffective at this speed.

The pilot on the starboard corner cracks his fingers, occasionally calls out some warning in Greek, and the captain then goes to his gyroscope and checks our course. We're flying four flags at the moment, the red and white flag emblazoned with the lion of St Mark, which is the flag of Venice, the red, white and green flag of the Republic of Italy, the red and white flag to signify a pilot on board, and the blue and white flag of Greece. Also up the masthead is Nigel Passepartout with his camera, ever in search of the Great Shot. His presence provokes terrific shouts and consternation from the crew below.

Just over an hour after entering the Corinth Canal we're through, saving ourselves seven or eight hours on the journey round the Peloponnesian Peninsula. As we emerge into the Saronian Sea the land to our left is burnt and bare, and the pine trees that do exist are scorched. There's obviously been a considerable fire. A coach at the side of the road below us disgorges a party of Greek ladies with handbags. They rush towards the canal side to watch us go by. Our tug turns and heads back through the canal. A launch comes alongside to collect the three pilots. A round of applause should really be offered, but they do this sort of thing ten times a day.

Three o'clock in the afternoon: Vast numbers of boats of all kinds around the port of Athens at Piraeus remind you that the Greeks still regard themselves as a seafaring nation. But in a bay almost out of sight are dozens of supertankers, laid up and rusting, a reminder that the golden days of the 1960s and early 1970s are over and may never return.

Mr Lalli is having a harassing time on the public address system: 'Transit passengers wishing to visit in Athens are reminded that we set sail again at nine p.m. Passengers *must* be aboard by nine thirty ... I'm sorry ... eight, *eight* thirty ...'

The Greek word for 'strike' is *aperghia* and we've already run into one. There are no taxis into Athens and as far as I can see no sign of a public transport alternative. For a moment on the dockside I feel a keen sense of isolation in a foreign land. A compatriot approaches: 'Saw you on Wogan!' Turns out to be a native of Manchester on her way to work on a kibbutz, and complaining bitterly about a 40-hour ferry journey from here to Tel Aviv.

A minibus takes me into Athens. Earthquakes or the threat of them seem to have knocked the stuffing out of domestic architecture and we pass row upon row of bland, unremarkable concrete facades. Sad in a city which contains two or three of the greatest buildings in the world.

What I've really come to see in Athens are the Evzones. Not sore throat pastilles, but the bizarrely dressed Presidential guards who, among other things, patrol the war memorial, and raise and lower the national flag at the Acropolis every Sunday. Enormous, specially selected, highly trained, superbly fit fighting men whose uniform consists of tasselled hats, embroidered tunics, short flared skirts, white stockings and clogs adorned with black pom-poms. Any temptation to see all this as rather twee is dispelled by one look at the giants who wear them. The outfit reflects the fierce national pride of the Greeks, for it was originally worn by the guerrillas who fought to keep the nationalist cause alive during 400 years of Turkish occupation. Nowadays the Greeks and the Turks are theoretically allies, as both are members of Nato, but the Evzone lieutenant I spoke to was in no doubt as to who was still the traditional enemy.

The Evzone tradition is that the guards dress each other, and I watch, feeling like a pygmy, as these huge, solemn young men, arms entwined around each other's waists, arrange the skirts (which they call *foustanellas*) so that every one of the 400 folds (one for each year of the Ottoman domination) hangs in exactly the right place.

We are entertained at the barracks with great warmth and courtesy by the Evzone commandant, a Cretan who offers us considerable slugs of tsikudia, his local spirit, which tastes like slivovitz. Maybe it's because of the taxi strike but the restaurants that ring the Piraeus waterfront are very empty and their owners seem prepared to go to suicidal lengths to stop our minibus as we drive back to the ship. We eventually stop at the only establishment whose owner hasn't flung himself into the middle of the road ahead of us. It's called The Black Goat Restaurant and features a special called 'Fish in Slic'. The sea water which laps gently at our feet is so full of oil and rubbish it's a wonder it can lap at all. (Perhaps this is the 'slic' referred to.) It's quite a relief to get back to the *Espresso Egitto*, and Mr Lalli's plaintive cries: 'Said Achmed Sabra from Egypt ... please call at the Purser's office; Mr Neekolas Russell from England ... *please* call at the Purser's office.'

He was smoking a lot when I passed his window on my way to bed.

Day 6 30 September

'This is my worst day ... this is my *worst* day.' Mr Lalli is referring to the arrival of 100 extra passengers at Heraklion, on top of the 100 who boarded last night at Piraeus (including, rumour has it, 31 unaccompanied German girls). I collect my shore-pass from him and at 7.30 on a clear hot morning I'm running along the sea-front past the low, solid battlemented fortress that dominates Heraklion harbour. On its wall the lion of Venice in low relief marks its origins in the time when Crete was part of the Venetian Empire.

This dusty sea-front has seen a few empires come and go. The Minoan civilisation, 3000 years before Christ, had already given way to Greek, Roman, Byzantine and Saracen empires before the Venetians arrived in 1210, and the Turks were still to come. I assume they all looted each other. A massively protracted exercise in the redistribution of wealth.

I rather liked the friendly atmosphere and human scale of the city. Everything seems to be half-finished, but there's an intimate little square in the centre of town where I rest and, over thick coffee, fresh orange juice, bread and honey, catch up on Olympic news in a day-old copy of the *Independent*. Ben Johnson's disgrace has followed his success with a swiftness the occupants of Mount Olympus would have been proud of.

I run at a gentle pace back through streets with unexpected names like Evans Street (after the Englishman who excavated the nearby Minoan capital of Knossos) and Duke of Beaufort Avenue ('Leoforos Dhoukos Bofor'). Back on board ship, Said Achmed Sabra is still wanted at the Purser's office.

Today's passenger intake has changed the character of the *Espresso Egitto* considerably. The leisurely sprinkling of smiling Egyptians and dour Scots with whom we left Venice has now been swamped by dreadlocked German bikers and package holidaymakers on 36-hour excursions to Egypt. There are a lot of thin, badly dressed Egyptians with plastic carrier bags and resigned, unsmiling faces. The sound of hawking and spitting is almost as frequent now as Mr Lalli's increasingly desperate announcements. As we pass the long, medieval harbour wall and ease into the eastern Mediterranean, we're still 200 short of a full complement of passengers. What it must be like when full hardly bears thinking about.

The highlight of my last day aboard the *Espresso Egitto* is a celebration dinner. The people from Adriatic Navigation have been extremely helpful to us and want to lay something on. Ann Passepartout suggests that we put two tables together, only realising later that they are bolted to the floor. But before she can stop them, Bruno, the Adriatic rep., Eros, the lugubrious maître d', several of the waiters and an engineer have begun construction of a wooden bridge from table to table.

In the afternoon I'm shown the galley where Franco and a team of 11 are preparing dinner for 300. Franco, a Neapolitan who's been 27 years 'man and boy' with Adriatica, gives me a rapid lesson in bread-making. The essence seems to be controlled panic. Once the dough is prepared Franco sets to at a furious pace, kneading, twisting, tying, folding, muttering, cursing and turning out, in the space of a minute, about 25 little rolls which an uncharitable observer would compare to a series of exquisitely formed dog turds. Egomaniac to the last I produce, after two or three attempts, a passable letter 'P' which I shall eat later.

5.30: On deck to watch my last European sunset. As the sun swells and sinks, a flight of small birds appears darting and diving in front of me. They're swallows. The sun has so dazzled me that they appear crimson.

The Great Meal this evening is to be filmed and all the waiters suddenly have crisp white jackets. Eros, in full dress, resembles a fifties matinee idol gone to seed. Champagne, risotto di gamberi, loup de mer, cheese and profiteroles, red and white wine come on inexorably, severely testing not just the diners but the structural engineering beneath the table.

As the *vita* becomes *piu dolce* the ship begins to roll for the first time in the journey. Eros looms over us, becoming more and more like Frankie Howerd. 'Not for nothing,' he declares with a twirl of the fingers, 'do they call me Eros,' and with an outrageous wink he turns on his heel and walks straight into a minion bearing more profiteroles.

To my cabin. Through eyes blurred by fine wines, I can just make out my copy of the BBC's *Get By In Arabic*. I'm on page 2, and Egypt's only 180 miles away.

Day 7 1 October

Dark, unsettling dreams from which I wake to the sound of throat-clearing, scratching and thick irregular breathing. It's not mine either. It's on the other side of the cabin partition but feels disturbingly close, as if this nameless heaving, unhealthy mass is on the other side of my bed. This all happens at 2.30, and I never quite recover. Four hours later I'm up, packing, deflating the inflatable globe which is the only way to get an accurate picture of the real extent of the journey. We hardly seem to have started, though Roger, trying to be encouraging, tells me that Cairo is 2,000 miles from London and when we get there we'll be a twelfth of the way home.

Up on deck for my first glimpse of the North African coastline. There's a smell of fresh bread oddly contrasting with the largely silent mood of passengers who stand staring mutely forward, their feet hemmed in by unwieldy boxes containing microwave ovens and Kenwood mixers. They're conserving their energies for queues and customs.

I talk to a lone Englishman who is travelling to Sinai and then the Sudan, scuba diving. He's addicted to the sport and finances his journeys by letting out grazing land he owns in Brecon. He grins apologetically, 'Not a very responsible way to carry on.'

Well, I'm not one to talk.

I'm now on the threshold of an uncompromisingly unfamiliar world. Everything is different, from the minarets on the dusty skyline of Alexandria to the blatantly shady behaviour of a small unmarked boat which sidles up on our stern port side, collects a pack of 200 Marlboros thrown down by one of the crew, secretes it and stands off for a while before returning for a few more goodies, all of which are swiftly stowed under the steering column in the wheelhouse.

Trying to sense a little of what drew Alexander the Great, Caesar and Napoleon to this place I shuffle down the

gangplank, barking my shins on a Magimix. I'm met by a very
charming lady in white who checks my passport and for the
first time I hear that soft, courteous Egyptian response to
foreigners, 'Welcome'.

The German bikers are wheeling their monstrous machines
from the ship's hold, a couple of middle-aged dock-workers
pass by holding hands and a shabby shuffling figure in loose
plimsolls dolefully works the crowd proffering a bucketful of
Coca Colas on ice.

Once on Egyptian soil, I feel a curious surge of adrenaline,
as if I've escaped from five days in cotton wool. There'll be no
such thing as normal for quite a while now. As if to underline
this I find myself in a fiacre, which is an open horse-drawn cab,
being galloped out of the port and into the hurtling traffic. A
gaggle of Egyptians, sipping tea, have presumably been told
what the camera's there for.

'You are Michael Caine?' they shout.

'No. I am cheaper than Michael Caine.'

They all laugh, beyond the limits of politeness. 'We want to
see this film very quickly.'

I just want to survive long enough to make it, but there's not
time to tell them this as Achmed the driver applies his whip and
we swing out into the streets of Alexandria. It's quite terrifying.
The horse, which for some reason is called Larry, seems
congenitally unable to move in a straight line and in a series of
lurches and wild whip-assisted sprints, dodging within inches
of passing cars, we eventually reach the famous Corniche – the
long curving sea-front. It's like Cannes with acne. A wide and
well-proportioned road and some handsome facades in the
neo-classical style, but everything blotchy and half patched-up,
giving it the odd air of a city that was abandoned long ago and
is now full of people gingerly coming back to re-inhabit.

On the sea-wall, itinerant street-sellers are curled up asleep,
their heads protected from the sun inside the baskets they'll
later sell. Achmed and Larry deliver me physically, if not

mentally, unscathed to the Cecil Hotel. Here hippies are having their shoes shined by ten-year-olds and within the space of a minute I'm offered sunglasses, black market currency and a trip to Alamein.

'Alamein ... you know ... Hitler! ...'

Midday: To the impressive Misr Station to pick up a train to Cairo. The noise is incredible. This is a horn-blower society. Egyptian drivers make New York cabbies sound like librarians. They must specially modify their cars to connect the accelerator to the horn. They never use one without the other. And now the muezzin has started, his raucously distorted call to prayer adding to the cacophony, and causing prayer mats to be laid down in the middle of an already packed ticket office.

A blazing row has erupted as to whether we're allowed to film or not, and about four people are shouting at each other, clutching their heads. You'd think there'd been a death in the family the way they carry on. It all reminds me of a big, slightly out of control boys' public school, everyone issuing different orders, a few people trying to be serious, but everyone else finding it frightfully funny.

Watching the crowds come off the trains it's interesting to note how the traditional garb – jellabas and turbans and fezzes for men, and veils and long dresses for women – is now mixed with Western dress – Levi's, jeans, slacks, shirts, dresses and skirts. The contrast is extraordinary: some look like Old Testament prophets, others like James Dean. Sometimes there's a mixture with the women, of the old Islamic headdress and a modern slightly blowsy Orlon two-piece. It may be chaotic but life wouldn't be as rich as this at airports, where people are much more conditioned, directed and cowed into submission.

Four o'clock: At Cairo station, half an hour late after a 135-mile train journey from Alex across the fertile, feudally farmed Nile Delta. The temperature is 91 degrees.

It's Saturday afternoon and I've been promised seats for the big football match between local heroes National Sporting Club and some tough-tacklers from Middle Egypt – Al Minya. I arrive at Cairo Stadium, in a grandiose complex called Nasser City, halfway through the second half. The stadium is a wide, comfortable bowl with an electronic scoreboard and lush grass playing surface. The terraces are clean and well cared-for and put most British grounds to shame.

I'm rather confused by the colours and enthusiastically cheer an Al Minya attack by mistake. I'm then taken in hand by some local supporters who explain who's who and offer me sunflower seeds. They are exceptionally friendly and as Sporting Club score twice only moments after my arrival, clearly regard me as having Bill Shankly-like powers.

The 60,000 crowd is well patrolled. Ten minutes before the end riot police with transparent shields, visors, helmets and long white sticks take up position around the touchline, facing the crowd like nervous samurai.

Outside, the army, consisting of thin and petrified teenagers, waits in trucks. But there seems to be no trouble. Indeed, some supporters produce prayer mats and fall to their knees as soon as they leave the ground.

On the way back from the match, traffic is so solid along a half-finished eight-lane super-highway that we are passed by an old woman in black on a donkey, leading a herd of goats up the side of the motorway. A red, rather unhealthily flushed sun descends slowly behind a hazy city skyline. Last night it was the crimson swallows; tonight, more menacingly, sunset brings the kites, flapping lazily around the eucalyptus trees.

I check in to the Hotel Windsor, which, like everything else in Cairo, is remarkable. It's run by two brothers called Doss. The Doss Bros have resisted any pressure to convert this unprepossessing pile into a characterless modern hotel, much to Passepartout's dismay.

I rather like its surreal atmosphere. The stairs and the stickily hot hallway are decorated with old Swissair posters of the Alps, so as you climb, perspiring, upwards you pass red, chubby-cheeked German children smiling in St Moritz and Alpine walkers in Zermatt with thick legs protruding from bulky lederhosen. The hotel was once under Swiss ownership and there are reindeer antlers and hunting trophies on the walls of the bar.

But the food is Egyptian. For dinner we have lentil soup, then a plateful of spring onions, cracked wheat, rice and fried onions, falafel (deep-fried vegetable balls), a chilli and onion salad and a thick and treacherous local wine, which is about the only thing that doesn't have onions in it.

Later, whilst Passepartout sorts out the film he's shot of this day's madness, I take a walk for a late-night look at the Nile. A brutal network of flyovers bars my way and I end up lost. A courteous Egyptian helps me out. He asks me where I'm from and what I think of the weather.

'A little hot for me.'

He laughs. 'This is very nice. It's the first time it has been below 95 for weeks.'

Back in my room, the bath tap produces only dreadful bronchial shudders and a thin trickle of water before sinking into total unconsciousness. There's a washbasin, but no plug, and the lavatory's unflushable. However, I work out an Emett-like temporary solution involving twisting a coat-hanger around the ball cock. Later discover it's my only coat-hanger.

Day 8 2 October

Sunday morning in Cairo.

I wake with a greater than usual feeling of sensory dislocation. Where am I and what is the horrendous noise?

Most of it can be attributed to my air-conditioning unit which changed gear during the night with a splintering crack that sounded as if someone were trying to batter the door down.

I silence the air-conditioner and throw open the windows only to find there's even more noise outside. I now know why they had laughed at me in reception when I'd asked for a quiet room.

'In *Cairo!*'

I suppose it's sheer weight of numbers. There are over 10 million people living in Greater Cairo and a further million or more unrecorded refugees and squatters – many of them living in the eerily beautiful City of the Dead, a huge and ancient cemetery. I passed by it with fascination, but on enquiry found that cameras are not allowed inside, so, with a day to kill before my next boat connection from Suez, Passepartout and I take up the invitation of a man I met in the bar last night to visit an Egyptian movie set. Crossing the Nile by the Tahir bridge I have my first sight of the more prosperous side of the metropolis. Hilton, Sheraton and Meridien hotels, skyscraper office blocks. From here Cairo could be anywhere in the world and I'm glad to be at the eccentric Windsor, in the as yet unsmoothed heart of the city.

The film is a political thriller called *Inar Gahined* ('Hellfire') and it's being shot in a Safeway supermarket in the tidy, tree-shaded Zamalek area. Foreign diplomats live here, so it's well tended, well guarded, and dotted with twee boutiques with names like 'Mix 'n' Match' and 'Genuine'.

It transpires that my contact is Egypt's leading lighting cameraman and I'm treated royally, meeting the stars and, without any audition, being given the part of Third Shopper In China Department. My six steps to the left as the gang pass by are executed so successfully that I am upgraded to the more demanding Man In Lift. The terrorists have a gritty scene here in which their recriminations are cut short by the arrival of the elevator, whose doors slide open to reveal yours truly. I'm not quite sure what I'm doing but I stare hard at the gang leader as I walk past him and he seems very pleased.

I talk to him afterwards. His real name is Noor-el-Sherif and he is very big in Egypt – where they make over 60 films a year. He admits only about six of these are any good and blames much of the blandness on the censorship that is necessary to make pictures saleable in the rest of the Arab world. I ask him what sort of things they censor.

'Sex, politics, religion …' he replies gloomily. 'That's all.'

Having arrived in Egypt 600 years too late to see one of the Seven Wonders of the World – the Pharos lighthouse – I felt I couldn't leave without seeing one that still exists – the Pyramids. I had always presumed they were in the middle of nowhere, marooned in the desert. In fact they are within five minutes' walk of apartment blocks in the suburb of Giza. My first view of them is from a traffic jam on Pyramids Road. The 4,600-year-old apex of the Great Pyramid pokes up from behind a block of flats. My first full-frontal view of the Pyramids provokes an heretical comparison with the slag-heaps which used to litter the South Yorkshire countryside where I grew up. They had the same solid bulk, shape and immovable presence. Once free of the straggling suburb we are straightaway in desert. There's no transition through savannah and scrubland, like in the geography books. The city ends, the desert begins, and it goes on until you reach Morocco. The dustiness of Cairo is explained. Every time a wind blows it dumps thousands of tonnes of desert on the city.

Closer now to the Pyramids and they are awesome. The blocks of sandstone at their base are twice as high as the small children playing around them. The structures rise serene and powerful above us, preserving an unmoving dignity, like great beasts surrounded by insects. Coaches ferry out an endless stream of human insects, deposit them at a tightly packed vantage point where they are assailed by camel-mongers, postcard salesmen, purveyors of trinkets and all the other free market forces which have ripped off tourists at this very spot for hundreds, if not thousands of years.

They have their patter well worked out, and very bizarre it sounds in the middle of the desert:

'You from Yorkshire? ... I am friend of Yorkshire!'

'You are English? Tally-ho!'

'What is your name?'

'Michael.'

'My camel's name is Michael!'

So it is that I find myself on a camel called Michael (or Ron or Julian or Nigel or Dwayne or Sheri-Anne) being flung skywards into the air as the creature raises itself on its forelegs. It looks and feels grossly unsafe, as it totters into the desert with me clinging on for dear life and feeling ridiculously conspicuous in an Arab headdress which the camel-owner, who I think is called Michael as well, has insisted I wear: 'Now you will be like Lawrence of Arabia!'

Behind me hot white people from all over the wealthy West are being given similar treatment. Every time they raise a camera to the Pyramids an Arab stands in front of it. The tourist adjusts his shot, the Arab follows. The air is full of the angry din of protest and dissension. This din is beginning to fade now as Michael, Michael and Michael wander further into the desert. In silence and sunset the Pyramids take on a potent, talismanic quality.

At supper at the Windsor, they appear to have unearthed a new and comprehensive wine list. Marked *Carte des Vins* and bound in thick, padded leather, it's presented to us proudly by Mahmoud, the small elderly head waiter. Inside it appears to consist of nothing but photos and press cuttings mostly featuring a squat, muscular man with very few clothes on surrounded by admiring groups of ladies. Mahmoud beams proudly. Of course, it's *him*. 'Yes!' he nods graciously and strikes a pose. He was once very famous for his body. We admire his pectorals, but would have preferred the wine. He retrieves the book, wipes its cover and presents it to an infinitely more appreciative group of Australian schoolgirls. They arrived at the Windsor last night, after a European tour which has left their teachers devastated. One of them tells me that Athens was the worst: 'All those sailors.' Then he shrugs and takes another gulp of Stella beer: 'So long as we get them home without any diseases.'

Seems a suitable epitaph for a long day, and I'm about to drink to it when Ann appears with a very long face. My onward connection from Suez – the SS *Algeria* – will not be leaving Suez tomorrow after all. Engine trouble. So it's back to the phone as soon as shipping offices open in the morning. Suddenly the schedule's looking shaky.

Day 9 3 October

Encouragement of a sort from my horoscope in the *Egyptian Gazette* (109th year of publication): 'Others may make demands on you today that you consider unreasonable, but you will come through with flying colours.' I wish I had their confidence.

My breakfast is served by a Nubian in a fez who was once a servant in the household of King Farouk. 'Nubians make very good waiters,' observes Mr Doss. What a dreadful reference for any nation. It's like hearing that Visigoths can iron well.

Better news from the shipping agent. Though I shall have to take a later boat out of Suez which will mean missing my planned connection from Jeddah to Muscat, a sister ship, leaving Jeddah later, has altered its itinerary to call at Muscat after all.

I leave the Hotel Windsor at 2. I was never able to have the bath I so much wanted and my coat-hanger remains a vital part of the lavatory system but there is an almost unreal individuality to the place which represents Cairo in a microcosm.

There is no train connection between Cairo and Suez, so I take a taxi. Within a few hundred yards I know that I should have gone by camel. This is going to be one of the most uncomfortable journeys of my life. The temperature is creeping up to the hundred degree mark. There is no air-conditioning, and the windows open onto a wall of noise and pollution.

The statue of Rameses II, discovered in Memphis in 1851 by French archaeologists, stands between two flyovers in front of the Rameses Station, moving no faster than we are. On my left is the railway line to Alex, which brought me in to the city what seems an impossibly long time ago, but is, in fact, less than two days. As if there isn't enough noise the driver flicks a cassette into his machine and loud Egyptian pop music fills the taxi. 'This was a very good song for Al Amkansoun,' he tells me. 'She was very famous lady from 15 years ago; she now very famous in Arab. More than 100 million population like to hear this song.'

We've been going now about 25 minutes, the heat, noise and smell of fumes still intense, but the roads have at last thinned out as we pass through Heliopolis. Lots of barracks around here, many soldiers. Howitzers and rockets are proudly displayed outside.

Suddenly we're on the edge of the desert, 96 per cent of Egypt's land surface, and mile upon mile of tips. All Cairo's rubbish; old furniture, rubble, twisted car wrecks, some of them burning. It seems to be an open dump. Pass a huge articulated truck which has swerved and overturned on the side of the road. The cab looks completely smashed in, and two men helplessly wander around the sacks of cement which lie scattered across the road.

Occasionally an advertising hoarding stands out in the middle of nowhere. We pass one which depicts a huge bidet and washbasin.

The meter ticks over. It shows about 40 Egyptian pounds – nearly £11 sterling. I pray that we keep moving. As soon as we slow down flies fill the car. Not a lot of traffic anyway. Trucks containing oil drums and pipes. At least there are some mountains now rising to the south, and a lower range to the north, something to look at.

Pass ten tanks and about thirty troop carriers by the roadside, with people playing on them. It's not really surprising the Egyptians were clobbered so often by the Israelis. They're not warriors. They're shy, rather jolly, humorous people. Can't imagine them taking military life and conquest very seriously.

It's 5.15 and approaching dusk when I catch my first sight of Suez, a flame high in the sky marking the first of many oil refineries. This does look a god-forsaken depressing place. What vegetation there is here on the edge of the desert, small scrubby bushes, blossom with a thousand plastic bags.

It's a quarter to six when I reach the gates of Suez port. We are not allowed to board tonight, and there seems some doubt as to whether we shall find a boat tomorrow. And we can do nothing until morning as the shipping office is closed. A battered sign in English at the entrance to the port gates reads 'Goodb'ye'. A harsh joke as we turn back and trudge into Suez to find a hotel.

In the centre of Suez two captured US-built Israeli tanks, taken in the 1973 war, are displayed. Alongside them can still be seen piles of rubble from the 1967 war when the town of Suez was almost destroyed.

Then all at once we are in an area of substantial houses with pillared porches and wrought-iron balconies, set along leafy avenues and around well-kept squares full of oleander bushes and Flame of the Forest trees. This is the Port Tawfik area and it was built as a cantonment for foreigners working for the Suez Canal Company.

Here we find the Red Sea Hotel with its plain, slightly depressing rooms devoid of any decoration. Worst of all it is 'dry' and more than anything in the world at this moment I want a cold beer. The receptionist, sympathetic to my plight, directs me to The Gulf Rose Restaurant and Bar where, creamed against mosquitoes, I sit for a while and take in the dark water ahead, the mouth of the Suez Canal and the busy flames of the refineries. A light breeze blows, and it has to be said that sitting in Suez is not at all unpleasant. Quite how *long* I shall have to sit in Suez is tomorrow's problem.

Day 10 4 October

Phileas Fogg arrived in Suez aboard the SS *Mongolia* six and a half days after leaving London. 'As to seeing the town, he did not even think of it, being of that race of Englishmen who have their servants visit the country they pass through.' One of the reasons for his superior rate of progress becomes clear this morning as I stand beside the Suez Canal just after dawn, watching the northbound convoy go through. There is not a single passenger ship among the fifteen or so which pass, one every seven minutes, rumbling away into the morning mist. The days when you could hop on a *Mongolia* or a regular P & O or Union Castle service are over. There are cruise ships and cargo ships and not a lot else in between. And that's why I'm already almost four days behind Fogg and every hour of this uncertainty in Suez puts me further behind.

There's no one else out here by the canal where the rusting sections of a pontoon bridge and the dug-outs, trenches and blockhouses are reminders of the bitter fighting that took place only fifteen years ago. The whole place is like one huge War Museum, through which ships pass at a stately pace, almost like mirages in the haze.

By mid-morning I'm back at the gates of Suez port. A steady line of brightly painted trucks and trailers is passing through, occasionally swerving to avoid a minibus packed to the gunwales which has in turn swerved to avoid a woman with her worldly goods on her head and a crying child on her arm.

Water-sellers clang brass rings together to attract attention, but vanish into thin air at the sight of a camera, which is a pity as their kit is extraordinary. It consists of what appears to be a long-spouted silver urn from which hang glasses and which is topped with a block of ice. A tin tray is worn on the waist to collect the money. Sometimes you can hardly see the boy inside all this, giving the odd impression of robot coffee bars whizzing around the dockside. On the roadside the beggars wait patiently, many with children sitting uncomprehendingly in their arms, flies buzzing at their nostrils.

At last it seems we are clear to go through. Reservations have been made for us on a boat carrying itinerant workers to Jeddah. At the immigration counters are long lines of people waiting patiently. Inaction is a fact of life, it seems. We are, I'm embarrassed to say, expressed through, but only as far as customs where we experience a lot of inaction.

There is nowhere to wait except in the minibus, and it's very hot. At the entrance to the dock they are preparing to resurface the road. The preparation consists of two men and a donkey drawing a small tank of liquid tar. One man holds a long leaky rod from which he sprays the tar on the road and his trousers whilst his accomplice shuffles alongside pumping a handle. The effect of the tar is wonderful to behold. Everybody treads in it. One man with green flip-flops discovers he's in it too late and each step he takes his flip-flops grow in size, so after a while he's walking like a huge duck. It affects everybody from the jellaba-ed peasant to the brisk, white-shirted self-important official. Soon all around us the dock is full of people scraping their shoes.

Can this be the same country that built the Pyramids, invented the column, the cornice and the capital?

After three hours of formalities we are aboard the M.V. *Qamar El Saudi II* ('The Saudi Moon II'). The II has, however, been roughly crossed out and I written in. Her sister ship, *The Saudi Moon I*, recently ran aground and sank on a reef outside Jeddah. The ship, of 5,342 tonnes, was built in Genoa in 1971 and began life as the *Dana Sirena* before being sold to a Danish outfit, DFDS Seaways, for North Sea ferry work. Now it's owned by an Egyptian company who bought it off the Saudis. The interior seems to have been left alone, and I find myself looking at a plan of the ship which still features the 'Hamlet Lounge', the 'Tivoli Club', 'The Mermaid Pub' and even the 'Dog's Toilet'.

Up on the bridge, beside an indicator with the ship's speed and direction in Danish – 'Frem', 'Bak', 'Halv' and 'Fuld' – the portly Egyptian captain is bent over charts of Suez harbour published in Taunton, whilst his first officer tends a radar scanner made in Bremen.

I've lost another half day on my schedule by the time we eventually pull away from the dockside, passing the stricken *Algeria* whose engine problems precipitated all these delays.

It's a 48-hour trip to Jeddah and our speed will not be much more than 15 knots, a much slower rate of progress than the *Egitto*. There are 650 passengers and 12 cars aboard (one of which is a gleaming Cadillac). Though Passepartout and I have comfortable cabins with plenty of portholes, we seem to be in splendid isolation, for most of the other passengers are squashed together in cabins below, and 200 of them are sleeping out on deck. The reason for this can be gleaned from a comparison of the per capita earnings of Egypt, 700 dollars a year, and Saudi Arabia, 8,000 dollars a year. Saudi Arabia is a magnet for labour in the Arab world, and many of these passengers have left wives and families to earn a year's good money in the still booming construction, oil and agricultural industries of their wealthy neighbour.

Sadly the Mermaid Pub is now much reduced. The bar and bar stools are still there, but only non-alcoholic drinks are available. Tea, coffee and things like Viva-Up and Santa – a dreadfully sweet fizzy apple confection. Stick to water.

Somehow drinking water in surroundings expressly designed for something more fun is a depressing experience.

Day 11 5 October

Ron tells me at breakfast that when his watch alarm went off on deck last night a lot of people woke up and started to pray. I had noticed yesterday that the deck passengers, who have very few belongings, do sport some impressive wristwatches. These are not only prestigious, but very practical for those who must remember to pray five times a day.

Apparently one is not advised to wear shorts. The sight of my knees would be frowned upon. I shall just have to get hot, secure in the knowledge that there is only cold water in the shower. And no towels.

There are four Arab women and a dozen men in the first-class lounge this morning. A video of expensive cars, prominently displaying 'Rothman's' signs, on some glamorous rally, plays in the corner. A group of children are chasing each other around the tables. The Arabs love children and when I show an interest in them there is a smile of contact from the parents. But that's about as far as it goes. Yesterday I had met some people on deck who were quite chatty. This morning with the camera about it is very different, and I sense a chill of hostility. A slim, intense young man with a beard and a brown third-world suit reads his Koran and very obviously avoids us. His attitude seems to affect a lot of the others.

The deck passengers all wear traditional clothes – tarbooshes or takaias (the white skullcaps), jellabas and sandals and have no interest in the small duty-free shop below with its VHS cassettes, lingerie, Lacoste shirts and bottles of 'Poison' eau de toilette.

I should assume no Arab, of whatever class, would have much interest in the information outside the main lounge that there was, once upon a time, a King of Denmark called Gorm the Old or that the present Queen, Margrethe II, is his direct descendant.

Lunch with Captain Abbas. He is a charming, enthusiastic and philosophical man. An Egyptian with fond memories of Liverpool, especially their football team. 'I follow the Reds!' he declares, beaming round at us, and scooping a little more beans and onion onto his plate. 'I am not a communist, but I love the Reds!'

He did not sleep at all last night, he tells us. He never does while going down the Gulf of Suez. It's a very busy waterway and now that they have discovered oil on both sides there are support craft flitting to and fro and fishing boats as well, for unlike much of the Red Sea the Gulf is only 50 metres deep. On the other side of Sinai, the Gulf of Aqaba is 2 kilometres deep, 'Which is why Moses decided to walk across the Gulf of Suez!'

Captain Abbas admires England: 'You have such a love for the sea.' Clearly he's not read the Greenpeace report on North Sea pollution. He regards himself and his fellow mariners as guardians of the oceans they serve, and is concerned at the way so many ships mistreat them, throwing unrecyclable rubbish overboard, flushing out oil tanks.

His ship may be tired, battered and grubby, but his love for his work and his affection for sea life and its special mixture of loneliness and comradeliness is very affecting. At the end of the meal he bids us all a most courteous farewell and excuses himself as he has to go to his cabin to listen to a football match on the radio. It turns out that his team is Sporting Cairo, whom I watched on Saturday. Today they have a midweek match against Ismailia ... 'Seaside boys, very young, very strong,' he winks and jabs both elbows out, dangerously.

By mid-afternoon the ship is beginning to roll quite noticeably in a six to seven foot swell. Jules Verne had noted that when the *Mongolia* rolled in the Red Sea, 'the ladies disappeared, the pianos were silent, the songs and dances ceased at once'. Not only was Fogg ahead of me, he was clearly having a much better time.

About six o'clock, as we are crossing the Tropic of Cancer, there is some bad news from Jeddah. One connecting ship which I had hoped might be delayed has left on time, and the next one will be missing out Muscat where I had fixed a dhow connection on to India, and going on to Dubai further up the Persian Gulf. Even if I were able to pick up a dhow in Dubai, the extra distance on both journeys would make me five days late in Bombay. The rest of the schedule would then fall apart like a pack of cards.

Meet Passepartout in the bar. Over water and Santas we discuss alternative possibilities. Unfortunately it's difficult enough to enter Saudi Arabia at all, let alone change plans whilst there, and all the shipping offices will be closed for the weekend. We are entering 'The Arabian Triangle', as Clem Vallance, director of this leg of the journey, puts it, where normal rules no longer apply.

We all need a drink: not a water, or a Santa, but a drink. At lunch Captain Abbas had eloquently defended the Muslim objections to alcohol. He reminded us of 'the phrase you drinkers often use – to get out of our minds'. Abbas wagged his finger and grinned sagely. 'This is not what we need. We need to get into our minds.'

Later I retire to my cabin and try to get into my mind. I can't concentrate, and head up on deck for a walk and listen to the World Service. Around me the 'deck class' are preparing for a second night under the stars. Some are already curled up, heads on crooked arms, others lying spreadeagled like dead men. In the stern the young man in brown, clasping his Koran, sits surrounded by a small group. He's making points on each finger, slowly, trying to bring in every one of his listeners. They watch engrossed.

I hold my short-wave radio out over the side, to receive the signal better. London comes through to the Red Sea loud and clear. They're talking about the Labour Party conference and Kinnock's fighting speech. Above me two shooting stars fall through a clear sky; below me a sleeping man's arms falls across my feet.

Day 12 6 October

Cheese, olives, omelette and hot rolls for breakfast. My system has been a little fluid recently. In fact everything I've eaten south of Cairo has turned to water. I dislike using drugs, but as I'm apprehensive about public lavatory availability in Jeddah, I've taken recourse to a couple of codeine phosphate. Ron swears by Imodium which, besides binding the bowels, apparently kept him as high as a kite in Cairo for 24 hours.

No sooner have we finished breakfast than the dining room is turned into a makeshift clinic. There is evidently a meningitis epidemic in Saudi and we must all be vaccinated. Soon the Elsinore room is full of children crying and adults screaming their heads off. It's all rather disorganised and I'm sure some people are vaccinated twice. I'm handed a certificate in Arabic which, they tell me, says I'm immune from meningitis until October 1990. As we approach Jeddah, we try to film the Saudi pilot coming aboard, but are asked not to. Later, on the bridge Captain Abbas has words of explanation for what he calls the prickliness of the Saudis. 'They are a desert people – and what do you get from deserts? Not roses ... cacti.'

Until five years ago, Jeddah, ringed by treacherous shoals, was one of the most dangerous ports to enter. Then, as part of his colossal investment in its improvement, King Faisal commissioned Gray Mackenzie, a British firm, to provide a decent chart. Now it's much easier and Captain Abbas has little time for the pilot, who looks about 16 and very nervous (as anyone with the expansive bulk and ironic eye of Abbas behind them would be). Pilots, he reckons, are very often a formality.

Any ship's master, with up-to-date charts, could make the approach himself.

As the sun burns off the morning mist, the skyline of Jeddah is clearer. If I shut my ears to the Arabic radio exchanges between the pilot and the shore I could imagine myself in America, Japan or Singapore. There's no minaret, dome or crescent moon in sight. Instead, the tall towers of a desalination plant dominate a waterfront of extensive jetties, state-of-the-art cranes and gantries, all set out spaciously and tidily, like an architect's model. Everything has been built in the last 15 years. It is the formidable face of a boom economy. I can't help thinking that this is what Victorian Britain must have felt like. Now it seems quite strange – the unfamiliar feeling of being in a country which can afford anything it wants.

In the last 48 hours I've grown very fond of Captain Abbas and we leave with regret. His boat I shan't shed many tears for, though. I feel travel-worn and grubby and haven't had a good bath since leaving the *Egitto*.

On the quayside at Jeddah we're met by Achmed, our man from the Ministry (of Information), and Nick, a young man from the British embassy in Riyadh. Everything is very formal here. Things have to be done the right way. The cheerful anarchy of Egypt is a thing of the past. For the grubby, flagged floor of the custom house in Alexandria substitute an air-conditioned plastic-finished international terminal. VDU screens shimmer behind colour-coordinated desks. The walls are covered with framed evidence of the Saudi boom – photos of dams, highways, power lines. For the Egyptian workers from off the *Saudi Moon* it's the Promised Land, but not *their* Promised Land. One of them has a last spit in a lined litter-bin before his passport is stamped.

Most of the menial work in Saudi Arabia is done by foreigners. As well as the Egyptians there are Yemenis and Filipinos and South-East Asians. The Saudis prefer to be behind desks, they don't really like to get their hands dirty. Difficult to know, quite inscrutable people, according to Nick from the embassy. As he says this I notice two men greeting each other with a rather delicate kiss on each cheek like a couple of French ladies in a café.

A Chinese boat, the *Cha-Hwa* of Keelung, is pulling into the harbour as we make our way through the white and grey marbled gatehouses and out of the port. The sign to the city centre is spelt in the American way – 'center'. Sony, Sharp and Panasonic signs abound. But perhaps the greatest shock is the Red Sea Palace Hotel. Not only is there hot and cold running water, there are valets in little hats and sachets of 'Foaming Bath Cream' and music seeping out of the ceiling. Nothing in the previous 12 days has prepared me for this, and I quite forget for a while that we have no idea how we're going to leave this place. Consult Dan Bannerman, a shipping agent and a Liverpudlian, born a football pitch's distance from Anfield. He confirms there is no alternative to the slow boat to Dubai, and indeed it's even slower than we thought, stopping to unload on the way.

The only way to make up time is for me to drive overland to the Gulf, a distance of about 1,120 miles. It will be very tricky to obtain permission for such a journey but Achmed agrees to try.

There is no such thing as a tourist in Saudi Arabia. Every visitor has to have a sponsor – a company or a government department – which guarantees his status and suitability. Saudi Arabia may look like America but it can behave like Russia. However, relations with Britain are good at the moment – we've just clinched a multi-million-pound defence deal – and Nick reckons we could be lucky. Achmed intervenes here to say that under no circumstances would a film crew be allowed to accompany me. Forward one step, back two.

Time to kill in the hotel bookshop. Look for something to follow *Stanley and His Women*. Find little more than a waterproof edition of *Red Sea Reef Fishes* and a stack of *Time* and *Newsweek* magazines on a shelf marked 'No reading please'.

I have to walk for a while before I find an echo of the conviviality of Egypt in the orderly Sony Panasonic world of Jeddah. It's a pavement café at No. 21 Tanaf Lane in the Al-Balad district, outside which sit two or three people smoking most elaborate hookahs. The old houses round here belonged to merchants who were very well off at a time when Jeddah was making money from two sources, one from the *haj*, the annual pilgrimage to Mecca, the other from the spice route to the Yemen. Most of these coastal areas would have been very rich, whereas Riyadh, now the capital, would just have been a collection of mud huts. In the middle of all this I chance upon the nostalgic sight of a manhole cover made by Brickhouse of Dudley, impressively inscribed 'The Pennine Drain Cover'. Pass a group of slim, bright-eyed smiling Sudanese guest workers touting for a bit of car cleaning. The Sudanese I've met on this trip I've liked very much indeed; they have a natural grace and wit and smile a lot, as though they like a good time.

To a courtyarded restaurant called El Alawey for supper. Delicious fresh fruit; and I eat couscous, with lamb, and then almond rolls and sesame seed rolls. The restaurant seems largely for foreigners – Saudis don't eat out much, and when they do they prefer Western-style restaurants. Very nice ambience here, with brass and silver pitchers. I sit with my shoes off and feet up, resting on my side, on a sort of carpeted pillow, like a Roman emperor.

A good chat with Nick from the embassy who used to be in Jordan. We talk about Middle Eastern affairs. Some foresee that Israel will cease to exist in 25 or 30 years because there are so many Arabs living within her borders and reproducing at a rate 50 per cent faster than the Israelis. In 25 years or so, half the population of Israel will be Arab. We walk back together and it's very hot and sticky. Still no word on whether I can move on tomorrow.

Day 13 7 October

I wake with sulphurous tastes emanating from my stomach and decide to kill or cure by taking some exercise. I am a regular four-times a week runner at home and yet, apart from hopping over the Heraklion waterfront, I've taken no vigorous exercise for almost two weeks. Out onto the Corniche, passing on the way the remarkable Jeddah roundabouts, decorated with huge and playful sculptures: at one a 25-foot-high bicycle, at another a series of enormous Arab lamps, at another a concrete block with the front and back ends of cars embedded in it. The presence of these light-hearted civic ornaments is one of the paradoxes of a country which takes itself and its role in the world very seriously, which can in many ways seem severe and intolerant, which won't allow theatres or cinemas but loves fun fairs and garden centres. Sculpture is everywhere. No human representation is allowed so the abstract and surreal flourish in exuberant childlike designs – spiky cacti, boxes of treasure with jewels inside, stranded ships.

Out on the Corniche beside the Red Sea, I can run in my shorts, which it would be highly disrespectful to wear in the centre of the city, and think myself to be in California, especially when polystyrene Big Mac boxes from the nearby fairground blow across my path.

And yet, though there are Big Macs and family playgrounds, the women of Saudi Arabia cannot drive, nor, for instance, can they find employment on their own airline, where the stewardesses are English or Canadian. In the shops I can buy every kind of sophisticated communications equipment and yet the *Observer* newspaper I buy in the hotel is crudely censored. A photo of Olympic athletes Mary Slaney and Yvonne Murray has been scored out with black Pentel below the women's necks. A half-page article on the drug Ecstasy has been partially cut out and a feature on Lord Lichfield's Pirelli calendar entirely black-pencilled. To a first-time Western visitor it is all most confusing, this mixture between the primitive and the sophisticated, the plutocratic and the austere, the open and the tightly closed.

Another night in Jeddah. To pass the time Passepartout and I visit one of the fairgrounds. It's family night, which means women and children only. Inside there is neon and music and bright lights, but only a few children, supervised by women in black. On one carousel children ride farmyard animals to the music of 'Old Macdonald Had A Farm'. Another, more energetic ride carries with it the warning, 'for your safety this game is not allowed for those who suffer from ... hearts, diabetics, nerves, high pressure and the pregnants'. Beneath the sign a group of Arab women, black veils flying, are sitting together in a huge teacup as it whirls round a teapot. Sadly it's too dark to film.

Above the Atallah Happyland flies the Saudi flag, unique in the world for having an inscription on it. It reads, 'There is only one God and Mohammed is his prophet.' I must hope both are on my side tomorrow.

Day 14 8 October

My *Arab Gazette* tells me it's the start of Fifth National Cleaning Week. For me it's the end of Second Travelling Week and nothing is getting easier. The word is that Achmed has been up all night at the Ministry, and at 3.30 a.m. finally secured permission for myself, Clem and Nick from the embassy to drive across Saudi Arabia. It's now eight o'clock in the morning and there is no sign of Achmed or the permission. Nick is anxious to be leaving, for we have an 1,100-kilometre drive ahead of us. This will take us to Riyadh, and after that there are still more than 1,000 kilometres to the Gulf. It's like driving from London to the Black Sea in one weekend.

At last Achmed, with neat beard and fresh white thobe (as the Saudis call the jellaba) enters the lobby of the Red Sea Palace waving our travel permission like a latter-day Neville Chamberlain. Profuse thanks, then into Nick's Toyota Cressida and we head for the hills.

Not far from Jeddah the road divides on creedal grounds. A huge gantry saddles the motorway, indicating two lanes for 'Muslims Only' and a slip road for 'Non-Muslims'. Only Muslims may look upon the Holy City, so we must take the Christian exit.

Here also we must leave Ron, Nigel, Julian and Angela Passepartout. They will fly on to Dubai and try and fix up a dhow to take us to India. It's a sad moment, as we were enjoying seeing the world together, and regard going on aeroplanes as a cheat.

The main road to Taif is closed for repair and for 50 miles or more we toil slowly up onto the central plateau behind a line of water-carrying tankers, past scrubby pasture where goats and sheep graze and higher up where a few crops are growing in neatly terraced fields. The trucks are nearly all grey-green Mercedes with ornate fifties-style curved radiators. The Saudi market is intensely conservative and apparently Mercedes continue to make them in the old style specially for the Bedouins.

Just outside Taif we come to a police road block, and the first test of Achmed's rather flimsy note of authorisation. The policeman reads it with intense concentration, his lips moving over every word. Time seems to stand still. The unpromising frown on his face proves to be a natural expression rather than an ill omen, and after one last searching look we are waved through. Nick says there may be two or three more such roadblocks. Now the road is straight and almost empty. What's more, it's a beautifully surfaced brand-new six-lane highway. The only possible hazard might be hitting a camel. There are 'Beware Camel' signs at regular intervals and fences along the sides of the road, yet clearly the ships of the desert haven't grasped the full implications of the Saudi road improvement programme, and insist on strolling across as if nothing had changed. Occasionally in the stony wilderness I see a camel herd being rounded up by Bedouin shepherds in Nissan pick-up trucks.

At lunchtime we stop for fuel, still about 300 miles short of Riyadh. I lay my portable thermometer on a wall as we fill up. When I pick it up it reads 50 Centigrade, 112 Fahrenheit, but the air is very dry and the temperature as bearable as 90 Fahrenheit was on the humid coast. The road continues straight and empty.

Most of the cars we see are wrecks, dragged off to the side of the road, bleached and rusting in the desert heat. I suppose it's cheaper for the owners (presuming they survive) to go and buy another car than haul the wreck off to a panel beater.

In the hour before sunset, the desert springs briefly to life. The slanting refracted sunlight, reddened by the dust, turns the blank face of rock and sand into a land of many colours – orange, deep reds, rich ochres and golds. This is the pitted, craggy, sandstone escarpment which leads to the plateau on which stands Riyadh. All around us are weirdly shaped pinnacles of rock, jutting up – like rotting teeth one moment, like the Sphinx the next. On top of all this is the city of Riyadh, built almost entirely in the last 15 years and one of the hottest capitals on earth. It is here because this central part of Arabia, the Nejd, is the home of the ruling house of Saud. It is as big, brash and booming as it is because the Saudis regard themselves as the natural leaders of the Arab world. That they have greater oil reserves and therefore more money than any other Arab country is not to them a coincidence, but a gift from Allah to help the country guard and preserve the two holiest places in the Muslim world – the shrines of Mecca and Medina.

So in this desert miles away from anywhere is this Las Vegas-like symbol of the fusion of the spiritual and commercial. In the neon-glowing streets, all spotless testimonials to the start of Fifth National Cleaning Week and the success of the previous four, glittering modern buildings rise above the old mud dwellings. There seems no attempt here to preserve the old city, as in Jeddah. Perhaps there was no old city. All is new and confident. It's Riyadh, Texas.

To the Al-Khozama hotel. Rather an anti-climax to have made our way to the heart of the Arabian Peninsula only to find that businessmen of every western country have got there first. In reception deals are being done and an English couple are arguing: 'The trouble with Arthur is, that Arthur's been out here too long.'

My spirits are revived by a lovely meal at a simple Lebanese restaurant. A meze with fresh radishes, mint, onions, lettuce and tomatoes as sweet and succulent as those we ate in Egypt, tahini, houmus with aubergine, then a mixed grill of tender and flavoursome shashlik and shish kebab.

Day 15 9 October

The *Arab Gazette* has a list of 'Today's Prayer Times', as well as the more valuable news that Sheffield United beat Wolves 2–0 in yesterday's League game. Nick is waiting for us outside Budget Rent-a-Car. He has arranged a car and driver to take us the 360 miles to the border with Qatar. We are not allowed to take a hire car across national borders, but he reckons that we should either be able to hitch, or pick up a taxi for the 60 miles across Qatar to the border of the United Arab Emirates. He has arranged for another hire car with driver to meet us there.

We leave Riyadh at 9.15. The temperature is 100 Fahrenheit, but dry and bearable. As we head out on another immaculate freeway – the Dammam Expressway – past the King Faud Security College and the Hyatt and Marriott Hotels, it's America again (but of course not *entirely* America, for no corporations, however rich and famous, are allowed here if they have any Jewish or Israeli connections). We pass modern tracking stations and more wrecked cars. Apparently there is no such thing as a driving test here and you can get a licence at the age of 13. Off the expressway and onto a single-carriageway road which bounces on interminably. Presently pipelines appear, my first view of the substance on which Saudi wealth is based, criss-crossing the landscape on their way from the refineries on the eastern horizon. Long-haired black sheep nestle up against the pipelines. The desert is whiter than anything I've seen so far. Bleached white.

We come to the town of Hofuf where the taxis are incongruous yellow Chevvies, like the checker cabs in New York. There is a huge centre here for the study of land reclamation, irrigation and fertilisation. One of the more encouraging aspects in a world which seems to be making every environmental mistake in the book is the Saudis' success in greening the desert. Plants are so tenacious. They cling desperately to life, and the grasslands outside Hofuf show what a difference a little help makes. I fall asleep. When I wake up I can hardly believe it, I'm looking out at the sea. My first view of the Persian Gulf. The air is salty and sticky again.

In marked contrast to most other public places in Saudi Arabia, the border crossing at Abu Samra is shabby and down-at-heel. As I crouch down at a window, proffering my passport and our authorisation, I notice a sniffer dog being walked along a collection of carrier bags belonging to some Arabs of little wealth going the other way. The authorities are very confused as to what we're doing here, and we are eventually shown into the presence of the top man. He motions us to sit down on a couple of armchairs, in whose arms large holes have been gouged, revealing torn and fleshy sponge-rubber beneath. He is a handsome, softly spoken man. His subordinates are progressively fatter and uglier leading me to wonder if promotion can be based on looks. With an elegant economy of movement he orders us to be looked after. A subordinate thrusts a form at us. 'Fill this!' he shouts. Another crosses to a rack of sports lockers on the wall, rummages around and produces an official stamp.

At 2.35 we are shown out of Saudi Arabia and into Qatar, country number ten in fifteen days.

The Qatari customs shed is not run down, just bare. I begin to wilt in the heat as we are slowly moved from desk to desk. One look around at this fly-blown place reveals a total absence of the hoped-for taxi. When we make enquiries, we're made aware of how much we need Nick, or someone with a little of the language. There is no taxi rank for 50 miles. Clem goes to try and phone up a car from Doha, the capital of Qatar, whilst I try my luck at cadging us a lift. Three friendly Qatari policemen let me share their hut. They assure me they'll find a vehicle going our way, with the two words that mean you're sunk in any language: 'No problem.'

They offer me their tea, and when I've drunk it, they order an Indian to fetch some more. Their names are Saalem, Omarj and Achmed. In between not getting me lifts, they ask about England. Omarj is going to London in December. I nod grimly: 'So am I, I hope.' They find this very funny.

Omarj holds his crotch unselfconsciously and talks of Princess Diana who came here a year ago. All testify to her beauty.

By now there are hardly any cars coming through and none want to take us. Clem is still in the guardhouse. We've been in Qatar for two and a half hours and moved fifty yards.

A truck driver from England pulls into the dusty compound. He's taken 11 days to drive his 40-tonner overland from England. (The thought occurs to me that if I'd come with him I'd be four days ahead.) He's not happy to be here at all. He had to go into Doha, to have his cargo inspected by a three million pound British Aerospace machine, for which he has nothing but contempt: 'They stick this vacuum tube direct to the lift to sniff for spirits. Well I've got half a hundredweight of paint-stripper aboard. It'll knock their bloody heads off!'

He waves a sheaf of customs papers in the direction of the guardhouse, now fading in the dusk: 'They're all new here. The old ones were alright. This lot don't know what they're doing.' It turns out that what irks him most of all is that he was asked to change into long trousers before they'd even look at his papers.

Neon lights flash on, off and finally on again at the top of the local minaret, bathing the place in a lurid blue glow. A pick-up truck goes through with two racing camels kneeling in the back. Amazing how neatly two camels fit in a Datsun.

At last our taxi arrives, and we are driven the 60 miles to Abu Nathil, the next Qatari border post. Here two bits of bad news are waiting. One is that though this may be the end of Qatar, it is not the beginning of the United Arab Emirates. There is another 60 miles of Saudi Arabia in between, and our driver is not allowed to cross this. Furthermore, the clocks are one hour ahead in the Emirates. The connection arranged for us by Nick will have given up and gone by the time we get there, and there's nothing we can do about it.

It's now 7.15 in the evening, and the Qatari customs here are even more obdurate. We wait our turn behind a Syrian truck driver, travelling with wife and children. More embarkation cards to fill in, more windows to be referred to. The sight of a cockroach at my feet making off with a crumb reminds me that I've only eaten a cheese sandwich since that far-off breakfast in Riyadh.

At last a piece of long overdue luck. A young Kuwaiti passes through with a brand-new red Mercedes 300, with the cellophane still on the seats. He speaks very little English, but his name is Hassan and he agrees to take us to the Emirates border. So we find ourselves racing across no-man's land, with the English channel of Emirates radio promising two hours of 'hard-driving rock' and Hassan tossing spent Pepsi cans into the desert.

Our next piece of luck is that our patient Indian hire-car driver, Vijay, is still waiting for us at the Emirates border, despite being treated shamefully rudely by a young, officious, Arab policeman.

We stop for a coffee at a transport café in the middle of nowhere. It's run by Indians, who sit outside, in the hot, dry night air, watching a Charles Bronson movie on video, at full volume. Sex and violence I can take, but sex, violence *and* noise is the worst of all. At one point the tape, obviously bootleg, mixes without an apparent break from the middle of a Bronson love scene to a wrestling match between two very fat Americans, before a crowd of many more very fat Americans. The Indians watching – slim, gentle people – appear not to notice the difference.

We drive off and I sleep again and in my dreams huge neon signs appear like mirages – 'Desert Springs Village', 'The Emirates Golf Club', 'The Dubai Metropolitan', 'Safeway Emirates', 'Beverage Filling Industries', 'The Princess Crown Beauty Centre, Specialists In Skin And Body Care'. But it's all real, and it's Dubai.

Uncrumple myself from the back seat. 2.20 a.m. We've been on the road over 17 hours, and travelled 660 miles. We're outside the Intercontinental Hotel, and I shall soon fall into the ninth bed since leaving London. And the most welcome.

Day 16 10 October

Woken from a five-hour sleep by the sound of a telephone at my bedside. Good news and bad news. The good news is that we have secured a dhow to take us to Bombay. The bad news is that it leaves at dawn tomorrow. No time for recovery before a six-day voyage on an open boat. On the other hand the sooner we move on the better. I must not forget that Phileas Fogg, aboard the *Mongolia* all the way, reached Bombay in eighteen days.

Walk out onto the quayside. My first sight of a dhow. Only nostalgic, crossword-loving Western romantics still call them dhows. To the locals they are 'launches' or 'coastal vessels'. They are wooden, built to a traditional design resembling in shape a slice of melon, with a high stern on which sits the wheelhouse, a draught of 15 or 20 feet, and a length of about 60 feet. There seems to be no shortage of them in Dubai. There are 20 or 30 lined up in this inlet of the river they call The Creek. One is loading crates of 'Tiger's Head' brand flashlights, made in China, 'Coast' full-cream milk powder, boxes of Tide washing powder, 'White Elephant' dry-battery cells, Sanyo radios and a twin-tub washing machine. Its destination is Berbera in Somalia.

Every one of the dhows is like a floating small business, and generally run by family and friends, though owned, as likely as not, by some shrewd import-exporter in a stretch Mercedes. They present quite a different dockside ambience from any I've experienced so far. Instead of cranes and gantries and hard-hats and bulk loads and lorries, operating behind guard posts and fences, the dhows are serviced, right in the centre of town, by small pick-up trucks, trolleys and men's backs. People bustle around, scrambling over the boats like ants, arranging, moving, heaving and hoisting the cargo. The reason for the great activity at the moment is that these are some of the first boats out after the monsoon season from May to August, during which the dhows are laid up because of storms.

In the afternoon we are taken by Kamis, an agent for the port and customs department, to see the boat that will be our home for the next week. The M.V. *Al Shama* (meaning 'Candlelight') is a trim, freshly painted ship, and her captain, Hassan Suleyman, bounds across the deckful of date sacks to welcome us. He smiles broadly and constantly, especially when giving us bad news, so it is a moment before it sinks in that he is telling us he will not be leaving tomorrow, but the next day, Wednesday, 12 October. Day 18.

All the time made up on the hectic scramble from Jeddah is suddenly lost again, but there is nothing we can do. Clem disappears to have words with the owners, Nigel and the other Passepartouts to the other end of the quay to film. I'm left with the taxi drivers. One nods towards the *Al Shama*. 'You go on that?' He clearly can't believe it. The other joins in. 'These boats no restaurant!' He shakes his head vigorously, mistaking my smile for disbelief. 'No clean, nowhere sleep!' Now they both shake their heads, like witches. 'It will be six, seven days, you know. Terrible ... Terrible! Three days on a dhow, fifteen in hospital!'

Day 17 11 October

A day's respite (which I am sure we will pay for later). Run along the side of the creek before breakfast, while the temperature is still down in the eighties. Much of Dubai is high-rise, prosperous and rich, but the area where the small ships unload must be much like it was before they first struck oil.

Kamis was telling me that the years of the Gulf War were boom years for these small boats. They could scuttle about the place, largely unnoticed, behind blockades, and away from heavily patrolled harbours. It was the dhows that kept Iran supplied throughout the war. I ask him who stands to gain from the peace, so recently broken out. The question perplexes him. 'For me ... they are all my people ... Iranians, Iraqis ... I see them all.' They're traders, not warriors, in Dubai.

Later in the day we visit the local supermarket for provisions. None of us is quite sure what we shall need, apart from my bag of rice, though drinking water seems a good idea. So in addition to 108 bottles of local spring water, we emerge with a motley assortment of Western delicacies, such as Spam, corned beef, tuna chunks, kitchen roll and digestive biscuits.

Buying bedding is more problematical. There seems to be no such thing as a camping shop and I end up buying a Czech Li-Lo from one shop, a soft cushion from somewhere else and at a third, a tastefully embroidered flowery pillow case, a stripy sheet and a blanket from China.

I make some phone calls home. Am I too garrulous? Do I betray in any way a nagging suspicion that I might never see anyone again? Steve at the office tells me that *A Fish Called Wanda* has now taken 53 million dollars in the USA. He must think my reaction ungratefully cool, but I'm wondering if I have enough codeine phosphate for the next week.

Day 18 12 October

Wake about 5.30. Recurring images of bags and baggage, loading and unloading, have filled my dreams. I'm tired but I can't go to sleep again. It's good old-fashioned nervous excitement. After all, I am about to experience something which nothing in my life has prepared me for. At breakfast an hour later even Ron Passepartout, who has been with the Pope to Paraguay and Madhur Jaffrey to Sulawesi, is strangely subdued.

According to the *Khaleej Times* the forecast for this part of the Gulf is a maximum of 99 degrees, waves 1 to 3 feet. Sea gentle and slight.

8.30: On board the *Al Shama* Captain Suleyman is beaming. Something must be wrong. It is. We won't be leaving quite as early as we thought, so plenty of time to settle in to our quarters. These appear to be on top of some boxes of sultanas where a flat space has been cleared and covered in a tarpaulin. The boat looks very spruce. The captain is proud of the fact that he has cleaned the paintwork, not just with ordinary water, but with drinking water.

Before we can leave, we must once again go through the tedious business of customs and immigration. Outside the immigration office several truckloads of gently bleating sheep stand in the sun. Inside a group of white-robed desert men cluster round our passports like surgeons at an operation. There follows the now familiar shaking of heads. Confusion followed by suspicion and aggression.

'What is *this*? Where is your Dubai visa?'

Kamis, dabbing at his face with a small white towel, argues wearily, brandishing papers. But like customs authorities the world over, these people always want the one extra piece of paper you never have.

On the wall above the unsmiling immigration officers are photos of the two sheiks of Dubai, who look worldly and cunning, with long, narrow noses and hard eyes. Clem says they live near Newmarket.

10.20: At last our dhow casts off. As we turn slowly out into the harbour I feel that regret at leaving which I've felt everywhere so far (with the exception of Riyadh and Qatar). Travellers depend so much on people, and have to place enormous trust in them. Strangers become friends quickly, but all too briefly, and I'm sorry to see Kamis with his ready smile and podgy, sweating face grow smaller on the dockside. Even our hard-bitten taxi drivers are waving.

We are flying the Indian red ensign, and a Muslim pennant with a crescent moon against a green background, and from the prow of the ship hangs a garland of flowers and paper decorations, an offering to the gods for a safe passage.

No sooner are we out of harbour than I am offered a glass of tea – of the kind Indians favour with evaporated milk and lots of sugar – by a burly man in a baseball hat who introduces himself as Osman. The rest of the crew, all Indians, Gujaratis from north of Bombay, cluster round me as I drink. None of them has more than a few words of English, but all insist on giving me their names, and they watch closely as I write them down, correcting my spelling punctiliously and sometimes gently removing my notebook and writing in it themselves.

There are eighteen of them, all from the same village, ranging in age from the two teenage cabin boys, Anwar and Hassan, to the venerable elders like Deyji Ramji, the navigator, who looks, in his brown corduroy cap, like some Oxford poetry don, and Kasim with the craggy face, beady eyes and stubbly grey beard of the Old Man Of The Sea. In fact there is a vaguely theatrical Arabian Nights air to the whole outfit. With their torn shirts and carefully patched trousers, shining teeth and wide smiles, they look like the chorus from a Christmas panto.

One of the quartermasters, Dahwood Adam, sets up two fishing lines trailing back on either side of the stern, making use of a hook, a length of nylon and a glittering piece of wrapping paper from a pack of biscuits. A huge container ship passes us. The bulky, top-heavy outlines of the stacked containers are so much uglier than the simple lines of the dhow. As she passes I notice her name – *Orient Express* – and feel perhaps there is a guiding and coordinating hand behind this crazy journey after all.

First lunch on the dhow: thick, juicy rice with lentils and curried vegetables; pears, grapes and apples (sliced) for us. The food is prepared in a galley the size of a large dog kennel by Ali Mamoun, whose hat says 'Buick'. We eat in a patch of shade provided by canvas sheeting slung across the boom and made fast to the temporary scaffolding rail which girdles the ship and is the only barrier between the date sacks and the deep blue sea. Beneath the tarpaulin it's 98 Fahrenheit. Eating a curry in such conditions is like taking a hot water bottle into a sauna.

Gingerly try out the lavatories which consist of two wooden barrels, open to the elements and suspended over the ocean on either side of the stern. The base of the barrel has two wooden footrests on either side of a T-shaped aperture. Both these appendages have been painted a tasteful pale blue. I clamber in and settle down, feeling slightly ridiculous, like a character in an Edward Lear drawing. Later I realise I was facing the wrong way. I should have been looking out to sea.

Talking later to Passepartout it transpires that what we all fear, even more than sharks, pirates or a resumption of the Gulf War, is to miss our footing whilst clambering onto the loo in the middle of the night. What a way to go.

In the middle of the afternoon Osman, with a shy, schoolboy smile which belies his bulk, brings us, not just tea, but a selection of Huntley and Palmers assorted biscuits which would not have disgraced a Knightsbridge soirée. We are nibbling at the corner of a Garibaldi when there is a shout and everyone rushes to the stern. Momentary anxiety that Ron may have fallen through the toilet is dispelled when it turns out they've caught a fish on one of the trailing lines. It's a *gedri*, which we think is probably tuna. The indefatigable Ali Mamoun has it cooked and served for us by sundown, with lentils and chapattis.

Afterwards, having ascertained that the captain will not be offended as the crew are Muslims and take no alcohol, we're enjoying a nightcap of gin and tonic or in my case a glass of Glenmorangie malt whisky when the engine cuts out. The captain and the engineer disappear down below. There are sounds of protest, indignation and recrimination from the engine room. Deyji Ramji lights two incense sticks and waves them before the flag, and Kasim and Sali Mamoun, a short powerfully built older man with a peaceful face, are praying in the bows. Suddenly, I feel a little vulnerable. It's getting dark, there's no wind to fill a sail, there's no radio or radar on board and we're drifting slowly towards the Straits of Hormuz.

Day 19   13 October

Sometime in the middle of the night the sound of the engine, now restored to life, mingles with shouts and the rustling of feet about the boat. Orders and counter-orders. Sounds like another crisis. Blearily look around me to find that there are enormous craggy rocks rearing up on either side of us. We are squeezing through a narrow channel, less than a mile wide, without the help of any navigational machinery, and in the dead of night. It's a considerable test of skill for the captain. What he seems most concerned about is the presence of other ships in these labyrinthine waters, hence his shouted orders to various watchers along the rails. None of this feels like the twentieth century at all. It's as if I'm back in some ancient legend, and I half expect the rocks to transmogrify into vast mythical creatures.

Wake again about six o'clock, with the first light of dawn. We are now through Hormuz and into the Gulf of Oman. There is nothing to see at all but flat, calm empty sea. Later, just to make sure that what I'd seen in the night was no dream, I checked the charts, and found that we had indeed made a complicated passage around the Mussandam Peninsula, past Perforated Rock and the Elphinstone Inlet, and other points in a ragged archipelago just off the northern tip of Oman.

All is pretty quiet aboard the *Al Shama* this morning, the crew lie curled up on various parts of the deck, sleeping off the night's activity. Ali Mamoun, of course, is awake, already making chapattis and brewing tea. A small rattan mat of many colours is produced for us, and our breakfast of omelette, chapatti, jam and fresh oranges laid out on it.

As we're eating the sea around us turns leaden and heavy. We're passing through the thick, viscous smear of an oil slick. It extends for several miles, and is so obscene it silences us all. Osman being flat on his back against a sack of pistachio nuts, Mahomet has taken his role as our guardian. Mahomet, wafer-thin and with a crop of curly black hair, is the father of Anwar, the cabin boy, and brother of the captain. He speaks more English than most because he worked for a while as an international seaman. He produces a carefully kept notebook which lists the details of all his journeys away from home. The time he left, the time he returned, all neatly rounded up to a grand total of nine years, seven months and three days away. He will receive 300 rupees for this journey, about £20, but he's much happier to be working for this company than for the P&O group. Here he's with friends and family and though no one gets rich, everyone is in it together. As they all wake up they're eager to see how we're getting on. First we practise the names. They try to catch me out, producing shy crew members whose names they think I'll have forgotten. 'Mi-kel ... who this?' The homework I did yesterday has stood me in good stead, and if in doubt I just say Mohammed.

They are fascinated by my map of Asia, and when I spread it out it gives the better-travelled crew members a chance to show off. Many of them have been down the East African coast, to Somalia and Kenya, and one has been as far as Madagascar. Only Mahomet and his brother, the captain, have seen the world.

The captain appears late, rubbing his hands through thinning hair and apologising for all the upheaval in the night. His ablutions are extraordinarily thorough, especially in the oral department. Using his forefinger and regular ingestions of water he massages the inside of his mouth with a zeal and ferocity which seems almost manic, as if devils are being expelled. I think he's quite concerned about health and hygiene for he comes and squats beside me later and says he is very keen to know if there is treatment in London for '(a) Cancer, (b) Diabetes, (c) Receding Hair'.

At about 10.30 Deyji Ramji produces his sextant and stands on the starboard side pressing the instrument to his eye and steadying it on his chin. Then he produces a small gold-backed pocketbook, makes a note, disappears into the wheelhouse, consults various charts and comes up with our position, which this morning, October 13th, is 57.30 E and 25.0 North ... about 100 miles south of the coast of Iran. The captain estimates our arrival in Bombay in six days. Ron groans. I don't think he's got into the spirit of the thing yet.

Kasim, The Old Man Of The Sea, is showing a marked interest in my Walkman. I'm listening to Springsteen. I offer him the machine and he seems delighted. Give him a quick rundown on the controls and leave him to it. A little while later I see him, face wreathed in a smile, head rocking from side to side, eyes wide with excitement. Only when I've taken the set back from him do I realise he's been playing 'Incident on 57th Street' at full volume.

Tonight there are flashes of lightning on the southern horizon. There could be storms tomorrow. To bed feeling a little apprehensive. Bad weather would hit a boat like this very hard.

Day 20   14 October

Somewhere a long way away it's my wife's birthday and *A Fish Called Wanda* is being shown to the British public for the first time. Here in the Gulf of Oman my chief preoccupation is avoiding seasickness. During the night I was aware of a freshening wind and a not unpleasant increase in the ship's movement. Now, at 6.30 I'm feeling rather ill. The waves are coming in at a height of five or six feet and the wind from the south is causing a sideways roll to add to the impressive pitching and rising of the bows ahead. We have some anti-sickness plasters which have to be stuck on behind the ear, from which a chemical called scopolamine is released into the system, preventing nausea. All of us stick them on, making ourselves look like initiates of some new religion, apart from Nigel Passepartout, who seems quite unaffected by the rise and fall of the *Al Shama*. He has his camera out already and is trying to set up a prize-winning shot of old Kasim asleep with the sun rising behind his nose. Unfortunately everyone keeps tripping over the recumbent old man and waking him. When he sees the camera he is delighted and turns and stares into the lens with a fixed grin. Nigel gives up.

The last few feet of the bow area are reserved for washing. A plank, laid vertically across the deck, serves to run the water away and allows a certain modesty cover, but basically, the bathroom, like the lavatory and the bedroom on the *Al Shama*, is al fresco. Once the morning ablutions are done (and the Gujaratis are compulsive washers) the bathroom becomes a kitchen extension and now (8 o'clock) Ali Mamoun is preparing the lunch, rolling red chillies on a stone, and then chopping aubergines and onions.

A fish bites and we all rush to the stern, where for a moment a *gedri* of Moby-Dickish proportions breaks the surface and skids and spatters along the water allowing us just enough of its time to create tremendous excitement before flicking off the line almost disdainfully and returning to the depths.

With breakfast before seven and very little to do for the next twelve hours, time passes slowly. I finish *Stanley and His Women* and wade into a thick Spanish novel called *Fortunata and Jacinta*. But mostly I sleep. The sun becomes so strong that most parts of the boat are too hot to stand on, and simply moving around is highly energy-consuming. There are regular false fish alarms. At these times the *Al Shama* resembles a Second World War aerodrome, with combatants suddenly scrambling into action, only to reach the stern, bearing cameras and tape recorders, to find that yet another has got away.

After yesterday's dose of Springsteen on the Walkman, today I offer the crew Oistrakh's Brahms Violin Concerto. Anwar listens for quite a while before pronouncing it, 'Great disco!' Anwar tries a little bit more English on me each day. He's learnt it at school. Hassan his colleague knows only two words, 'Mi-kel' and 'Jack-son'. Whenever he sees me he grins manically and shouts, 'Mi-kel! Mi-kel Jack-son!'

I, in turn, press on with my Gujarati. I'm pretty handy with 'Thank you' (*mehrbani*), 'Good morning' (*salaam aligam*) and today, after a very good lunch, I embarked on 'Congratulations'

(*Mubarakhi*) and the less problematical *Thik-Thak* ('Hey man! Everything's OK').

Weather conditions improve during the day and seasickness is avoided. The captain informs us that we have just left the Gulf of Oman and are now in what he calls the 'Big Sea', the Arabian Sea. There is no land south of us now until Antarctica. Only ocean, through which we are making our way, at eight knots an hour, a pace at which many marathon runners could overtake us. The natural world assumes a much greater significance out here. The sky and the sea are watched anxiously. Apart from the fish alarms, the sight of a school of porpoises loping by or flying fish skimming across our bows can be the highlight of a morning, and now, at five o'clock, I find myself waiting impatiently for the next entertainment – the sunset. It's quite a short show, only about half an hour, but on a clear day like today, the view is immaculate and of course quite unobstructed. I watch every detail down to the five-minute climax when the golden ball comes to rest magnificently on the horizon before being squashed, squeezed and distorted out of sight, returning for a final brief manifestation as a shimmering disc on the surface of the sea, signalling that it's time for the infidels to get amongst the gin and Glenmorangie.

There's no lights out, because the lights never go out. So we're in bed by 7.30, looking up at the stars. Ron tunes in to BBC World Service for the 8 o'clock news from London. Gorbachev's proposed reform of Soviet agricultural policy seems wonderfully irrelevant.

I drift off to yet more sleep with a last lingering image of Nigel's head, with a miner's lamp-style torch strapped around it, protruding from his sleeping bag reading about another dhow trip in Gavin Young's *Slow Boats to China*.

Day 21 15 October

Fourth day on the dhow and life increasingly resembling that of a nursing home – waking with the dawn, then visiting, first the barrel, then the bows, making sure we take a bottle of our 'Jeema' mineral water for cleaning the teeth. Like invalids, all our movements are a little unsteady, what with the roll of the boat, the unevenness of the sacks and the necessity of having to virtually climb overboard to reach the loo.

Our Gujarati nurses have meanwhile prepared us a morning cup of tea which we drink slowly, comparing our sleeping experiences. Having compared notes and confirmed to an increasingly despondent Ron that there is absolutely no chance of us being in a nice comfortable hotel for at least four days, we then tidy our beds away (to the self-contained Gujaratis, with their neat bedrolls, our elaborate deflating of Li-Los and folding of striped sheets must look ridiculous) and turn the bedroom into the day-room. Our mat is laid out and breakfast taken. The crew will let us do nothing to help with the running of the boat, further fostering the nurse–patient relationship.

It's mid-morning. A fish alarm goes unheeded by the camera team who are playing backgammon. It turns out to be a whale, about a hundred yards off the port side spouting water every twenty seconds or so.

What have my books taught me today in my odd waking moments? That *tertulias* were, in nineteenth-century Spain, semi-informal meetings for conversation. We have a *tertulia* over lunch, the upshot of which is that it's decided we should film the sail going up this afternoon. The captain checks wind direction and speed with a quick look at the flag and seems unenthusiastic. He's clearly more comfortable with his 280 h.p. British-made Kelvin diesel engine.

Good news – we have travelled 204 miles in the last 24 hours, as opposed to 197 the day before. But there are still 720

miles between us and Bombay. Like a model patient I'm in bed
and tucked up at some ludicrously early hour. The soft lapping
of the waves and the steady chug of the Kelvin set a soporific
mood and the last detail I remember of the world is that
Sheffield United have won 2–1 at Blackpool.

Day 22 16 October

The boat really comes to life at first light which, as we are
moving east and have not yet adjusted our watches, comes a
little earlier each day. I'm awake today at 5 a.m. The wind has
dropped and the sea is flat and calm. Over the reassuring
rumble of the engine I can hear the soft sound of singing. Pull
myself up on an elbow and look towards the bows. There is
Kasim, standing motionless and in perfect silhouette, looking
out to sea and chanting. Beside him two or three others are
gathering in the small foresail.

"ello Mi-kel!"

'Mi-kel, Mi-kel Jack-son!'

As soon as they see we're awake someone is taken off
foresail lashing and sent to arrange some tea for us. One of the
things this traveller has learnt is that those who have least are
prepared to give most. This crew has given up a lot for us –
sleeping space, living space and precious fresh water – without
ever making us feel obligated or tolerated. Their life is
communal, they depend on each other rather than machines,
and maybe because of this their attitude to us materially
overstocked and somewhat stand-offish Westerners has been
unfailingly generous and helpful.

The captain takes a look at the sea and removes his cap,
scratches his head and shakes it respectfully. 'We are lucky
men,' he says. He's rarely seen it quite as calm, and he knows
the power of the sea, for in a storm last year, his brother's ship
was sunk and 18 drowned.

The captain and his navigator sleep in the back of the wheelhouse. A new music centre and a pair of speakers are the only luxury. The only printed books appear to be navigational charts and almanacs. The front of the wheelhouse contains, apart from the wheel, a compass, a clock that's stopped, a throttle control and a bell that's rung every time the fish-line is sprung. There is also a panel of dials indicating engine r.p.m., water temperature and oil pressure. None of these is working.

Under the wheelhouse is a fetid, windowless airless cabin which I hope we never have to make use of. The temperature in there hovers constantly at 100 degrees, and Julian and Ron, who have to go in to load film and change stock, emerge pounds lighter. The corresponding aft cabin is full of the crew's trunks. They are allowed one each in which they can import certain items free of duty. A perk of the job.

Captain Suleyman says the Indian customs are very strict. No gold or guns.

'Is there then much smuggling?' I ask him.

'Oh, plenty smuggling … in clothes, wristwatches … but,' he reassures me, '*we* are not smugglers,' and laughs uproariously.

Midday: 92 Fahrenheit under the awning. We're due south of Karachi. Looking at my map I observe that it has taken us a day to travel between the 'A' and the 'R' of 'Arabian Sea'.

Sunday afternoon on the *Al Shama*. The crew sit round watching us read or sleep or listen to our headsets. They're curious but never intrusive. My fat Spanish novel intrigues them. How could anyone hold a book of such size, let alone write it, and why does it make Mi-kel's eyes close so frequently?

Suddenly there is some sea-borne entertainment. Dahwood, at the wheel, has spotted dolphins approaching the boat. They gather ahead of us, lazily and luxuriously rolling around in the bow wave, weaving in and out, diving, backtracking, returning and always keeping just ahead of the boat. The crew encourage them with drumbeats and whistles. As soon as they know there's an audience the dolphins show off shamelessly. For a magical few minutes they stay and play. The sea is so blue and clear it is one of the most remarkable and beautiful sights of the journey so far, rivalled a little later by the raising of the huge sail.

All hands are needed for this task, for there are no mechanical pulleys, no cables or electric winches. It's all done by human effort. Rather as they encouraged the dolphins they now encourage each other, chanting and singing as they pull on the rope. Once it's up, Kishoor and Haroun shin deftly up to the top of the 20-foot mast and release the cords that bind the sail, which billows down, revealing a much patched and stained canvas. But against the sky at night with a big moon shining it looks impressive and very beautiful. Indeed this is the most pleasing evening so far. Lying in bed beneath the boom with the sail spread out above and beyond it the clearest of night skies is almost perfectly peaceful. There is a request from Nigel to make it totally peaceful by turning off the engine. This produces a sharp cry of horror from Ron's bed! But engine or no engine it is the sort of moment when you would be quite happy for time to freeze.

Day 23 17 October

Having overdosed on happiness and contentment I pay the price a few hours later when an ungrateful stomach has me out of bed and swaying dangerously toward the barrel soon after midnight. Fierce acidic discomfort persists and I have to make three visits to the stern during the night. Each time I feel worse and each time I'm greeted warmly by the crew. Any hopes of slipping quietly by and enjoying my misery in private are out of the question. They all seem to be awake, and as I totter across the sacks of dates, on the point of nausea and clutching my lavatory paper, a chorus rises from the darkness:

'Mi-kel! ...'Ello Mi-kel ...'

'Mi-kel, Mi-kel Jack-*son*!'

And even more poignantly, 'Mi-kel ... 'ow are yoo?'

The first time I react very Britishly, with a complete fib: 'Fine ... fine, thank you!'

But later when my resistance is lower it's not so easy to be British about it: 'Mi-*kel*, 'ow are yoo?'

'Not at all well!'

'Good, Mi-kel!'

It doesn't really seem to make a scrap of difference what I say. They're just pleased to see me, whether white as a sheet and carrying an ever-decreasing roll of loo-paper or not. On my third and most traumatic visit they actually ask me to come and eat something with them, which at that moment is a bit like offering a vegetarian a job in a butcher's shop. I clamber back into my pit feeling sorry for myself and a cockroach walks over my head. By the time dawn comes the idyll has gone. There's nothing like feeling ill to make you want to be at home, and the smell of the morning omelette and chapatti induces a sudden feeling of imprisonment.

But outside the boat things are happening this Monday morning. We are now in the much shallower waters of the continental shelf and the captain shouts as he sees the marker buoys of a large fishing net. Apparently there are always fish to be found on the periphery of these nets. He orders the quartermaster to turn the ship smartly about.

Soon both lines are twitching and a 25 to 30 lb *arbrous* practically falls into the ship. No one seems to know quite what to do with it especially as a *gedri* has been caught at the same time, and the wretched fish lies panting in the bows, its tail flicking ever more weakly until an expert can spare the time to kill it.

By 8.30 a.m, four sizeable fish have been caught and everyone's looking not only pleased but relieved. Up till now the sea has not been fruitful. Ali Mamoun sets to producing his much-vaunted fish biryani and suddenly all the talk is of food.

They must notice that I'm not joining in with my customary ebullience, and Kasim seems especially concerned. He stands over me like some craggy bird for a while then indicates my stomach and rubs. I nod and offer the appropriate grimace. Kasim then indicates that I should turn over on my stomach. The accumulated wisdom of many years at sea is not to be questioned, but I'm certainly not prepared for what happens next. Kasim starts slowly and agonisingly to walk up and down my body, starting at my ankles and working his way along my spine. He's surprisingly light, but when his prehensile feet come into contact with my tender muscles the pain is excruciating. Kasim, quite unmoved by my cries, continues his walk.

There's no doubt about it, Kasim's feet are precision instruments, even if they are applied rather ruthlessly, and inasmuch as I can no longer remember which parts of my body hurt before he began, he's been successful. As he was busy realigning my spine, and Passepartout, with a certain amount of sadistic relish, was recording my cries, the prospect of a new form of TV chat show occurred to me, in which the host would talk to famous people whilst walking on them.

We are 200 miles from Bombay. Ron gloomily observes that this is the distance from which planes begin their descent into Bombay airport. *Our* approach is going to take two days. I must say that I am now beginning to feel very Ronnish. A dhow is not a good place to feel unwell – there really is nowhere to go and lick the wounds. The thought of Bombay, bed and bath seems irresistibly attractive.

The captain is concerned about me. 'You are sick, sick man,' he says and orders me to be brought his patent remedy, a glass of 7-Up with drops of lemon, knocked back in one go. This causes me to belch thunderously, after which all is well for a while.

*

Evening: Have not eaten today and worst of all the Glenmorangie has lost its attraction, so I am ill-prepared for the news that I shall not be in my bed in Bombay tomorrow night after all. The reason is that we shall reach Bombay at 7 in the evening and the Indian customs (keeping British Raj hours) close at 5. The captain does not want to spend the night in a busy harbour and is proposing we cut speed and wait a few miles out, dragging out our final approach until the morning of Wednesday, 19 October. I'm now likely to be a week behind Fogg at Bombay. I've lost so much time since Suez that an extra day doesn't seem to matter any more. By the law of averages we must have some good luck too.

Day 24 18 October

An air of anticlimax hangs over the boat. The elation of the first few days has been replaced by impatience and now resignation. At one time on the dhow I wanted time to stand still; now that it is, I just feel frustrated.

Our speed has been cut to four knots, a pervasive odour of fish hangs over the boat, for most of yesterday's catch is being dried for the return voyage. *Fortunata and Jacinta* is a terrible translation and I'm going to have to abandon it after 150 pages, which I always feel is a bit of a defeat. As I'm not eating I feel my energy reserves dwindling. Nowhere on the boat is comfortable any more. The clear bright skies are gone and it's cloudier, humid and very still. Even the weather seems to be waiting for something to happen.

The captain is less relaxed the nearer we get to Bombay. An Indian navy vessel passes slowly and he eyes it unhappily. Apparently they occasionally come aboard and ask awkward questions about gold wristwatches, especially if they know you are from Dubai.

The navy boat disappears over the horizon. The captain has a new stomach-cure for me today, 7-Up and black pepper.

Kishoor, the slim, dark engineer with big sensuous eyes, erects a screen in the bows before having a shower. This occasions the only real guffaws of the day. Apparently he is going to shave his entire body. When I ask why, I'm told, with much giggling, that his wife prefers him that way. At dusk more oil platforms sprout on the horizon, flaming away like mini-sunsets. Kasim walks on me again, and perhaps because I'm prepared for it, I don't react quite so pathetically.

Our seventh and last night on the dhow should be celebrated but, as the *Al Shama* turns in aimless circles, wasting time, Passepartout and I are subdued and quite soon get our heads down, taking refuge in the world of personal stereo whilst the crew sit round in groups, talking, for most the of the night. There's an end of term feeling aboard, and I feel that our inertia must be something of a disappointment to them.

Day 25 19 October

Wake to the sound of crackling cooking oil. Ali Mamoun is making puris (deep-fried fluffy pancakes) as a farewell meal. My stomach has now recovered sufficiently to make me feel hungry for the first time in 48 hours, but there's precious little time to eat. The captain shouts and points into the teeth of a welcome easterly wind.

'Bombay!'

The engines, which have been idle most of the night, are restarted.

Anwar is very excited. 'Indies ... Indies!' he keeps shouting to me.

The grey mist is lifting and revealing a long, tall, unexpectedly modern skyline, which surprises me – I'd expected Bombay to be low-rise and cluttered. I can now make out my destination – the Gate of India, a triumphal arch erected for the visit of George V in 1910. But first we have to go on, southwards to the Hay Bunder, the dhow port, passing a lot of ill-kept and rusty-hulled freighters and the navy base containing the largest warship I've seen so far, the 16,000-ton ex-British aircraft carrier *Vikrant* (née *Hercules*).

At about ten o'clock we are opposite the port, but as the dhow cannot go alongside until customs and immigration have come aboard, the crew prepare to weigh anchor. This procedure, like raising the sail, involves all hands – old men and boys, side by side, releasing the anchor and lowering it into the murky water. Scavenging crows board the ship, followed by three well-built customs men in dark glasses.

So the time comes to say goodbye to the people in whose hands we have entrusted our lives for the last week. It's been a unique relationship, for I can't imagine any other circumstances in which we would have become so close so quickly to people like this, and of course it's hard to come to terms with the fact that it must end so peremptorily. But I clutch a batch of addresses and Kasim clutches me and I climb down the rope ladder to waves and smiles and 'Goodbye Mi-kels!' Then my launch speeds me to the quayside and I know I shall never see them again and I shall miss them.

Into Indian customs 'F' Division hut. Seeing men in unpatched shirts is quite a shock. Their uniforms are clean and crisply pressed, which is something of a contrast to the general condition of the hut, which looks like somewhere commandeered behind the lines in wartime – dusty with cracked walls and a sackcloth ceiling. There is no door, but a curtain. The officers are very charming. Then outside to meet the owners of the dhow. There are two of them, sharply dressed in the manner of international hairdressers – Cuban heels, expensive shoes, Afro haircuts. They stand holding hands on the quayside and seem to have little to say to us.

Then back into a small launch to take me to the Gate of India. Despite its name no one enters India through it any longer, apart from royalty I suppose, so it's a very curious feeling to scramble off here, with my bags, clothes crumpled from seven days in a dhow. There are snake charmers and drug pushers and men with monkeys and women with babies and outstretched hands. Indian life is no respecter of great monuments, especially one so prominently associated with alien domination, nor does Indian life have to be sought out in back streets and certain quarters of town. It begins, like the heady, warm smell of spice and manure, as soon as you set foot on the land.

A hundred yards further on I am confronted by a completely different world again – a world of turbaned doormen, Mercedes limousines, air-conditioning and American Express. The world of the Taj Mahal Hotel. I'd been dreaming about its soft beds and clean sheets for days but now I'm here, grubby and unshaven in the lobby, I find it sour and rather objectionable. For a week I've been in a world where rank, class and social distinction don't exist. Now I see it all around me. Of course I'm happy to be comfortable and to be looked after and to enjoy the style and splendour of the hotel but I hope I never forget the values of simplicity, honesty and unselfishness which I associate with the *Al Shama*.

A copy of the *Indian Express* is in my room. The government is thinking of lowering the voting age to 18. A stay of execution has been granted on two assassins of Mrs Gandhi and on the entertainments page I see there is a play in Bombay called *No Sex Please, We're Hindustani*. It's billed as 'The Ultimate Laugh Riot'.

Spend an afternoon unwinding, and checking my onward plans. I hear that all is not well for the next connection in Madras. The ship I was relying on has been delayed to mid-November and the only alternative, so far, has no room. All the timetables have been disrupted by a dock-workers' strike in Bombay.

In the evening I walk along the Apollo Bunder, which extends along the waterfront from the Taj, enjoying the street life, the old-fashioned and ubiquitous Ambassador cars, the smells, the crumbling hotels on the front called 'Evelyn' and 'Shelley's' – the ever-present parody of Britain. It's better than being a parody of America, which is what Saudi Arabia was. There's a big, bright noisy party being held out on a pier. Folk dance inside which looks like an Indian Morris dance. Much striking of sticks. Sends me to bed happy, on my first night in Asia.

Day 26 20 October

'It's out of the question for a sane man to spend his life jumping from one steamer onto a train and from a train onto a steamer, on the pretext of going round the world in eighty days! No, all these antics will come to an end in Bombay, you can be sure of that.'

I pondered on Passepartout's words as I lay in bed after waking at dawn from a night during which my room had very gently rocked from side to side. Passepartout's gloomy prediction is nearer to my experience than his own. He and Fogg arrived here in eighteen days, and left on a train across India within three and a half hours, during which time Fogg saw nothing of the city save for the inside of the station restaurant, where he was served with cat disguised as rabbit.

I'm eight days behind Fogg, and as yet I have no onward passage from Madras to Singapore. The dhow was a wonderful week out of life; now the realities must be faced and some clear thinking done. But somehow Bombay is not the best city, nor India the best subcontinent for clear thinking.

It's quiet now on the quayside below me, though I'm sure I heard marching bands and a confusion of drumbeats and explosions in the early hours. All I can see from my window are children and street sellers around the Gate of India and pigeons wheeling and flapping about the façade of the hotel. The fussy little balconies and turrets which project from every sea-view room are a pigeon's delight and, judging by the thick encrustations of bird lime, have been since the hotel was opened eighty years ago. Walk down to breakfast. The layout of rooms along open galleries leading off a central staircase gives the impression of a sumptuous prison. There are huge arrangements of flowers about the place and I make the mistake of asking the lady who's setting them out if they're real.

'Of course they're real,' she replies admonitorily, 'this is India, not Hong Kong.'

I glean from her the reason for the unnatural quiet on the Apollo Bunder, and the noises in the early hours which, like another traveller in the Indies, Waugh's Gilbert Pinfold, I'd begun to think were my imaginings. Today is a festival day called Durga Puja, the climax of a ten-day celebration of the triumph of good over evil. There are at least seven different New Years in India, depending on when the harvest is brought in. Effigies up to 50 feet tall will be carried through the streets and destroyed to commemorate the killing of the evil king Ravenah of Sri Lanka by Lord Rama. The celebration of myth and the belief in the supernatural is an important part of Indian life, and on this festival day it is customary to bless whatever brings you your livelihood. So the soldier garlands his rifle and the photographer his camera and the farmer his plough and so on. This is called *puja*, meaning worship, and would probably explain the garland on the prow of the *Al Shama* as she left Dubai.

I venture into the streets of Bombay in search of someone to remove eight days' growth of beard. If you look around with only reasonable diligence you can find someone on the street to do anything for you. I end up opposite the grand Gothic pile of Victoria Terminal – one of the most gushingly elaborate station exteriors in the world. Sandwiched in between a professional letter writer and a man who organises mongoose and snake fights, I find a barber who shaves me then and there on the grubby pavement with a cut-throat razor. Not something I shall tell my mother about, especially as I'm convinced from the way his fingers rather than his eyes seek out my face that he is blind. By the time he's finished shaving me, a crowd has gathered that would not disgrace a third division football club. The barber completes the shave by rubbing my face with a smooth piece of alum, a crystal-like stone which is used as an antiseptic.

Passepartout is more interested in the mongoose and snake attraction next door, but as soon as the presence of the camera is detected, the snakes are popped back in their baskets and a furious row ensues. It seems their owner knows all about world television rights and he negotiates with a single-mindedness that would assure him of a vice-president's job in any Hollywood studio. A man with a hooded cobra in one hand has to be listened to. The 'fight' itself is a pathetic and ugly affair. The mongoose, looking terrified throughout, is not only chained to a stone, but has its front legs tethered so that it couldn't kill the snake even if it wanted to. The snake man tries to introduce a note of danger by continually ordering back the fly-blown street children who are his chief audience. But the mongoose is clearly not interested in exterminating any snakes today and has to be forcibly yanked upwards to simulate aggression. Of the five snakes kept in baskets, only the cobra looks fit; the rest are dry and docile. This whole grubby spectacle takes place only a few hundred yards from the bewhiskered bust of Lord Elphinstone and his fellow Victorians whose idea of civilising India was to build massive public buildings in the architectural style of a continent five thousand miles away.

The oldest surviving English building in Bombay is a more modest affair than the Victoria Terminal. It's a church, with a simple perpendicular tower, completed in 1718 and full of sad memorials to those who, by and large, died young and far away from home. Of 'cholera, aged 32', of 'wounds received at Lucknow, in the mutiny, aged 23'. Now it is St Thomas's

Cathedral, the main Christian church of Bombay. I assume
wrongly that it is frequented by the English community, but the
priest in charge tells me that the congregation consists entirely
of native Christians, and that Christianity, far from being a relic
of the Raj, is the third most popular religion in India, after
Hinduism and Islam.

The key to India's remarkable success as the world's largest
democracy is, he says, tolerance. There are 16 different
religions in India and all respect each other. There are, on one
Indian banknote, 14 different languages, all of which are
protected.

On my way back to the hotel I find the road blocked by
chanting crowds who are milling around slow-moving trucks
carrying effigies of the goddess Kali and making a lot of noise;
banging cymbals, dancing and singing. They have crimson
powder all over them and the Indian photographer who is with
me says that their wild stares are probably the result of a certain
amount of ganja. 'Join in!' he urges, and leaving me to be swept
along towards the Gate of India he rushes off to get some shots.
I don't know what's happening, except that I'm the only white
man there and I'm being carried along in the crush toward the
great arch and the sea. At about the spot where I landed
yesterday they begin to submerge their goddesses, tossing in
garlands, offerings in small clay pots and, very often,
themselves. Some of the more intense disappear beneath the
muddy waters for a minute or more, to reappear jubilantly
soaked. There is an edge of hysteria which I'm glad to escape
from unscathed.

Day 27 21 October

Extraordinary night of dreams. A series of benevolent
nightmares on the theme of travelling but never arriving.
Recurring images of friends and home veering wildly from the

modern (new information systems being installed at Swiss Cottage Underground) to a Hardyesque world of country pubs and masques and morris dances. An Indian postal official dumps his sports bag in my car, I try desperately to ring my wife and tell her why I'm in Washington D.C. with George Harrison and the next moment I'm driving a Mini over a ploughed field. The reality is that I'm in India, which is more bizarre than any of my dreams. I read in my *Times of India* at breakfast that fourteen people were killed yesterday in a stampede at Jamshedpur during the immersion of their goddess in the local river.

Taxi to Victoria Terminal to collect my rail tickets for tomorrow. On the way we pass a shop called Dogy Items and another mellifluously named The Lovely Steel Centre. Traffic conditions in Bombay are anarchic. Pedestrians and cows have as much right to be in the road as cars and this makes for a constant disorderly fight for space. My cab has a sticker on the dashboard which reads 'Trust in God'.

Despite the noise and heat and smell at Victoria Terminal, the faces in the crowd show none of the tension, anxiety or pent-up anger which you can see any morning or evening at a London main-line station. I think it boils down to tolerance again. The Indians do not betray impatience. They accept everyone's right to be wherever they are. Thus poverty and appalling destitution, malnutrition and deformity are on public view, but nervous breakdowns are almost unknown. The ticket office presents the modern face of India, all smoked glass and VDU screens. They're very proud of it and I am asked if I will sign their Distinguished Visitors Book. The head man stands over me as I write and prompts me. 'Yes, just there please … Staff all very cooperative, very good conditions … nice and modern. Thank you.'

And I'm out again, clutching my seat reservation, into the street with its blind and limbless beggars alongside red pillar boxes and 1930s-style double-decker buses.

There are more aspects of British India left than just the buses and the pillar boxes. The world's largest democracy drives on the left and plays cricket. The English language unites north and south and east and west of a country that has no other common tongue. But India remains, like few other countries in the world, its own place, the archetypal non-aligned nation, putting self-sufficiency before luxury, a social and economic buffer-zone between the thrusting certainties of Western and Oriental capitalism.

I end the day at the Chowpatty beach. From here the tower blocks of Nariman Point make the Bombay skyline twinkle like Manhattan. Here on the beach at night is a public massage school, where students try out their technique on anyone willing to take the risk. I settle for a scalp massage. It's so powerful that I actually worry at one point that his fingers may enter my head, in a sort of digital acupuncture.

Day 28   22 October

In order to convince some of the sceptical friends who haunt my dreams at night that I am not mocking all this up in a BBC studio I have undertaken to try and bring back various items as proof of travel. One has asked for an Indian astrological chart for their first child, expected next April. It so happens that the Taj is the only hotel I know of in the world which has a resident astrologer. So this Saturday morning I repair to Mr Jagjit Uppal, a pleasant, soft-spoken man with a serene but disturbingly impenetrable smile. Astrology, he confirms, plays a big part in Indian life and he is regularly consulted by businessmen, politicians and film stars. He needs to know only dates, places and exact times of birth to give a fluent prediction. Having collected my friend's chart I ask him about my own prospects, especially for the next 52 days. Fixing me with big round eyes he assures that as bright stars, Jupiter and Venus, govern my future, all my problems are over. My journey from now on will be smooth and I am destined to arrive on time or even early. I see the director's face drop. It may be good astrology but it's bad television. Personally I'm rather relieved.

Having put the cost of predicting my future down on my hotel bill, I venture out for a last look at Bombay before I take the Madras train this afternoon. I find myself in one of the poorest parts of the city. For several hundred yards along a high wall are clusters of dwellings assembled from bits of old cardboard, corrugated iron, sacks and assorted pieces of wood and metal. It looks like a long rubbish tip but it is, in fact, the most basic form of terraced housing. Yet, as I walk along past these rickety tenuous little coverings, I see very little sourness and despondency. There is dignity in the faces of mothers washing in the water from the standpipe. Eyes are not averted in embarrassment or shame, the children are responsive, lively and curious. Once again I'm confused and surprised by the way India works. Poverty seems not to be judged as failure, as it is in the West. Here it is a fact of life. There are too many people and too few jobs. Those who have little or nothing are not cleared off the streets or shoved out of sight. To make something out of almost nothing, as in the case of these families huddled against the high wall, is an achievement, and that shows in their faces. But as soon as we start to film, and I cease to be a solitary wandering foreigner, the relationship changes and children who have hung on my arm and laughed when I've pulled silly faces become suddenly inquisitive. Some bigger children join the group. One feels in my pocket. By now the word has gone out that I have money, and money changes the group from hanging on to me in good humour to clinging menacingly, and with frightening speed inquisitiveness turns to anger.

Just before we leave the Taj Hotel I take a last walk by the sea. I'm approached by a man who says he'd seen me dancing at the Durga Puja festival yesterday. Had I enjoyed it? Having ascertained that I had, he falls into step alongside and proceeds to try and interest me in other aspects of Indian life.

'You want woman?'

We walk on for a bit.

'I can show you fifty thousand women.'

This is a bit of a leap. 'Fifty *thousand*?'

'More, more,' he adds hastily, misinterpreting my surprise. He is referring to the red light area of Bombay, known as The Cages, which someone had wanted to take me to on the first night off the dhow. I wasn't really interested then or now. He goes on to offer 'Good boys', 'temple carvings' and 'a joint' before giving up.

I feel like a paragon of virtue, but really I'm just trying to take in, on my own, some last impressions of the atmosphere of Bombay – like most of India, enticing, elusive, imprecise, uncertain and seductive. But a foreigner, strolling on his own in Bombay, will not be alone for long.

Now we're on our way to the station passing, outside the 'Ear, Nose, Throat, Deafness and Vertigo Clinic', a huge Bruce Springsteen hoarding, and a big rather ugly statue of Mahatma Gandhi, much less affecting than the modest one in Tavistock Square in London. This one appears to be made of shiny brown plastic and makes him look like a Martian.

We pull up at Dadar Station at two o'clock, our minibus driver sliding in beneath a sign reading 'Parking For Four Bullock Carts Only'.

Train travel in India is not restful, and the shredding of the nerves begins as soon as you enter the station. The Indians seem to revel in the arguments and mis-arrangements and hustle and heat and chaos. Though my name is clearly spelled out on the computer-printed list of passengers, posted on the platform: 'Michael Palin ... male ... 45 ... 194/64', it appears that there are two other people called Michael Palin in 194/64, and one of them is a woman.

Part of the problem is that Indian Railways is the largest civilian employer in the world, and for every single problem you have there are about eight people all with different ideas of how to solve it. A hapless man called Mr Nitti has been detailed to accompany us and look after all our needs. He is nowhere to be seen.

We leave on time at 2.30. Our journey across 775 miles of India will take 27 hours and we shall make 30 stops. The implacable couple called Michael Palin sit resolutely surrounded by BBC equipment, quite unmoved by the entreaties of the recently located Mr Nitti. I sit in the corridor with the window open, glad to feel a breeze on my face and glad to be circumnavigating again. I could well do with a cool Kingfisher beer but the only bars on this train are across the windows.

The suburbs of Bombay slip by, presenting a Caribbean or West African aspect, with a cover of bamboo and palm trees amongst which are tethered cows and goats on small scrubby patches of land beside stained concrete shacks. These give way to battered shanty housing of great ugliness in the midst of which are people walking hand in hand, talking, smiling, sharing loads and generally behaving most cheerfully.

The train is progressing comfortably but unspectacularly, at 50 or 60 miles an hour. The lines are busy, with much more freight being moved than in Britain. Our meals are ordered ahead, so we have to decide on tonight's supper at 4.30 and tomorrow's breakfast about an hour later. Details are phoned through to the relevant stations, so if the train is late so is supper and breakfast.

My compartment is First-Class non-air conditioned. First-Class air-conditioned are apparently very cold and have windows tinted so thickly that you can hardly see out. There is a 'Western-Style Latrine' at one end of the carriage which has a sit-down lavatory and a push-button water dispenser that fires straight over the basin and into the trousers. As we begin an eye-catching climb out of the humid, tropical plain into the cool red hills of the Western Ghats, I'm allowed to ride in the cab. The locomotive, a diesel-electric, was made in Newton-le-

Willows 31 years ago. Though it would have been long retired in England, it heaves and shudders powerfully up the gradients and through the tunnels. Sweeping views of softly sunlit, wooded slopes below.

I notice that though every window on the train, even the small, thick side-windows of the engine, is barred, the track ahead is completely unfenced and clearly used as a public highway. Apparently oblivious to the oncoming presence of a 17-coach intercontinental express, a group of 20, mostly women, are picnicking between the rails at Karjat Station. Goats graze suicidally on the track until we're almost on top of them, cows amble across the line and even in the middle of a tunnel our headlight picks up a man in a white dhoti coming towards us carrying his shopping.

As the engine works harder and the air swirling into the cab becomes fresher and cooler I think of my father taking this train 60 years ago, for he visited the regatta at Poona when he worked in India as an engineer. A silver mug celebrating his part in a coxless fours victory and inscribed 'Royal Connaught Boat Club, Poona 1929' stood on our mantelpiece throughout my childhood, and now, as daylight fades, I find myself crossing the river where it was won. But Poona is now spelt Pune and it's an awful anticlimax, grey and industrial and no sign of flannelled fools.

At Daund our meal arrives on a tin tray, neatly portioned with yoghurt, dhal, chapattis and a small vegetable curry and rice. As we eat a station official peers in from the platform and advises us to shut our window, lower the bulky steel shutters and to sleep with our feet facing the window.

Part of the exhaustion of Indian travel is the profusion of things to see. At every station there is something going on. Some fierce argument, a pair of monkeys scouring the platform, a steam engine with *puja* garlands draped over its boiler, a line of military tanks on low loaders, their barrels hung with washing.

At Kurduvadi at ten past ten. We're now up on the wide central plateau, the Deccan, as I remember from 'O' level geography, and running about fifteen minutes late. I'm not much reassured by a board on the station which reads 'Trains Running Late May Make Up Time Or Loose Time'. No bedding has come aboard for us and Mr Nitti has disappeared again. I feel absolutely exhausted and fall asleep using my bag as a pillow. About 12.30 I'm woken from deep sleep by the arrival of our bedding at Solapur. Never really get back to sleep again.

Day 29 23 October

Another Sunday, and into my fifth week away. At this moment home seems very far off and the prospect of seeing family and friends again in 50 days utterly remote. But at least we are moving east, and there is daylight through the shutters. There's also an insistent pounding on the door. I open it and find a small, grubby, bearded man standing there looking disgruntled. He demands to know what I want for lunch:

'Chicken biryani very nice,' he proposes briskly, and when I don't show instant enthusiasm (it *is* seven o'clock in the morning) he looks irritated: 'Egg curry, Western style, very nice.'

An order for several biryanis, accompanied by payment, is all that will get rid of him, and I hear him go on to the next compartment. He knocks at this door persistently for at least 15 minutes, too afraid to open it, too dogged to give up.

Not wanting to wake the rest of the compartment, I visit the Western-style latrine, then consult the two railway officials sitting in the corridor as to our whereabouts. Guntakal Junction is the next stop. How long would that be?

'Fourteen minutes,' says one, very positively.

'Half an hour,' pronounces the other authoritatively.

We pull into Guntakal Junction 45 minutes later. When I next look, both men are gone.

Outside there are rain clouds in the skies. A boy waves at the train, further on an older man pulls his trousers up after depositing another load of what is poetically known as night soil.

The bird life is rich and I wish I knew what they all were. Egrets perch on bullocks and the rest pose on the telegraph lines as if in an ID parade – parrots, hooded crows, shrike, kite, humming birds. Some of the bullocks' horns have been painted bright blues and reds. Pride of ownership, I'm told. Like putting 'Les and Christine' across your car windscreen. There are no tractors in the fields, not even a bicycle.

Crowds of passengers disembark at Guntakal's 'Bathing Cubicals', which are lines of basins with a cold water supply running along them. They clean their teeth vigorously and wash themselves. I buy a newspaper. 'Punjab Ultras shoot dead 12 Harijans', '8 Killed in Lanka Violence'. Tolerance clearly has its limits. Inside there is a small piece on the arts page about the government's recent ban on Salman Rushdie's *The Satanic Verses*. The writer seems to think that the authorities have over-reacted and that the book is difficult and probably quite inaccessible to those it's being banned to protect. There's also a long letter of complaint about the number of soaps on Indian TV. *Ramayan* and *Mahabharat* (sponsored by Dunlop) come in for most criticism.

Mr Nitti is still with us and, as he couldn't find any room for himself elsewhere, is installed in our compartment. He's now been joined by his counterpart from Southern Railways, a Tamil. He has nowhere to sit either so we all move up. The irony is that they're here to make sure we're comfortable. They talk to each other in English as Mr Nitti has no Tamil and the Tamil no Hindi. The first thing they do is cancel my lunch order. Apparently I should not have given in to the small bearded man, however much he knocked on my door. He is not a good man and his lunch will not be good. They propose instead a Southern Railways Special, and are justifiably proud of what arrives. It's a thali, which is a sort of south Indian vegetarian meze, with all sorts of different fruits in pickles and curries and dhals and raitas, fresh and sharp.

After lunch we descend slowly from the plain to the hot coastal strip. We're now in the province of Tamil Nadu. The complexions are darker, the earth a deeper red, and the settlements less drab. Much smiling, from slim graceful faces, and a characteristic rolling wobble of the head as they speak. I talk to a much-travelled lady from Madras, a paediatrician in her mid-forties, brought up on English literature. She says that southern Indians feel infinitely superior to the northerners. It starts to rain. Gentle showers. More like sweat than real rain, and soon past. I buy a bag of nuts at one stop, to find that the paper cornet they're served in is made from a page of *Alice in Wonderland*.

Arrive in Madras 45 minutes late. I'm thrust aboard a rickshaw and pedalled off to the Connemara Hotel. A parting glimpse of Madras station. Imposing scale, big pink Gothic tower and a loggia on either side. The neo-Renaissance effect spoilt by an extensive corrugated-iron roof. Over a foul-smelling river we go, my straining Tamil and I, past lots of adverts mainly for films and cigarettes, past The Convent School of Commerce and over a succession of speed-breakers in the road – rather a cruel obstacle to throw at my driver, as he's only doing about three miles an hour anyway.

Down Marshall's Road and Monteith Road and into the gates of the Connemara Hotel – a low thirties-style building, which looks more Croydon than Madras. As soon as we pull up, we're waved out of the way by an officious doorman to accommodate a white Mercedes, from which descends a very well-dressed couple indeed. I have arrived in the middle of a wedding party. Rich Indians fill the foyer as I walk through. I catch sight of myself in the mirror. I look like a scarecrow.

Unshaven, unkempt, clothes crumpled after a night sleeping in them. A burgeoning cold sore. The manager pushes through the crowd towards me. I'm sure he's going to take me round the back and fumigate me. But no, someone has told him that this tramp is a VIP and I find myself garlanded, given the mark on my forehead by a beautiful woman, and led to my room by the assistant manager himself. I find myself gushing apologies for my appearance.

The bath and the cold beer that follow are two of the most wonderful experiences of the journey so far. I feel, perhaps prematurely, that I have survived India.

Day 30 24 October

Not out of the woods yet. The earliest boat to Singapore doesn't leave for 48 hours. It's a Yugoslav freighter chartered by a German company called Bengal Tiger Lines. The chief, and as far as I can see, insurmountable problem is that the ship has no space for passengers. There is a crew of 18 and only 18 places in the lifeboat, so it would be illegal and uninsurable to take any supernumeraries. There is no other sailing to Singapore until the end of the week. We have to try and put pressure on Bengal Tiger Lines for a compromise. Added to this uncertainty Roger Mills, director on this leg, who, like me, felt pretty lousy on the train, has come down with sweats and a temperature. So a day off is called, our first non-filming day since we left.

After a breakfast of paw-paw, fresh pineapple juice and brown toast I nose around the hotel. There is a pool and a small bookstore called Giggles, which doesn't sound promising but is a treasure trove inside. Though only the size of a couple of cupboards it seems to contain a comprehensive selection of all the latest novels, but the chatty, intelligent lady who runs it is still not satisfied. 'I'm after them every day for *Bonfire of the Vanities*, and every day they let me down.' She will stock *The*

Satanic Verses. 'After the elections the ban will be lifted. It's all so political.' I ask her why she called the place Giggles.

'Because I started it for a giggle,' she replies very seriously.

I buy Ellman's Oscar Wilde biography, a Ruth Prawer Jhabwala and a J. L. Carr novel, *A Season in Sinji.*

Meet two southern Indians who are staying at the hotel but working abroad, one as a bookie in South Africa, a country he thinks most highly of, and another in Singapore.

'What's so good about Singapore?' I ask him, a little peevishly.

'They work hard. Nobody cheats.' And he proceeds to warn me against the greed and duplicity of his fellow Indians.

The day passes most agreeably, reading, sleeping and generally behaving more like Fogg.

I attempt some sightseeing later on, but don't get very far. It's Mohammed's birthday and already hellish traffic conditions are augmented by processions and truckloads of flag-waving Muslims driving about, horns blaring. Retreat back to the hotel to find a crowd outside in the street, peering over the wall. A feature film is being shot in the hotel grounds by an outfit called Prasad Art Pictures. It doesn't look like an art picture. The leading actor is on the chunky side and dressed very early seventies in a black shirt with collar turned up and white pants stretched tight across his bottom, flaring to white leather boots with Cuban heels. He's obviously a big favourite with the crowd and a ripple of excitement goes through them when he occasionally glances over towards the wall and waves. When he's not looking a security man sprints across to the spectators and whacks them viciously with a stick. The star casts his eye cursorily over a script held up in front of him by a minion, whilst another pats periodically at his perspiring face. His female co-star wears almost as much make-up as he does. She too is on the stout side, but an undeniably good-looking lady. Their hands remain entwined after the take.

Whereas many hotels have taken to providing the freshly tooth-washed guest with a nice little chocky on the pillow, the Connemara provides instead a small but intriguing package with the words 'For Your Comfort'. Inside are two cotton buds and a nail file. The nail file is a bit chewy, but the cotton buds are delicious.

Day 31   25 October

Extraordinarily good English Sunday lunch at Roger's beautiful house on the Suffolk coast. Even as I scrape away at a meagre slice of paw-paw it's hard to believe it was another of my British Tourist Authority dreams. I've described the house to Roger and he's promised to get one like it as soon as possible. He's a pale shadow of himself this morning, having sweated through a day and night's fever, but at least he's up and about and we all go off together to film the news as it happens in two shipping offices.

It's nine o'clock when we leave the hotel and Madras is already, like its curry, hot and lively. The big film on the hoardings is *Grunt – The Wrestling Movie*. We pass the oldest Christian church east of Suez, St Mary's. It was built in 1680 and designed by a British gunner, who built the walls four feet thick and the roof a foot deep. Then we swoop down into a four-lane underpass which is being swept with a single straw brush by a lady in a green sari.

The office of the agents for the Bengal Tiger Shipping Company, Babuji Jetsea Freights, is located on the corner of Ebrahamji Street, where the countryside has come into the city. Wandering goats pick up what they can from broken sidewalks and sleeping dogs and naked children sit about. When we arrive Vikram, a young, personable Tamil who is in charge of our case, is talking to Lloyd's of London to try and effect some insurance deal for us on the Yugoslav freighter the *Susak*. He fails. Our only hope now is a plan of Clem's which involves substituting myself, the cameraman and sound man for members of their crew who would be flown to Singapore at the BBC's expense. Vikram promises to put this to the owners.

We go on to check out the next possibility at the New Indian Maritime Agency in Armenian Street. The street is a director's dream. Every image of India apart from the Taj Mahal is gathered here. There are street sellers and bullock carts and cars and stalls full of aromatic garlands of rose and jasmine and there is, across the street, St Mary's Cathedral in whose forecourt, beyond a sign reading 'Take Care Of Your Money Jewels And Things', an Indian priest in a white surplice is blessing a long line of supplicants. The beggars are everywhere. One man has a piece of string around his big toe and is tugging at it. Others display mutilated hands and limbs. The cathedral bell tolls.

Three floors above all this I'm shown into the office of a Mr Arul, who has another Yugoslav ship, the *Kamnik*, on his books. He is a most singular man, an ex-chief of police in Madras, living out his retirement as a shipping agent. He tells me that the bell is the sound of the angelus and on Tuesday anyone of any condition can come along to be blessed, hence the lepers and cripples. He describes all this quite matter-of-factly. He goes on to bemoan the water shortage in the city. Because the monsoon has failed here for the last three years water is desperately short and available on alternate days only. I ask about the hotel, feeling guilty about my luxurious baths.

'Oh, they will have private suppliers, of course.'

He assures me that the *Kamnik* will be our very best way of proceeding to Singapore. There is room for everybody and it leaves in three days. The catch is that whereas the *Susak* is a container ship, the *Kamnik* takes break-bulk, i.e. mixed, uncrated cargo, subject to much last-minute delay. I ask him what sort of thing they carry.

'Oh ... granite, quartz, hair ...'

'Hair?'

'Oh yes. Indian hair is highly prized in Japan. Many in India go to the temples to have their hair shaved off as a penance. The hair is sold for wigs in Japan. The temples pocket the money.' Here Mr Arul spreads his arms and raises his eyebrows as only an ex-policeman can.

Later in the afternoon: In a rickshaw, 94 Fahrenheit and humid. I've been looking at the grand imperial statues which have not been removed from sight in Madras as quickly as elsewhere. There is an equestrian statue of Munro, a governor in 1820, with stirrups missing. They say that the sculptor took his life as a result of this omission ... Edward VII (1903) stands in a well-tended garden whilst George V is slap in the middle of the flower-market and has bills stuck on him and families living around his plinth. Both the royal statues were given to the city of Madras not by the British but by local Indians. Back at the hotel, hot and tired again, we're revived by good news. The *Susak* will take two of us – Nigel Meakin, the cameraman, and myself. It looks as if I shall have to take a crash course in sound recording. Nigel says it's not difficult. Ron says it's very difficult.

So with the way ahead looking clearer my last meal in India is something of a celebration. I eat in the open air beneath a full moon and beside an enormous raintree, in the gardens of the hotel. The food is excellent. A buffet full of mixtures of yoghurt, carrot, coconut and aubergine, tomato, chillies, coriander, spinach, onion and peanut. No meat but plenty of fish. There is a fierce crab curry which is irresistible.

All this is accompanied by classical dancing of extraordinary precision, complexity and beauty. Folk dancing usually has me reaching for my room key, but this display is quite superb. The girl dancer speaks good English. She is fifteen, and has been learning classical dance full-time since the age of six. She reckons it will be another five years before she's any good.

Day 32 26 October

The Hindu reports yet another air crash. There has been one a day for the past week, two of them in India. Any tendency to smugness on the part of the non-air traveller is countered by a small headline at the bottom of the front page: 'Ferry Overturned By Typhoon In South China Sea. 500 Lost.' If all goes well I shall be crossing the South China Sea next week.

My more immediate problem is to get aboard the *Susak* by 10 a.m. The highly efficient Mr Vikram is out of town today and has deputed an assistant to help us. We wait for him outside his office for over half an hour, before deciding to try and enter the docks ourselves. We arrive at a level-crossing beyond which is a railway, a high wall with barbed wire and the gates to Madras Docks. Two trains roll by but the level-crossing gate remains lowered. One or two dockworkers amble across the line, but we have a vehicle so we're stuck.

Indians seem to have a knack for sniffing out agitation and discomfiture, and a small crowd has gathered staring patiently but implacably at our every move. This in turn adds to our agitation and discomfiture and the crowd, duly rewarded for its patience, grows. The level-crossing barrier is still down after 45 minutes and since no one can be found with the authority to raise it, we execute a rather grumpy three-point turn, and leaving a satisfied crowd behind us return to the goats, the naked children and the office of Babuji Jetsea Freights. We are half an hour late for the *Susak*.

Of course when Mr Vikram's assistant – a cool young sharply dressed Tamil called Jacky – eventually turns up, he is completely unflustered and assures us that ships never leave on time anyway.

4.15: Still in port. We are having a problem with immigration. Having been through the usual number of confused junior officials we are now in the senior immigration officer's presence. On the wall is a gaudy, gold-trimmed clock, hung up, but still in its wrapping paper. A metal cupboard is covered in violent stains, as if cans of paint had been hurled at it in some kinetic frenzy. In front of him is a desk diary for 1985. He sits examining our papers critically, like a headmaster with a bad report. His hair is thick and grey, but on closer inspection is growing out of one side of his head only and spread artfully across the rest, Bobby Charlton-style. He sniffs. Obsequious attendants lurk in the background. After he's finished a brief phone call one of them steps forward, uncoils the telephone wire and replaces the receiver for him. We are losing time, and I notice on a blackboard behind us that our only alternative out of Madras, the *Kamnik*, has been postponed five days. As if sensing our restlessness, the officer becomes even more leisurely. He asks me the purpose of my journey. 'Jolly,' he says, 'jolly first class.' He smiles across at me, pleased with his grasp of the colloquial idiom, then returns to my papers: 'But everything must be pukka you see.'

A separate letter, explaining yet again the intention to substitute two of us for two of the *Susak*'s crew has to be drawn up and brought to him. By this time it's five o'clock. Sailing time. The officer reads the letter very slowly. Beside him another acolyte stands, with a huge stamp in his hand, for at least ten minutes, after which, at a nod from the officer he brings the stamp smartly down onto the paper, and retires into the shadows, never to be seen again.

5.30: Finally cleared to leave India. We are shown aboard the *Susak* and meet the captain, a handsome man with greying hair and a face of infinite melancholy. He tells us they're still loading and will not be under way until ten o'clock. So, another twelve hours wasted. Nigel and I are shown to our quarters. A sign on the door reads 'Hospital and Medicine Locker'. Inside are two beds, high off the floor and equipped with various adjustment devices. There is a washbasin, complete with single, nonturnable hospital tap, a couple of lockers, two portholes and a bedside cupboard which contains the only evidence of medicine in the place – a litre bottle of Ballantyne's Scotch. Next door is a bath, lavatory and another washbasin. The room is air-conditioned, clean, and two towels are laid out on each bed. I ask the captain what will happen if someone has to go to hospital. He shakes his head wearily.

'No one will go. They are all young.' And here he smiles, a smile well worth waiting for, bleak and quite unexpected.

Midnight. Still loading. Nigel is down in the engine room with the effusive second engineer Ivan, who has limited English and unlimited supplies of slivovitz. I'm in the hospital, talking to Jacky. Indian shipping agents and their representatives are lolling about the officers' mess. Much Ballantyne's is changing hands, plus the odd video and gold timepiece. It's a seedy time of the night and Jacky is telling me about sailors and their needs. A man called P. C. Alexander, an ex-Indian High Commissioner in London, has cleaned up Madras. There's a very Puritan atmosphere here now, and the seamen are not happy.

'All ships crews very happy with Calcutta. Can bring many girls there. Bombay too – no problem.' Bombay is apparently the only city in India to license prostitutes. The girls are very often procured from local villages, where fathers or uncles are paid maybe 5,000 rupees by travelling pimps. This is a lot of money to a poor villager and the girls don't stand much chance. They are brought to the city and installed in a pimp's bungalow. He trains and looks after them for a year. Then they may have outlived their usefulness to him, and he turns them out. Indian girls are naturally very shy and nervous, says Jacky, and Western crews can be disappointed. Good prostitutes can be found, oh yes. The big companies, and here he names a prominent British-owned tobacco producer, will provide girls who will do anything for buyers.

It's a dispiriting conversation, and it seems likely to go on for a while, as through the porthole window I can see containers still being swung aboard. The operators in the huge gantries seem unable to get a trip on the containers first time. It all looks awfully amateur.

Jacky explains to me what is going on. Incentives are necessary for these workers. 'Speed money', it's known as: 25 rupees per container and the dock drivers will move at 40 miles an hour rather than 20.

I walk on deck. It's limbo time. No one is really comfortable. A solidly built, dark-haired Slav called Marenko, who is the Donkeyman on the ship, unburdens himself, in very limited and slightly slurred English, about the political situation in Yugoslavia. He's a Catholic and a Croatian and can't see why the people of Kosovo should not have their own republic, when the Montenegrins have theirs. He can't stand the Serbs.

'They are ... the secret police ... the controllers,' and he emphasises his distaste with a curious gesture – a flick of the back of the hand up the neck and out under the chin.

There are two communists on the boat, he tells me, the chief steward and the chief engineer. I ask if the captain is a communist. Marenko looks shocked 'No. He is a Catholic! Like me.'

It's when he begins to tell me of his prostate problems, 'but sex is still *goot*', that I know I've had enough. Apologising, I turn to go back to the hospital. Marenko presses upon me a little gift. It's a magnetic badge on which is a picture of the Virgin Mary and the words, in English, 'Christ Came Into The World To Save Sinners'. I stick it onto the door of my locker but it drops off in the night.

Day 33   27 October

The *Susak* seems more firmly attached to the Madras dockside than my badge to the door, for sunrise comes and we've still not moved. Nigel was up and out with the camera at a quarter to six, and an hour later, feeling rather guilty, I grab hold of the clockwork handbag, as Ron calls his tape recorder, and go out on deck to help him.

7.15 a.m: We finally set sail. Striking juxtaposition of thin, wiry, almost black Tamil stevedores, unlooping the ropes and huge, blond Schwarzeneggerian Slavs hauling them in.

So I sail away from the Coromandel Coast of India, in a Yugoslav ship, owned by a German company and registered in Cyprus. It's a Thursday morning, the delays in India have put me ten days behind Fogg's schedule, and unlike him I have no Indian princesses to show for it – only Nigel, who is not as far as I know of royal stock, and 30 pieces of BBC film equipment under my hospital bed.

The only ray of hope is that Fogg sailed from Calcutta, away to the north, so we should catch up a day or two by Singapore. Not that the *Susak* is a fast ship. Though only launched 18 months ago at the May 3rd Shipyard in Rijeka, she is making a mere 13 knots, slower than any ship I've been on so far, with the exception of the dhow. Doubtless there are sound commercial reasons for this fuel economy, but it's frustrating for the circumnavigator.

Breakfast is at 7.30. We are served it in the officers' mess (there is strict dining and accommodation segregation between officers and crew) beneath a photo of Marshal Tito, which emphasises his spectacles so strikingly that he looks like an optician's model. The various officers come in at various times and the food, cooked by Nino, is served by Szemy. The crew divide neatly into physical types. Either they're tall, blond and clean shaven or short, dark and bearded. The short, dark and bearded ones are the most jolly and whereas Nino has a twinkle in his eye, and has indicated that I can come into the galley for a snack at any time, Szemy (best pronounced like the Glaswegian 'Jimmee') seems not altogether pleased about our presence. Breakfast consists of two fried eggs on a bed of greasy luncheon meat (which I wolf down), thick slices of Nino's home-baked white bread with butter and jam, washed down with strong Turkish coffee.

It's hard to conceive of what sort of life it must be for Yugoslavs ferrying goods they hardly ever see between three Asian cities they know nothing about, and two of which – Calcutta and Madras – they clearly dislike. This 15-day round trip will be their lot until May next year. The young radio officer has already had enough and will be transferred back home in January.

The *Susak* is, at 4,000 tonnes, classed as a feeder ship, distributing containers, off-loaded from the big carriers, to secondary ports. It has a capacity of 330 containers and is carrying about 300 at present. Many of them seem to contain onions, and to prevent these rotting these have their doors kept open during the voyage, so a gentle shallotty aroma accompanies any walk on deck. The captain claims to have a computer print-out of all the contents of the containers, but is vague as to what their cargo might be.

'Cotton fabrics ... leather ... some dangerous cargo.' These are the ones with skull and crossbones markings and the word 'hazardous' stamped on the side.

We have 1,500 miles to go to Singapore. The sea is calm, the sky clear and sunny.

Lunch on board the *Susak* is at 11.30, and supper at 5.30, which takes a bit of getting used to, but it's all based around changing watches.

The cuisine is relentlessly carnivorous, and comes as a complete contrast to the delicate vegetarianism of southern India. The tea and fruit juices of India and Arabia have only limited appeal on the *Susak*, which amongst its cargo has 3,000 cans of Zlatorog Export, a high-quality Yugoslav lager which sports a cheery-looking mountain ram as its trademark and is available at most times of day, as of course is Ballantyne's Scotch, a bottle of which seems to be in every cabin, storage locker and maintenance room. With some of the meals, according to Jimmee's mood, there is Yugoslav wine, bearing the government name Vinoplod.

Much of the talk at the meal centres around shopping. Where did you get that watch? Did you know that you could get 17 track, triple re-wind, simultaneous play-back Dolby stereo music centres for 43 dollars in Singapore?

I find a place in the sun after lunch and lie on an unvisited deck high up beside the smokestack and listen to Billy Joel and Leonard Cohen on my Walkman and read the excellent *Travellers* by Ruth Prawer Jhabwala, which tells me a lot about India, a country which it's not easy to put out of mind.

At half-past five an intense golden sun sinks beneath the horizon drawing with it all the light from the sky, which changes from off-pink to lemon to light eggshell to murky grey. The long evening, which stretches from 6.15, or earlier if Jimmee is being brisk, is devoted to Zlatorog, Vinoplod and backgammon lessons from Nigel.

Day 34 28 October

The clocks have gone on by one and a half hours, so sleep later. Nigel and I try our most technically ambitious adventure this morning – an interview with the captain on the bridge. This necessitates me holding the tape recorder and mike (and remembering to keep both out of shot) whilst checking the level on the recorder and answering questions. The captain has chosen this moment to give long, discursive replies and my arm is practically breaking by the end.

Finish *Travellers*, a gentle, sensitive, sensuous tale, which has restored my faith in writing. Now embark on Anthony Burgess (*Little Wilson and Big God*) and a book on Islam, about which I know woefully little. On the *Susak* mental exercise is not as problematical as physical exercise. There is nowhere to run off the effects of the Zlatorog.

The sea and weather conditions become the main source of interest. There are no other ships to be seen, only a squall of rain and a sensationally prolonged sunset, during which the surface of the Bay of Bengal seems molten.

Spend an hour or so at the prow, screened by the containers from the noise of the engine, just gazing out over the glassy silent surface of the sea, and looking down at the wash from the bows which is filled with phosphorescent pin-pricks of light. I am taking a last walk around the ship when a door opens at the stern, letting out a long strip of light, into which a huge bull-shouldered deckhand steps, lifts his arm and sends a bottle of Ballantyne's arcing high into the ocean.

Day 35 29 October

Today is Jimmee's 32nd birthday and the celebrations start early. I've just finished my toast and jam at a quarter to eight when he produces two bottles of what appear to be a Yugoslav version of grappa, one of which is colourless and the other the dark brown of an amontillado sherry. I plump for the latter, which is called Pelinkovac and has a bracing taste like Fernet Branca. Two of these before 8 a.m. produce a warm interior glow to match the warm exterior glow from clear sunny skies and a deep-blue sea. We seem to have the Bay of Bengal to ourselves and the captain confirms that this is a little-used route, the main shipping lane being further south, on a line from the Red Sea to Singapore. I ask the captain who is doing the job of the two crew members we've been substituted for. The captain says he himself is covering for the 3rd officer by doing an extra watch. The other was a deckhand and in an excess of zeal, brought on I'm sure by the early application of Pelinkovac, I find myself offering to swab decks and help out with some painting. Ships are always being painted. It's a continuing battle against the sun and salt. I'm given a roller on the end of a very long pole and told to paint more or less anywhere. Nigel's efforts to capture this on film make him look like the one-man bands that used to entertain cinema queues. He balances precariously on a deck rail, a sheer drop into the sea behind him, with camera on one shoulder, tape recorder on the other, headphones over his ears, microphone between his knees and clapper-board in his teeth.

Mid-morning and we're 620 miles out of Madras, the sea calm.

We go below to film a sequence in the laundry. A crewman who doesn't speak any English is showing me how to work the washing machine. Unfortunately he keeps pouring the soap powder in before Nigel has the camera focused or the tape recorder on, and has to repeat the action. Eventually he times it right, but by then about six loads of powder have gone into my washing and we leave the scene rapidly before lather engulfs the entire below-decks area.

To the engine room, which is pristine compared to the last one I saw – on *The Saudi Moon II* (crossed out and *I* written in), which shuddered and rattled and leaked oil from the cylinder casings, where Filipinos worked at temperatures of over 100 Fahrenheit. The *Susak* engine room is like a library by comparison and the control room is cool and spacious. The chief engineer is anxious to show me how they can re-bore piston rings in their own workshop; Ivan, his assistant, is anxious to show us the comprehensive display of beverages in their fridge.

The engine room is unmanned from five in the evening until eight in the morning. The whole thing operates automatically, but has a system of alarms which ring through to the cabin of the engineer on duty. It's a far cry from the cinema image of the engine room, which always had Richard Attenborough or Michael Medwin about to be engulfed by seawater. Stuck to the walls are pin-up photos of great-chested ladies. One for each of the engine-room crew, according to Ivan, who seems to have picked the most statuesque for himself.

One would think it's a bachelor life at sea but the captain tells me at lunch that 80 per cent of the crew are married men. He has a wife and two children, whom he last saw in July and will not see again until next May. It's hard, but the pay isn't bad and his wife comes from a seafaring family and is used to the separations. Jobs are scarce back home, he says. Many young people, qualified as lawyers or doctors, are forced to make a living selling newspapers. I ask him if he would advise his own son to go to sea. He shakes his head.

'It's all changing,' and he smiles. Sadly, as ever.

In the middle of lunch, the young 2nd officer with the swallowtail of hair down the back of his neck suddenly bangs the table and points at me: 'You are Monthy Pyton!'

I have a dim recollection that the series was at one time sold to Yugoslavia. He looks awfully pleased with himself, but the captain rather spoils things by recognising Nigel as Bill Oddie.

'And you do all those bird programmes!'

This evening there is a certain amount of nodding and winking and leaving the table early. A blue movie is being run in the crew's dayroom. Everyone quite enjoys it to start with and there are the same shouts of encouragement, gasps of appreciation and groans of incredulity that you might hear at any Sheffield United game. Eventually the jollity wanes with the sheer relentlessness of it all, and a rather morose silence descends. Post porno omne triste est. The captain is one of the last to leave. He gives a hint of an ironic smile and a shrug of the shoulders.

Clocks on an hour again.

Day 36 30 October

Nigel says I moaned tragically in my sleep. He says it was like a horror film, each sound more heart-rending than the last. I try to tell him that that's the sort of thing he should expect, sleeping in the hospital. The real reason for my performance may have been a sea-swell, which appeared from nowhere and had us both rolling across our beds, perilously close to the edge.

After breakfast land is sighted on the port side. Radar and satellite navigation systems have made crows' nests and cries of 'Land ahead!' obsolete, but there's still a frisson of excitement when you've seen nothing but empty ocean for four days. The land in question is Great Nicobar Island – 27 miles long, the same size as Singapore, but almost uninhabited. Though we are now 950 miles from Madras the island is still Indian territory. On the bridge the captain has the Admiralty charts laid out. However exotic the location the names remain incorrigibly British. Wherever you look there's a Dreadnought Channel or a Ten Mile Channel or a Carruthers Deep. At the end of Great Nicobar is written 'Densely Wooded' and the highest point is marked as 211 metres.

Up onto the topmost deck for a better view. Great Nicobar does look like the stuff dreams are made of. Dark, wooded hillsides run down to the sea. No smoke to signal a settlement, no sign of a building, and what looks momentarily like a flash of light reflected on a window is the white foam of a wave breaking on an empty beach. (Later in my journey I was told of an outrageous but apparently successful attempt to bring tourists to Great Nicobar. During the monsoon torrential rain comes down spectacularly. A bright Indian entrepreneur advertised a tour for rich Arabs from the arid Gulf who could sit on their hotel balcony and watch rain for a week. It was a sell-out.)

Today's big event is a barbecue. The tireless Ivan has once again been the moving force, and the captain has agreed to pay for the drink.

Preparations start after lunch (i.e. about midday) when an oil drum, split in two and laid end to end, is filled with driftwood and set alight. Two 7 lb turkeys, skewered on a long metal rod and basted with salt and olive oil, are laid across the fire and turned continuously for about four hours. Everyone takes a turn, fortified with Zlatorog and mournful singing. Cans of Zlatorog tumble into the Andaman Sea and the singing becomes so awful that a huge cassette player is fetched out and a tape of Croatian songs blares out. More melodic than the deckhands' dirges but still no match for the sound of a 2,800 horsepower engine

The pathos in all this is that these are love songs, sung by a Yugoslav woman, and it will be seven months before any of the crew see Yugoslavia or a Yugoslav woman again.

3.15: First sight of the islands and coastline of Sumatra, and of a succession of vessels, 15 or 20 miles away, emerging from the Malacca Strait to head across the Indian Ocean to Socotra Island, Aden and the Red Sea. For a long time the land is a smudge on the horizon, barely distinguishable from the sky, but the moment when it becomes definably land, when features can be picked out, is for me one of the most exciting moments of sea travel, especially when it is a new land. Sumatra was just a name I'd pored over in stamp albums and inky school atlases and read about in explorers' tales and quite probably Biggles stories. Now as I sit with the smell of wood smoke, roasting turkey and diesel fumes wafting gently about me, it is slowly becoming a reality beneath a low band of dark rain clouds on the south-eastern horizon.

Along the deck two of the crew are fashioning a long table (for we all eat together at the barbecue, officers and crew alike). Jimmee produces acres of red cloth from somewhere and drapes it tastefully over everything, including one of the capstans on which the bottles of wine are arranged. The islands ahead loom slowly larger – silent, dark and peaked. The captain takes his place rather languidly at the head of the table.

He's in a T-shirt as usual. I ask him why I never see him in his uniform.

'Only in the port,' he grins. Can't imagine this happening on a British ship.

It is a wonderful meal. The turkey is succulent. Thick tender meat and a crackly skin. It's served at sunset, which is another beauty. 5.9 from all the judges. Smiling, singing, laughing and sharing incomprehensible confidences we enter the Malacca Strait. The music is an incongruous mixture of Yugoslav songs sung *a capella* and Kenny Rogers, Bob Dylan and the Beatles on the cassette. As the sky grows darker so does the conversation and after a while the sexual exploits of the small 3rd engineer, whose squashed face resembles that of a satanic baby, become a bore and I wander off to the bows, full of good food and too much drink and sober up with the football results from London. Wednesday lose at Charlton, United beat Bury and we are heading south to Singapore.

Back at the table a previously quite unobtrusive deckhand has seized a broom and is miming guitar to a Dylan song. He does it very well and after a final flamboyant riff hurls the broom overboard to a standing ovation from those who can still stand. This encourages him to delve into a maintenance locker and produce a shovel with which he does the same thing. It's only with difficulty that he's stopped from flinging my long paintbrush into the sea.

Day 37 31 October

Now we are in the Strait the swell has eased, the ship is once again on an even keel, and I can think of no explanation for a vivid dream of snakes beneath my feet. All I know is I wake kicking.

There is an air of melancholy about the *Susak* this morning. It's as if yesterday's conviviality was an aberration, and today life is back to being what it probably always is on board a cargo ship, slow, listless and repetitive.

On the bridge the captain indicates the print-out screen on the satellite navigation system. This is a relatively new but radical improvement. Eight satellites orbiting the earth send down signals against which the ship's position can be checked. The vagaries of the weather – clouds or fog – have been defeated, the days of the sextant superseded. This morning the screen indicates that our speed is down to 11 knots. A strong northerly head current is responsible. Time of arrival in Singapore has been put back to midnight tomorrow.

On deck the weather has changed completely, from the sunny to the surly, and from the Malaysia shore a low grey mass of cloud swings towards us from a pitch-black horizon. I realise how fortunate I have been so far. Since Day 2 the sun has shone from cloudless skies and the only complaints have been about the heat. I've forgotten about rain and lowering skies and thought we'd left them behind in Northern Europe. Now, as we draw near to the most southerly point of the journey, only 300 or 400 miles from the Equator, they're back.

The rain hits the *Susak* about two in the afternoon. Grey, flat and prolonged, dampening spirits and disrupting radio communication so that I'm unable to reach the rest of the crew in Singapore to tell them of our further delay. A succession of container ships and car-transporters pass us going north whilst others rapidly overhaul us going south. The effect of the weather on the visibility makes me uncomfortably aware of how potentially dangerous busy shipping lanes can be. Ferries and fishing boats from both sides of the Strait weave in and out of the transporters and supertankers, most of which cannot be brought to a standstill in less than half an hour. Even the little *Susak* would take two miles to stop.

Late afternoon: Playing Scrabble and looking out over grey seas and rain puddles on the containers. This should be one of the most exotic parts of the journey, slipping down between Malaya and Sumatra. Instead it's like a wet Sunday in Sheffield. Ironically the ship has run out of drinking water. On our last night on the Bay of Bengal, the rolling of the boat mixed residue from the bottom of the tank into the water supply, which is why Nigel's bottle of drinking water looks the colour of a prop from Dr Jekyll and Mr Hyde.

At dusk I take a walk on deck. A pair of dolphins has homed in on the ship, and, as usual, make for the bow wave. I hurry to the bows to watch them and whistle encouragement. They play for a while, but the sea is no longer blue and translucent, and they have to dodge polystyrene fragments, swirling tissue paper and bobbing cups – the trail of debris that heralds the approach of civilisation.

Even the meals fail to lift our spirits. Meat, meat and more meat, and the officers (apart from Ivan) seem dragged into a pit of Slovene moroseness in which nothing gives them pleasure. The news that we shall be later into Singapore compounds their gloom for it means even less time ashore in the only port they can bear.

If Nigel and I can be so desperately bored after six days, what can it be like for the crew after six months? I suppose they become numbed, their responses reduced to the minimum necessary. *They* don't rush to the rails every time they see a dolphin or climb to the highest point of the ship to strain for a view of a distant island. They just want it to be over. For them Singapore is not the gateway to new unvisited lands. Singapore means Calcutta and Calcutta means Madras and Madras means Singapore again, and this will be their life long after I've finished going round the world.

Day 38 1 November

At breakfast the captain announces that the *Susak* will pick up the Singapore pilot at 11 p.m. tonight, and will be in berth by midnight. 310 containers will be unloaded and 150 loaded. Departure from Singapore will be 3 p.m. tomorrow. Audible groans.

The crew disappear to their various jobs. To pass the time (breakfast having been cleared away by 8 a.m.) I look for a while at the framed map of the world, courtesy of Transjug, Rijeka. Looking at my route from London to the Equator I can see a symmetry. The Adriatic, the Red Sea, the Persian Gulf and now the Strait of Malacca, are all splits in a landmass, all aligned N.W. to S.E., giving the impression of progress, by a series of down escalators, from sea to sea – the Mediterranean, the Arabian, and, to come, the South China, where it's typhoon season.

A small seabird is trapped for a while in the kitchen. It flies, foolishly, into the oven. But before Nino can turn the gas on, Jimmee has chased it out with a brush (the only one that survived the Dylan impersonations). It flies down towards the engine room, then up again, fluttering along the passageway until one of the engine crew (who looks like Trotsky) happens to step in off the deck, whereupon the bird flies out past him, leaving him quite confused.

In the radio room, where tapes by Tiffany and Samantha Fox lie about the desk, I at last make radio contact with Singapore. Odd to hear guttural Yugoslav talking to tinkling Chinese using English alphabetic identification. I become 'Mike India Charlie Hotel Alpha Echo Lima, Papa Alpha Lima India November', and Roger, whom I'm calling at Raffles Hotel, becomes, much more exotically, Romeo Oscar. The news is that I shall not be spending a night in Singapore. A container ship, the *Neptune Diamond*, leaves for Hong Kong at 11.30. I tell Roger that we shall not berth until 11.30, and explain the problems of the head current. He says I shall just have to ask the captain to put his foot down.

Last lunch with the captain, Ivan and the radio op. The conversation ranges from the idiosyncrasies of the Albanians – at an Albanian port the crew of any merchant vessel is confined to the ship and soldiers with rifles patrol the dockside (the Yugoslavs seem to think it quite a good thing that Albania is cut off) – to a warmly appreciated recitation of the different brands of Scotch: 'Chivas Regal ... ah, yes ... Dewars ... yes ... Johnny Walker ... ah, yes ... Famous Grouse ... what is that?' I ask the captain if there are any restrictions on travel for Yugoslavs. 'Only money,' he smiles. 'If a Yugoslav have enough money he can go to Seychelles.' The captain himself is living with his mother-in-law but has bought a small apartment in Rijeka which he's doing up. Somehow I can't imagine him in the Seychelles.

We have a long and faintly surreal discussion in which the words 'cheap', 'ship' and 'chip' become hopelessly muddled. I ask the radio operator how he'd heard of Samantha Fox. He is surprised I should even ask the question. Every full-blooded male in Yugoslavia has heard of Samantha Fox. 'After Mrs Thatcher, she is the best-known woman!'

At this, the conversation lapses for a while. The captain sits, head on one side, toothpick in his hand: 'So, you will be home by Christmas.' I feel a pang of guilt as I nod.

We've talked about more at this last lunch than at any previously, and as always seems to happen you get to know people a little better just before you have to leave them. Both Nigel and I have grown to greatly like and respect Captain Sablic. He's a man of quiet authority and considerable understanding and I've never heard him raise his voice in anger. Significantly, that goes for the rest of the crew.

This afternoon the wind drops. A feeling of lassitude hangs over everything. A long, lumpen, heavy day, in a lazy, hazy sea. The sort of day when you fear you could stick fast here forever. The sort of day when the Ancient Mariner was 'sad as sad could be, and we did speak only to break the silence of the sea'.

Down in the engine room Ivan is getting very drunk. 'I believe in whisky,' he confides to me. 'But in my cabin you will see Jesus picture and the Virgin Mary.'

At a quarter to eleven after a last round of backgammon Nigel and I would normally be taking a last Zlatorog and heading for bed, but tonight an adventure is about to begin. The solitary days on the Bay of Bengal seem like another life as we make our way slowly closer to Singapore, just one in a long line of southbound ships, whilst another line, northbound, slips past us on the port side. There is very little noise but an enormous, almost frightening amount of movement. Our maritime progress is mirrored in the skies above as a constant succession of jets, their navigation lights flashing, descend to the airport. There is a feeling of heightened excitement – we are coming into the centre of things.

At eleven o'clock precisely a launch emerges from the darkness and puts the pilot aboard. Two hundred ships are processed every day through Singapore and things are done in a brisk, businesslike way.

Up on the bridge the pilot and the captain are lit by a spectral blue glow from the instrument panel. The pilot speaks softly but clearly into a walkie-talkie. We are to be taken straight into our berth at Keppel Harbour, which is good news for those of us hoping to catch the *Neptune Diamond* before she sails, but it'll be a close thing. I can see no sign of her at the dockside.

Down on the deck, I'm grabbed by Ivan who is soaking wet. There had been a leak in the engine's seawater cooling system, but he had plugged it. His face shines with achievement but his eyes are red and tired. He insists we have a last rum together in the engine room. When it's time to go, he says to me, 'You know for me the best sound in the world? Is the motor of aircraft,' and he looks up to the flashing lights in the sky, which one day will be for him.

After fond and emotional farewells all round I totter off the *Susak* and onto Singaporean soil at a quarter past midnight to be told the *Neptune Diamond* had already sailed.

I feel rather glad I've had that last rum. It helps to cushion the blow. But Roger, who has taken over the direction from Clem, is rushing me away from the dockside as if my life depends on it. What's going on?

They tell me as our minibus rushes Nigel, myself and our baggage to customs and immigration. It's to be another night at sea. Such is the power, might and influence of the BBC that the *Neptune Diamond* has agreed to wait for us, four miles out in the roads.

At 2.15 in the morning, after two hours in Singapore, all is cleared for our departure and we are at Clifford Pier, boarding a small but sturdy launch called *Carnival* which sweeps me in a curve past the prosperous, boomtown skyline – the Oriental Hotel and the Westin Raffles, which they tell me is the tallest hotel in the world. But at the pier itself I have seen some litter and a drunk or two – neither of which I thought were allowed on the streets of the city.

2.45 a.m.: Hurrying past all manner of ships in the harbour. First the section they call Smuggler's Corner, where the smaller, less conspicuous boats come and go with surreptitious cargoes, then out between the cruise ships, festooned with lights, past a surveillance ship with two bulbous deck structures, and in among a crowd of cargo vessels riding at anchor. Then voices are raised, the engine tone deepens and sputters and ahead of us is a sheer wall of steel, rising 40 feet above our heads. This is the *Neptune Diamond*. We've made it.

Climb aboard, up a 30-step ladder at ten past three. Met by a Singaporean officer who takes me upstairs to meet the captain who turns out to be a reassuring Geordie, Norman Tuddenham. His wife Pat, who's Scottish, is in her dressing gown. She fusses around us – showing us our cabins and offering us chicken salad and Tiger beer. My cabin is enormous after the *Susak*. The whole ship is enormous after the *Susak*. It carries 2,000 more containers than the *Susak* and travels twice as fast. There is a lift to carry us the six floors from the deck to our quarters. To transfer from a Yugoslav 'tramp service' (as Ivan once described his ship) to a Japanese-built, Singaporean-owned, British-captained 35,000 tonner between midnight and three in the morning in an unknown foreign port is overloading a sensory system already full of rum and Zlatorog, but as I fall asleep I can feel the throb of the engines and I know we're moving round the world again – and that's really all that matters.

Day 39 2 November

The ship as hospital analogy which first occurred to me on board the dhow is becoming remarkably literal. On the *Susak* Nigel and I shared the hospital, and on the *Neptune Diamond* I'm occupying the Doctor's Bedroom. The ship's doctor seems to be a largely fictional character these days. Norman and Pat Tuddenham seem capable of anything and I'm sure minor surgery wouldn't be beyond them.

Despite not getting to bed until the small hours I'm awake early. A new bed, a new ship, a new movement, a new engine note, a new set of circumstances, a new crowd of people to absorb and process into the film, together with my natural curiosity, all conspire to keep me from a lie-in. I have to realise that until I reach London in December everything that surrounds me is potential material. I'm on full filming alert for eighty days – or however long it takes.

A look at my copy of *Around the World in Eighty Days* is not encouraging. Fogg, aboard the *Rangoon*, was in and out of Singapore as fast as I was, but ten days ahead of me. He hoped to accomplish the 1,400 miles from Singapore to Hong Kong 'in six days at the most', but Captain Tuddenham is quite confident that we can accomplish it in 67 hours. Fogg was crossing the

South China Sea at the same time of year and hit seriously bad weather. Tuddenham checks his radar and his daily weather charts and says we have nothing to fear. Perhaps this is another chance to catch up.

Unlike the *Susak* which pottered along at 13 knots to conserve fuel, the *Neptune* ships earn their money by getting there fast and arriving on schedule. Gone are the days of pleasant lackadaisical dawdlings on the Bay of Bengal.

Norman and Pat Tuddenham try hard to inject some human interest into what is essentially a cool and unsentimental business operation. They show us the swimming pool, which has the brightly painted figure of Snoopy on the bottom. 'My wife says that's what I look like,' cracks Norman. They're both very game and go for a splash around for the cameras.

There was, as we know to our cost, no extra room for super-numeraries aboard the *Susak*, but on the *Neptune Diamond*, perhaps to compensate for the factory-like existence, wives are allowed, even encouraged, and Pat is one of three aboard.

We meet the others for a drink before supper up in the captain's cabin. The room, with patterned sofas and family photos on the table, is neat, tidy and domestic and could, one feels, be as easily at their home in Broughty Ferry as in the middle of the South China Sea. The chief engineer and his wife and the radio operator and his wife remain shyly silent throughout. It's a new crew. They mostly joined the ship at Singapore and are as familiar with the captain as we are. On deck earlier today I encountered a painter who asked me my nationality. 'British,' I told him, 'like your captain.' He looked surprised: 'Is captain British?' Norman and Pat propose a party for tomorrow night so that everyone can get to know each other.

'You've got to tell a story, sing a song or show your bottom,' he tells them. The Singaporeans look suitably terrified.

Dinner is a mish-mash of British specifications and Singaporean application. The captain's attitude is to resolutely avoid too much foreign stuff. 'I've ordered steak, because at least they can't muck that up,' he reassures us, inaccurately as it happens. It's interesting that someone who has spent most of his life abroad should be so inimical to foreign cooking. But I must stop making the mistake of confusing being at sea with being abroad. Being at sea is really being nowhere and I suppose you have to create a cultural cocoon in which to live. The Tuddenhams have chosen to survive by replicating familiar home conditions as thoroughly as possible.

On the charts earlier today I notice the words 'Many sightings of unlit sampans,' added in pencil. These presumably refer to the refugees from Vietnam, whose coast we are approaching fast. Captain Tuddenham's attitude to the boat people is as pragmatic as one would expect. He would set a course 20 miles longer to try and avoid them but 'of course I'd pick them up if I had to, poor buggers'.

Roger, who's recently completed some filming in Vietnam, scents a photo-opportunity, and tries to persuade the captain that it would be in everyone's interest for him to divert towards the coast and see if he could find any boat people to rescue. 'You'll bring glory to the company and a medal for yourself – you'll probably get the O.B.E.'

'The P.U.S.H. more likely,' replies Captain Tuddenham drily.

Day 40 3 November

My eighth consecutive day at sea. Exactly halfway through my ration of days, but far from halfway round the world. Ron wakes me with a cry of 'Mi-*kel*! 'Allo Mi-kel!' and a cup of coffee. We're 160 miles off the Vietnamese coast and a big sea is running, whipped up by a Force 7 wind from the north. The Beaufort Scale, on which these things are measured, is still internationally accepted as the wind speed criterion. On the bridge is a display board of photographs illustrating the various

CROSSING THE SOUTH CHINA SEA DAY FORTY   119

conditions. Force 7 is white caps and 10 foot waves. The hurricane that struck southern England a year ago was Force 11. The top of the range is 18, though it's hard to find anyone alive to talk about a Force 18.

I find a gym with table tennis, some weights and a rowing machine, and row for a quarter of an hour. At least I can say I've rowed across the South China Sea. I even manage a run on deck. I get soaked with spray every time I pass the bows, which is most refreshing.

The captain has to admit that the current is running against us and has forced a cut of one and a half knots per hour and our ETA in Hong Kong is now 2 a.m. on 5 November. But we are still in less of a crisis than Fogg, whose vessel had also hit strong North-Westerlies and Passepartout had begun to panic:

'Until then everything had moved on so well! Land and sea seemed to be devoted to his master. Steamers and railways obeyed him. Wind and steam combined to favour his journey. Had the hour of mistakes finally sounded?' On the *Diamond* the only precautions the captain advises is that not more than two of us should use the lift at the same time.

I ask the captain why he joined the Merchant Navy. Like most seamen he's been in the business all his life. (No one seems to drop chartered accountancy and run away to sea, however romantic it may sound.) His father was in the Merchant Navy too – which was true of the *Susak*'s captain and Abbas of the *Saudi Moon* as well. Merchant seamanship is an hereditary condition.

Captain Tuddenham remembers when he was a junior purser in Hong Kong in the 1940s, it was his job to supervise (i.e. lower the ladder and take it up again rapidly if the captain appeared) the embarkation of Chinese ladies, whose company you could then purchase in day-, week- or two-week lengths. 'Very civilised in those days,' he adds provocatively, and Pat is duly provoked:

'*Nor*-man!'

'Long before I had you, my love.'

Outside, the character of the sea has changed totally since we left. Now it's ceased to be a supportive friend or a calming influence – it's fierce and powerful and agitated. 'Only a moderate swell,' the captain insists, in between coping with telexes from the shipping agents in Hong Kong who want to know why he was hanging about in the Singapore roads until five in the morning.

The party starts, unhopefully, after supper, at seven. Shreds of streamer and strands of tinsel from the Christmas decorations remain stuck to inaccessible parts of the bar as Pat and Norman personally set out bowls of crisps, twiglets, prawn crackers and, for the Singaporeans, fragrantly roasted peanuts. 'They won't eat them unless they're like that.' One of the married couples arrives. The wife of the radio operator has been seasick and won't be here. Disco music blares out across an empty floor. Passepartout waits patiently to film whatever might happen, but without him probably nothing will. At last some of the 25-strong crew begin to filter in. The beer and the whisky begin to flow, and much to Tuddenham's relief there is talk, laughter and even dancing – albeit led by the captain himself. I talk to a Singaporean, aged 28. He joined the navy to see the world and is not disappointed. He loved distant places, different cultures, and asked me if I knew Felixstowe. It's only 20 miles down the coast from the little Suffolk town where my mother lives, but I can't imagine what it would offer a hot-blooded oriental. It turned out that when he was there he was doing Captain Tuddenham's old job and dropping the rope ladder down for the girls. Suffolk girls are evidently carrying on a time-honoured tradition. The rate of change is a common theme in conversations with the older officers. Smaller crews, more automated ships, tighter commercial pressures and the shift of the centre of trade to the Pacific Rim, all add a certain poignancy to the captain's reminiscences of the days when Britannia still ruled the waves and the depth of a continental shelf was determined by a weight dangled over the side until someone shouted 'Bottom!'

I ask him if he thinks the British Merchant Navy is in terminal decline.

'It's already dead. We only run ferries now.'

He starts on another reminiscence: 'A man came to my cabin one night holding his hand in his hand ...'

Time for bed.

Day 41 4 November

A rough night. Wake at 5.30, with a sore head and the boat pitching and plunging. Unsteady progress to the bathroom, trying to time my movements to the roll of the ship. First Alka-Seltzer of the journey.

Later, on the bridge, last night's party is judged a success. The captain sounds surprised. 'They all came!'

Ascertain that 'they' comprise 18 Singaporeans, 1 Burmese, 1 Filipino and 5 Malaysians. I ask the captain what size of crew he thinks will be needed to run ships like this in the year 2000.

'One. An educated monkey.'

What is sad is that so much folklore will die with Captain Tuddenham and others like him. No one else could tell so richly the story of the woman who knocked on the door of the captain's cabin in the middle of a voyage, said she'd fallen asleep on the toilet after saying goodbye to her man, and could he drop her off at Cardiff.

'Well,' I said, 'I'm not goin' to Cardiff. We're in the middle of the Bay of Biscay and the next stop's Brazil.' She had been quite unfazed by this and in the end he'd had to put into port at Madeira and pay her fare home. 'She walked off that ship lookin' immaculate!' I ask him if he has any legal redress and he shakes his head. 'At sea, Michael, everything's legal after seven days.'

*

5.00: I try to run round the deck but the wind has shifted to the North-West and is hitting the ship at 50 knots (speed of wind plus speed of ship) and waves are crashing over the bows. There is a tropical storm heading north at Latitude 5 and the captain is hurrying for Hong Kong on full power. There's also news of a 'very severe' storm developing to the East of us. (This was the genesis of Typhoon Tess, which we missed by 48 hours and which was one of the fiercest in living memory.) Roger, thwarted of boat people, is gnashing his teeth that we seem once again to have just missed something truly dramatic. We all blame the astrologer. On my way to supper, I mention the smell of some unpleasant gas.

'Could be from one of the containers,' observes the captain. 'There were five seamen killed quite recently inhaling toxic fumes.'

(Twelve hours after we left the *Neptune Diamond* in Hong Kong, one of her containers exploded, starting a fire so severe it could not be controlled with the CO_2 on board, and Captain Tuddenham was forced to bring her back to Hong Kong.)

Day 42 5 November

At 5.30 Ron wakes me with a coffee. Counting six days pre-filming in London this is our 48th day together and our last. Nigel, Julian and Ron will hand over to another Passepartout today and by Monday will be back in England, having taken 14 hours to retrace the steps which have taken us 42 days. To have come this far and shared so much and still be brought morning coffee in bed is more than I could have hoped for. I lie and consider the days ahead. Confronted with the prospect of two weeks' intensive travelling through China and Japan with a rested director and a fresh and eager new Passepartout, the temptation to fly away to some beach or simply sleep for a week is momentarily strong. But having come this far, I mustn't weaken, especially as, for the first time since leaving London, I have gained some time on Phileas Fogg. His ship, the *Rangoon*, arrived in Hong Kong battered by storms, and 24 hours late, on Fogg's 36th day out of London. The gap between us is now reduced to six days. Fogg, however, left Hong Kong for Shanghai by sea, and I shall be taking a more tortuous railway route across China, which may be more adventurous, but offers little immediate chance of catching up time.

Physically I've held up well so far, with only the gripes on the dhow coming anywhere near immobilising me. A tan from five weeks' unbroken sunshine covers up some of the creases and helps to make me look better than I feel. Despite the lack of hard physical exertion since running in Dubai, I've managed to take some exercise every day, though much of this counteracted over the last few days by far too much to drink. Travelling light has paid off. There are only two casualties. Of my six trusty shirts one was aborted in Bombay, when the hotel laundry washed it in acid rather than soap, and another is terminally covered in oil from the rush through Singapore docks.

We disembark at 8 a.m. Verne observed as Fogg landed in Hong Kong that there is 'a track of English towns all around the world'. It's now reduced to one, and after 1997, none.

My bag breaks. The strap, unable to take the strain any longer, rips away as I set foot on British soil for the first time in six weeks. Unfortunately the camera has a fault as well and I am required to walk down the gangway twice more, pretending that the bag isn't broken. By this time I'm anxious to be away from the container port – so empty of people and full of the smell of diesel engines and the clang of metal resounding. Above my head huge gantry cranes are off-loading a 40-foot container every 80 seconds. I find that the Peninsula Hotel, where I am to stay for two nights, has sent a green Rolls-Royce, complete with chauffeur and champagne, to the dockside to collect me. The driver shows me, somewhat distastefully, into the snug, white leather seats, and soon we are in a traffic jam on a flyover. Somehow after ten days at sea a traffic jam seems singularly pointless even if you *are* in a Rolls-Royce. Ships may move at less than 30 miles an hour, but at least they're moving. You never find yourself pulling up behind another vessel. On either side the tall apartment blocks are huddled together, side by side and back to back, scrambling for space. The city feels unbearably claustrophobic, but my eyes are wide, taking everything in – the Chinese signs and the Union Jacks. Down into Kowloon, past sparkling and expensive hotels and office buildings. I'm back in the world of security men, outside prestige entrances with their two-way radios and swivelling suspicious eyes. Haven't really noticed this breed since they chased us and our camera from the front of the National Bank in Jeddah.

Outside the handsome period frontage of the Peninsula Hotel, Passepartout One take their last shot of me. As I come through the doors into the lobby Passepartout Two take up the story. The cameraman is still called Nigel (Walters, not Meakin). His assistant has become Simon (Maggs) and Ron has metamorphosed, and lost a stone or two in the process, into Dave (Jewitt). Far from looking fresh, Passepartout Two is grey-eyed and thick-headed, having struck a run of mini-flu since arriving a week ago.

There is hardly time to be introduced before I am led with an ever-increasing entourage into the lift and up to Room 417. The door is opened before me to reveal a small hallway with an antique table on which stands a bottle of every kind of sophisticated refreshment. A bottle of champagne nestles in ice and beside it is an invitation to a black-tie party tomorrow night to celebrate the halfway point of my journey. My broken bag is swiftly removed to be repaired, laundry is whisked away and, after some shell-shocked pictures of my reaction are taken for hotel publicity, I'm left alone for fifteen whole minutes!

Then to the Bird Market, a long narrow street devoted exclusively to the sale of birds and their accessories. The only other creatures well represented are grasshoppers – sold by the pound in plastic bags as bird food. Songbirds are very popular here, and punters looking to buy one bring with them birds they already have, for the birds won't sing unless there is another to sing to. Not all the birds are bred for choral purposes. Some are for fighting, and one stall has a large number of small angry birds, about the size and beauty of shabby starlings, which are specially bred for this purpose and imported from mainland China. There are also some very fine parrots and macaws if you want conversation, and while I am trying to teach one of them to say 'John Cleese is rubbish' I feel an affectionate tug at my trousers. A beautiful white cockatoo on a lower perch has taken a shine to my faithful cotton trousers and is shaking them at the knee.

I call the camera over to witness this charming rapport between man and beast only to find the hard-beaked little zygodactyl has bitten clean through the trousers and is now going for the kneecap. He is as tenacious as Norman Hunter and eventually has to be pulled off. Everyone seems to find this a lot funnier than I do.

This unprovoked assault on my costume reminds me that I have to acquire a black tie and suit to match before tomorrow evening – and it's the weekend. But Hong Kong is a 24 hours a day, 365 days a year city. The only reason for cramming onto these islands is to make money and do business, and if you want a new suit on a Sunday, Sam's tailors will make you one. Sam's shop is no Savile Row salon. It's a cramped narrow unit in a featureless arcade, but its fame is worldwide. It's full of westerners who've maybe heard about the place from Henry Kissinger or Cyrus Vance or Bob Hawke or Prince Charles or David Bowie or Derek Nimmo or George Michael or any of the illustrious names who appear in photos displayed around the mirror at which you have your fitting.

Within about seven minutes I'm measured for jacket, trousers and shirt, all of which will be custom-built for me in 24 hours.

Back to the hotel. As in any fast city, the traffic moves incredibly slowly, and there is no time for a breather before going into a press conference. I have been happily unrecognised for most of the journey, and it's disconcerting having to play the celebrity again. I agree with Paul Theroux and Norman Lewis that travel is best enjoyed by being as inconspicuous as possible. The newspapers want funny stories and lots of incident, but I haven't edited the journey down yet. It's still a big, rambling, extraordinary experience, not easy to sum up in headlines. Clem says there has been keen interest in the journey here and when he was talking to a radio station earlier in the week he was introduced, with an apt slip of the tongue, as the producer of *Around the World in Eighty Delays!* Thank God for the trouser-eating cockatoo. It's just what the press want to hear – and it even ends up in the London papers.

After a quick lunch I'm onto the Star Ferry from Kowloon to Hong Kong Island. I'm surprised that the enterprising Chinese haven't slung at least one bridge across the downtown area, but heartily glad they haven't. Today the water of the unstraddled bay ripples in bright sunshine. They call this millionaire's weather, and I'm off to millionaires' territory – the Happy Valley Racecourse. I reach it by tram, a well-worn vehicle of character that used to run in Glasgow in the 1940s.

Happy Valley is an extraordinary phenomenon. Billions of dollars change hands here on the two days of the week when there is racing, because it is the only legalised gambling in Hong Kong, and the people of the city love to gamble. (Living here at all is a gamble, I suppose.) The Hong Kong Jockey Club, a very exclusive and traditional band of gentlemen, have found themselves sitting on a goldmine, which they are permitted to continue sitting on if they redistribute a certain amount of profit in good works around Hong Kong. So everyone's happy and the place is aptly named.

Buildings all around the course form a natural amphitheatre. When it gets dark and the floodlights bathe the lush green turf and the shining outfits of the jockeys, it becomes curiously intimate. Thousands of spectators are easily absorbed in clean and comfortable surroundings, and there is, in the centre of the track, a huge video screen which gives up-to-date information and a simultaneous TV picture of every race. I'm given a tip by the racing correspondent of the *South China Post*, an amiable Australian. Though I don't much go for the name I do win 600 Hong Kong dollars (about £50) on a horse called Supergear. After a couple of hours, despite the cool clarity of the evening and the spectacular location, the crowds and the standing and the sheer weight of the day's activities get to me, and I return to the sybaritic clutches of the Peninsula.

My bag and my parrot-molested trousers are waiting for me, restored to life. I play the laser disc of David Byrne's movie *True Stories* and eat pigeon breasts and Dover sole. I ring my mother, secure in the knowledge that, at this moment, I can tell her how completely safe I am.

Day 43 6 November

Sunday morning. The only thing that irritates me about this marvellous room is that I can't pull the curtains open. Nose around behind chairs and up and down the walls searching for those pulley systems that hotels like to torment their guests with, and am about to give up in disgust when I notice the word 'curtains' on a space-age control panel beside the bed. One press and they soundlessly swing apart. The start of my seventh week away from home. Almost halfway round the world and yet so much about Hong Kong is familiar that I feel closer to home than at any time since I set out. There's an article about Jamie Lee Curtis and John Cleese in the arts section of the paper, talking about the film we all made last year. The *South China Post* leads with Maggie Thatcher and her triumphal visit to Poland. A long and sycophantic piece, and it comes as no surprise to learn that the *South China Post* is owned by Rupert

Murdoch. Breakfast of muesli, fresh orange juice, croissant, brioche and coffee.

Even the weather is passably English. The humidity and high temperatures that have dominated much of the journey have given way to dry, cooler, crisply fresh air as I walk to the ferry to Cheung Chow – an island known as the Hong Kong Riviera, where live my friend Basil Pao, wife Pat and baby Sonia – born almost to the minute as I left London.

Hong Kong harbour is, like the Happy Valley Racecourse, a great outdoor arena. In the centre of the stage are ships of every shape and size. Coasters, sampans, powerboats, tugs, hydrofoils, yachts, ferries, barges with two or three containers aboard, intercontinental carriers with two or three thousand, junks and rowing boats, floating restaurants, cruise liners and police launches, tankers and motor boats and frigates and rickety wood-built fishing vessels which look as if they have come out of the Middle Ages. (Clem says this is very deceptive and many of them are smugglers fitted with 200 horsepower motors which can move at 30 knots and outrun any police launch.)

I meet Basil at the Cheung Chow Ferry Terminal, an hour or so out from Hong Kong. The island has a Mediterranean feel. The low, white-painted jumble of houses and particularly the richness of produce in the market heighten this impression. Basil selects scallops, prawns and crab which we will take to a local restaurant and have cooked for lunch.

We wet Sonia's head with champagne overlooking a beach on which the Hong Kong Open Windsurfing championships are being held. They look to be dominated, as was the racing last night, by the Australians and New Zealanders. One feels the Chinese have more important things to do than windsurf.

Way beyond the windsurfers and tucked away almost out of sight on another island are the long ugly prison-like blocks that provide temporary accommodation for Vietnamese boat people. There are still thousands unhoused, and a repeated point of issue with the Mother country is her reluctance to take what Hong Kong sees as her fair share.

I have persuaded Basil to come with me to Shanghai. He speaks Mandarin, understands film, is a well-informed guide and brilliant photographer, and we have for many years intended to do a book together on Chinese railways. We celebrate with one of the best meals I've had in 43 days, at a very un-fancy restaurant, known locally as the Bomb Shelter. Basil tells me it's the only one on the island that doesn't use monosodium glutamate. Our scallops are cooked in garlic sauce, the prawns with black bean and chilli sauce, like the crab, and we also feast on calamares fried in spiced salt with black pepper, spicy bean curd and a large and delicious white fish (name unknown). All washed down with Tsingtao Beer, from the mainland.

Reluctantly back to Hong Kong Island after this pleasurable unwinding in a quieter place. The ferry is much busier than when we left this morning. Tourists, many of them German, fight for deck places in the sun. The local Chinese stay inside with the air-conditioning.

By the time we land there is no time for a wash and brush-up before the party. So straight to The 1997, a small, smartly furnished club which doubles as an art gallery and trebles as a jazz club. There to meet me is Sam with my suit. Before I can even try it on a photo has to be taken of the two of us together. The fact that I'm hot and a little irritable doesn't seem to matter, and I now understand why the smiles on so many of his celebrity photos look a little cracked. A fashionable young man sits at the bar and, taking him to be the manager, I ask where I might go to try on my new outfit. He indicates a door which turns out to lead to the gents. I am beginning to bitterly regret this whole enterprise when the door to the gents swings open as I'm in mid-change, catches me off balance and sends me spinning, and half de-trousered, into one of the cubicles.

Eventually all is well. I cool off with a beer and the reassuring attention of the club's real owner, a young man from Austria called Christian. He came to Hong Kong in the Foreign Service eight years ago, quit the job and has been running the club since 1982. He fully expects to be running it after 1997. The bubble of enterprise and energy and self-belief that sustains Hong Kong must not be pricked by premature speculation. I suspect that everyone is looking to the business community. If *they* can operate with the new regime then Hong Kong will probably stay much as it is. A young Italian at the party, confident and prosperous, says that the great attraction of Hong Kong is that almost every financial and commercial practice is legitimate. Stacks of money can be, and are expected to be made. There is a fierce battle for mainland Chinese business, with most governments standing firmly behind their companies in offering substantial discounts on loans. But the Japanese have so far pre-empted everybody, offering the Chinese money at zero interest.

Back at the hotel, the feeling of being back in London persists. There are two messages on the video screen in my room. One to say that Douglas Adams called and the other that Mr Alan Ricker *(sic)* was at the Mandarin. Alan, who was once approached by the BBC to do this journey and who gave me some advice before I left ('Faced with any trouble, I become *tremendously* British'), has rung to check if I'm still alive and Douglas is quite upstaging me with something like a two-year journey to various remote parts of the world for a BBC radio series.

None of the travellers meet tonight though, as I am off to a farewell dinner with Passepartout One at the Kowloon Hotel across the road.

Day 44 7 November

Up at six. Pay my bills and am asked, 'Taxi for airport, sir?' Glad to shake my head and notice momentary concern cross the faces at reception. Can one trust the credit card of a guest who doesn't travel by plane?

Eight o'clock at the Tai Kok Tsui ferry terminal, waiting in a queue beneath a sign 'To China'. Tour groups are pushed through ahead of us. Dishevelled and overladen and in need of sleep we may be, but at least we're not in a herd. Ron and Julian have sacrificed a lie-in to come and say goodbye. We shuffle through. Final farewells. I shall be in Guangzhou this evening. Julian will be in Fulham. As we board our twin-engined catamaran for the 110-mile journey up the Pearl River I talk to Nigel Walters, our new cameraman. He thinks we're doing it right. Travelling by ship, I mean. 'At least your mind gets there at the same time as your body this way.' A customs inspection. 'No spitting', 'No smoking', 'Keep clean please', read the signs. An American girl is worried whether she'll get on. I ask her why she's going to China. She looks nervously around: 'I'm going to Beijing to collect some stuff.'

At 8.20 a.m. the ferry *Long Jin* pulls out into the hyperactive waters of Hong Kong harbour. She was built in Norway two years ago and has a maximum speed of 30 knots. Soon we're passing the New Territories north of Hong Kong, leased from China in 1898 for a 99-year period. These are what will revert to China in 1997, and there is bad feeling here that Mrs Thatcher should have thought it necessary to include Hong Kong Island and Southern Kowloon in the deal.

Now, from the windows of the air-conditioned cabin I catch my first glimpse of Hong Kong's prospective owners. A huge country, but everything is on a smaller scale. Thatched huts stand in the water at the shores of the estuary, beside them long, low, elegant pencil-thin fishing boats. The river is as busy as the harbour in Hong Kong but less glamorous and cosmopolitan –

the boats here move more slowly, and produce is more likely to be shifted in slow-moving lines of multiple barges than in shiny new bulk containers. Most of these barges look as if they're also people's homes. One is black and grimy, straining under a pyramid of coal slack and coke waste, but beside the wheelhouse a man is doing his washing. Clothes hang on a line and pot plants decorate the grubby superstructure. Everywhere I look, on land or on the water, are lines of washing and potted plants. Launderettes and garden centres could be the businesses to get into in China.

Even before we reach Guangzhou (or Canton, as it used to be known) I sense a similarity between China and India, as strongly as the similarity between Hong Kong and Singapore. Though China has factories and modern docks, and even, I'm solemnly informed by the captain as we pass beneath them, the tallest pylons in the world, it's a land of small enterprises, highly labour-intensive, with most of the work being done by human rather than mechanical effort.

Down in the cabin the passengers are riveted to a beauty competition beamed out on Hong Kong television. Basil says the Chinese love beauty contests. He thinks maybe it's an identification with the rags to riches story, the refugee's dream of making it into the glamorous life; which is the motivation of Hong Kong.

As we draw closer to the centre of Guangzhou I notice that the tallest structures are not offices and apartment blocks but something I never saw in Hong Kong – factory chimneys. And they're all belching smoke, lending the skyline a Victorian aspect.

On TV Miss Chinese International 1988 has been chosen and her two dry-eyed rivals attend her simperingly while she, radiant and sparkling, allows a tear or two to trickle deftly onto her left cheek. Whatever is the Chinese equivalent of patriotic music surges and chord-changes its way up the emotions and rings in my ears as I step out onto the soil of the People's Republic for the first time in my life.

One thing a land of over a billion people does not have is staff problems, and this small, rather homely ferry terminal is manned by countless young people in Ruritanian uniforms – peaked caps, lots of braid and buttons and gold-trimmed epaulettes, bottle green for the police and navy blue for the Customs. Unfortunately none of these ornate uniforms fits very well, and no amount of twirly stripes and badges can disguise the cheap and shapeless material, nor can Dan Dare-style peaked caps disguise unflattering lumpy haircuts. But the set-up is extremely efficient and courteous and we are processed through in just 40 minutes, which must be a world record.

Taken to the White Swan Hotel. This is the real thing. A real replica of a Western luxury hotel complete with bellhops, receptionists dressed like lady barristers, a floor of polished granite, a marble-topped reception desk and a hanging gallery of trailing plants surrounding a waterfall, four storeys high, that spills into a little garden with bridges and paths that lead to the coffee shop. I sink gratefully down beside a gurgling pond, in which goldfish laze comfortingly. A lady barrister approaches and waves me away, 'No sit here!'

A constant stream of ruddy-faced, wide-eyed visitors perambulate around the lobby. Some of them are soldiers, some family groups up from the country who gaze about in awe. They all gravitate towards a peach tree made entirely of jade, and here they are photographed. There is a card beside this remarkable object with information in English. It is called, a little baldly: 'Big Sculptured Jade Article'. The blurb continues effusively, 'It has more than a thousand jade peaches and 15,000 jade leaves. It is beautifully shaped and it looks really lifelike. It is the biggest potted landscape in our country at present.'

Mingling incongruously with the Chinese proletariat are huge bronzed Western athletes, glowing with hairy good health and carrying sheaves of tennis rackets. They have come to take part in the first professional tennis tournament ever held in China. They look like men from outer space.

I have a room on the 16th of 28 floors with a stunning view down onto the Pearl River where it bends and is joined by a side canal. I could easily sit and watch the ebb and flow of craft along it all afternoon, but we have a film to make and after a bland international buffet lunch I'm out in the streets. The commonest, nay almost universal, form of transport is the bicycle. No racing bikes here, no sports bikes, mountain bikes or drop-handlebar affectations. These are solid traditional sit up and beg jobs, with wheelguards and racks on the back. Housemasters' bikes. There are occasional cars and the way they are driven suggests an apocalyptic future for China when the millions decide to forsake their bikes for Toyotas. As it is, rush-hour, apart from the occasional tinkle of a bell, is pollution free and wonderfully quiet.

As in India, there are enormous numbers of people about, but the Chinese behave very differently. They're more purposeful, they always seem to be on the move or intent on doing something. There isn't much of the drifting, gazing, eye-wandering of India. Nor are they particularly curious. Whereas Indians are always catching your eye eager to exchange a smile, the Chinese tend to avoid eye contact and it's difficult to get any response from the faces.

Just behind the White Swan is an area called the Shamian. This is where the foreigners who were allowed to trade with Canton in the eighteenth century were confined. I walk along its leafy avenues of cinnamon trees before supper. The great merchants' houses in elaborate Western styles – classical, rococo and baroque with wrought-iron balconies and pillared porticoes – still exist, but the people have taken them over. They have subdivided the huge rooms and hung their washing out on the balconies on bamboo poles and their plants have filled the window ledges and they've lit open fires in the porches.

Three little girls are running up and down an impressive staircase playing a game which involves energetic activities and

much shouting at each other. I ask Basil what they're saying. '…
and the next competitors are the Americans,' he translates. I
remember that it's only a few weeks since the Olympics.

Basil points out several small shops offering earthenware
bowls of what looks like stew, heated over a charcoal fire. I am
quite tempted to indulge, until he tells me the attractive folksy
bowls contain dog.

But greater gastronomic adventure lies in store in the
evening. We drive down endless dimly-lit streets, some dark
because of low voltage, others because of power cuts, all
intriguing and full of atmosphere, to a restaurant at which
snake is the speciality. There are one or two in the window,
twined around a dusty branch in a cursory attempt to re-create
a natural habitat. Inside there's a bustle of waiters and a family
atmosphere at the tables. The Chinese, who take their food very
seriously, like to select a snake of their choice before it's killed,
and accordingly a number are brought to your table, or rather,
thank God, to the floor beside your table. They are in circular
baskets from which they are extracted and deftly displayed. Not
wanting to see them twist and writhe in the air any longer than
necessary, and having no clue as to what to look for in a snake,
I leave Basil to choose. He selects a nice bit of cobra. The waiter
makes a small incision in the chosen one, and deftly removes its
gall bladder which is laid neatly upon a white saucer and which
will later form the basis of a highly prized liqueur, available here
but not in Hong Kong, from whence special tours are laid on to
taste it. I'm told it's good for rheumatism and speeds up blood-
cell regeneration. Once the gall bladder is removed, the head is
cut off and, its forked tongue flicking desperately at thin air,
laid beside the saucer on which the gall bladder nestles. The
waiter then slits the snake's skin from top to bottom, and with
rather too much pulling and tugging for my liking peels it away
from the body. Spots of blood splatter onto the floor, but the
whole operation is over in less than a minute and is watched,
admiringly rather than sensationally, by the other diners. A

moment or two to recover before the cooked snake appears (in many forms) at table. It tastes like rich chicken, and is served as part of a long, and I have to say, delicious meal of which I can do little more than relate the menu:

Snake bladder liqueur
Cat and snake soup
Shredded snake with broccoli
Snake balls (tender morsels of deep-fried snake)
Rice birds (these are the smallest birds I've ever eaten, and they come whole, but plucked. None of our party ate the head, which to the Chinese is the supreme delicacy)
Ginseng, chicken and mushroom soup (served from a silver steamer with coiled-snake handles)
Fresh fox (fruit-eating foxes, which live only on bananas and taste of venison)
Noodles
Melons

The proprietor assures us that all his snakes are free-range, from the warm and humid province of Guangxi, and that autumn is the best time of year to eat them, as they've fattened themselves for winter hibernation. And in case we still have any doubts, the Chinese Olympic team trained on snake and ginseng – and they were the most successful in Asia. There's a lesson there somewhere.

When I get back to the White Swan it's a little after eleven o'clock. I notice that people are still working on the building site next door.

Day 45 8 November

Up at 6.15. Misty half-light over the Pearl River. To Guangzhou station for the 8.30 train to Shanghai. Through the cycle rush-hour. Only older men still favour Mao jackets. Otherwise it's Western 1950s or, amongst the young, American casual. A Turnerish sunrise spreads over the city, silhouetting the forest of TV aerials turned, despite official discouragement, in the direction of Hong Kong.

The long, elevated motorway to the station is a Western commuter's dream; almost empty at peak travel time. At the station, an immense characterless building in a side square crowned with neon signs advertising Sanyo, Seiko and State Express 555s, there are few vehicles but a huge swell of people. Many are squatting in groups on the main concourse, their baggage consisting of two plastic or string bags, looped around a bamboo pole, and carried on their shoulders. They scan a state-of-the-art matrix indicator for news of their train.

Ours is already at the platform, which is clean and well-swept. The eighteen coaches are green- and cream-painted, of chunky old-fashioned design, ridged along the outside with air vents on top. A stocky girl with a pretty face and pigtails stands, in the uniform of the railways, at the entrance to our 'Soft Class' coach. Attendants in peaked caps abound (there are fifty to serve this train). One feels that part of China's achievement has been to put as many people as possible into uniform – of any kind.

The 'Hard Class' coaches are already full, their occupants leaning from open windows to buy sandwiches, orange juice and cola, or drinking their tea from big enamel mugs. The 'Intermediate Class' have bunks, but in an open-plan arrangement, and without the homely touches of 'Soft Class' compartments, which include four berths, complete with duvets and fluffy pink cushions, a small table with an embroidered red cloth on which is set a reproduction oil lamp with cut-glass shade, and, of course, a pot plant. Lace curtains are drawn back at the window. It's very cosy, an odd mixture between a bordello and my grandmother's.

We leave on time and are quickly out of the city and into a landscape of fields still worked by families with hoes and rakes. Our smiling, pigtailed lady appears with an enormous steaming kettle and fills up my thermos jug. Another attendant follows up with some cups and jasmine tea-bags.

Talk to a helpful railwayman who tells me, among other things, that we have 13 stops ahead of us on our 35-hour, 1,130-mile journey. He's called Mr Cha and has worked on the railways for more than 20 years. I ask him if there were foreigners riding on Chinese railways 20 years ago.

'Oh yes, indeed. But only from countries we were friendly with.'

'Such as?'

'Vietnam, North Korea ...' He can't think of any more names. He gets off at the next stop and leaves me his cap badge as a memento.

At 10.30 plastic bags are brought round to collect our rubbish. Outside, the landscape is still, serene and peaceful. Every stage of rice production is in evidence: planting, growing, harvesting, winnowing and threshing, all non-mechanised, like a series of period tableaux. A couple of perky dogs march across a field, tails in the air.

'Lunch on a lead,' says Clem.

Lunch turns out to be dog-free and extremely good. There is one restaurant car, which appears to exist mainly to service the huge staff, who are to be found in there most times of day, with their caps off, laughing and gossiping. The kitchen is solid and heavy and full of people, with the cooking done by five chefs on cast iron ranges in woks the size of Jodrell Bank. The tablecloths are plastic and two bottles are at each table, one marked 'China Red Wine' the other 'Chinese Brandy'. I presume they're ornamental as I never see either drunk by anyone throughout the journey.

Those who don't want the restaurant, and haven't brought their own food, can buy carry-on lunches in white polystyrene boxes, which they then throw out of the windows.

At Ganzhou station a wall is being erected at enormous speed, by a workforce consisting of old men, young men, women and boys. Fourteen-year-olds are straining under bamboo yokes from which are suspended pails full of bricks. I counted 30 in one load.

We talk to some of the passengers in Intermediate, including an infectiously enthusiastic lady who has learnt English off the BBC World Service. When asked for an interview she agrees politely and just before we turn over cries, 'Wait a minute!' and rushes off to put on her lipstick.

Mid-afternoon and feeling drowsy as we pass into Hunan province – Mao's province. I talk to Mr Xie, one of our minders from China TV. He's very earnest and calls me 'Mr Mike'.

'Lot of people have deep feeling for Mao,' he says, 'but there have been economic changes that are visible, and the political changes must accompany economic changes.'

'Do you think there will be free elections in China, say, ten years from now?'

'Yes,' nods Mr Xie, frowning with concentration, 'is historical tendency.'

Now we are in amongst walls of rock rising sheer from the fields, eroded into fantastic shapes. Then we run along a narrow gorge beside a mud-brown river, down which stacks of bamboos are being punted. At Zhenzhou a couple of grimy steam engines stand tantalisingly close to our train. I hop out and ask if I might climb up into the cab. (For train buffs, the engines were 2–10–2s with smoke deflectors, built in 1981.) Whilst in the cab I notice that the engine is parked level with the roof of a long engine shed, roofed with small earthenware tiles, of the kind which Terry Gilliam, one of my timekeepers, requested I bring back. Very gently I prise one loose and return to the train, very pleased with myself.

At sunset *Swan Lake* is playing over the PA as we head out of Hangyang. The chef excels himself and provides the best train meal in 45 days. Pigeon in soy sauce, squid on a hot plate, with tomato, pork and sea-turtle casserole, fish cutlet, and in the Chinese manner, just as you think the meal is over, soup – in this case cucumber and egg-white. In Intermediate Class they're playing draughts. A lot of people are smoking. The land outside is very dark. The stations we pass through are dismally lit, though large crowds still wait patiently on the platforms.

At Zhuzhou station at 10.15, Dave Passepartout goes in search of digestive biscuits, a man goes along checking the axle temperature with his bare hands and Mr Xie wants to draw me into conversation about the book I'm reading: *The Horse's Mouth* by Joyce Carey.

'This look very serious book, Mr Mike.'

When I tell him that much of it is raucously funny, he seems very disappointed.

Later: I'm comfortable under the thick duvet but lie awake for quite a while, listening to the ever-changing sounds of the train. It seems wrong to waste any of China in sleep.

Day 46 9 November

Hot water arrives at twenty to seven. Hawaiian music is playing over the broadcasting system. Beyond the lace curtains the fields are already full. The countryside is like a Thomas Hardy novel come to life. One man is hoeing, another cutting the rice. A woman is washing, someone else is fishing, another feeding rice stalks into a thresher which two others pedal. An old man is setting the cut rice up in stooks, a woman tills the soil, two men pass carrying a threshing machine on a pole slung between their shoulders. A brick kiln is already smoking. The Chinese seem to have an insatiable appetite for building.

Into the loo for a wash. Only cold water and that is sporadic. The smells have increased overnight, and my Armani soap, a memento of what seems like days long ago at the Peninsula Hotel, adds an unlikely whiff of Beverly Hills to this stained and shabby place. As I return to the compartment, I find my way blocked by our attendant who is sloshing a filthy old mop across the floor of the corridor. It's a painful process to watch, as the floor is carpeted.

At Yin-Tang in Jianxi Province I alight from the train and take the morning air. I realise, with quite a start, that it is cool, even cold, and riffle through my bag for my short-sleeve sweater, which I haven't worn since the night we left Venice. There's an edge of autumn in the air which I suppose is to be expected as we've been travelling due north since leaving Singapore – from 150 miles off the Equator six days ago to over 2,000 miles north today.

More steam engines up here. One passes slowly in the dusty low sunshine, double-headed with a diesel. Interesting comparison. What makes steam engines so good to watch is that you can see them working.

The countryside continues to be fascinating. The Chinese manage their water carefully. Every village has its central pond (with ducks and geese in attendance), and a nearby river with channels and canals and waterwheels and stout stone bridges that Devon would be proud of. The water always seems to be still, reflecting the life that goes on around it, and setting off the constant movement of figures on the landscape. Tufted haystacks, tufted rice stooks, tufted children.

Our latest estimate of arrival is four hours late in Shanghai. Mr Xie can see I want to be left alone, so he slides up to me: 'What are you thinking, Mr Mike?'

Last night I gave him *Travellers* by Ruth Prawer Jhabwala and Graham Greene's *Ways of Escape*. He was absolutely delighted and has probably read them already. But I haven't enough stamina for a literary discussion and I mime exhaustion so effectively that he nods understandingly, like a hospital visitor, and settles down to watch me.

From the compartment next door comes the rasping prelude to a good spit. The Chinese are great expectorators and very often a hideous deep-throated rumble will belong to a petite lady.

I visit the train's DJ. She is a petite lady but would, I'm sure, never be heard to rasp. One of the qualifications of her job is 'impeccable Mandarin' and besides record requests and on-train information *and* pre-announcing every station, there's precious little time for a rasp even if she wanted to.

Her compartment is papered in dark-blue brushed suede. There is a tiny bed and a stack of cassette players, amplifiers and a mike. She has 30 cassettes, two of which are Western. One is classical, another contains an amalgam of such memorable tracks as 'Let's Go' by Magazine '60 and 'Scandal Eyes' by Fesh. Requests to play a track from my Springsteen and Billy Joel tapes have been vetoed by her superior, the Director of On-train Broadcasting, so I suggest a Mozart flute piece instead. She eyes my tape doubtfully. They don't know who Mozart is, so it's privately played first, approved and, much later, relayed to the rest of the train.

Talk to two journalists from Shanghai. She is 32, he's 33. In the last ten years they have seen their salaries increase and the freedom of the press widen. They are proud of the fact that their newspaper – *The People's Evening News* – is not a government mouthpiece and has a circulation of 1.8 million. The view of Shanghai people is that the process of opening up – Chinese *glasnost* – should continue. The irony is that it has not changed Shanghai, which always enjoyed a privileged and independent status, even under Mao. The recent improvements have allowed the rest of the country to catch up and Shanghai's privileged position is now threatened.

At Xiaoshan industry intrudes onto the Arcadian landscape, dust and smoking chimneys, coal heaps and piles of ballast everywhere.

I meet the nearest thing to a Chinese yuppy, a 24-year-old girl in smart Western-style outfit who has learnt English with an American accent. I ask her where she works and she replies, without a pause for breath: 'China National Light Industrial Products Import and Export Corporation Shanghai Branch.' She's returning from the Canton Trade Fair where she has been selling hurricane and kerosene lamps. I ask what she thinks of the Chinese one-child policy.

'Well, *I* don't want *any* children,' she says with great determination. 'We have too many people.'

But she concedes that most of her fellow Chinese wouldn't agree with her. She works a six-day week and for relaxation likes the cinema and going out with her old classmates. She likes Western films but *Waterloo Road* was the only title she could remember seeing recently.

One advantage of running four hours late is that we have time for another dinner. A lot of the standard ingredients have run out and the chefs are making the best of whatever they can find. So tripe and eels (in soy sauce and chilli) and duck's gizzards are presented.

It is a tired and travel-worn Passepartout who partakes of a whisky with me as we roll in darkness through the interminable hinterland of China's biggest city. We have been moved out of the corridor, and the much-mopped red carpet has been rolled up. We have been shifted around our compartment so they can collect the towels and sheets. It's the end of journey treatment which I have observed many times on British long-distance trains, that point at which you switch from being a customer to being an encumbrance. When there's nothing left for you to buy, you're in the way.

Nigel returns from the loo with a look of deep shock on his face. He's just seen all the plastic bags, into which they so punctiliously gathered our rubbish, being emptied out of the window.

9.30: At Shanghai. Cannot see any porters. Maybe people aren't allowed to be porters here. So long walk with bags down densely packed, featureless walkways, smelling of chlorine.

Then an hour's wait in a cold car park for all our film gear to be checked through. A female voice echoes across the emptiness from the station loudspeakers. I ask Basil what she is going on about. He says they are public service admonitions – advising people not to smoke within the station area as it pollutes the air for others and polluted air makes you dizzy and so on ... It doesn't seem to make much difference.

Midnight: In bed at the Peace Hotel, formerly the Cathay Hotel, built by the Sassoon family between 1926 and 1929. Noel Coward may have slept here. I *certainly* will. Slightly regret the gizzards.

Day 47 10 November

My room is spacious, but there isn't much to fill the space. The curtains don't quite meet in the middle and the carpet bears some prominent stains.

Down to breakfast, only to find it's being served on the eighth floor. As I climb back into the lift I'm horrified to see one of the uniformed attendants clear his throat vigorously and deposit a glob of spit, quite deliberately, in a rather attractive brass bowl which sits on a pedestal by the lift doors. Later I see someone else doing it and feel foolish that I didn't know such a beautiful object could be a spittoon.

The Peace Hotel is a curious mixture of dark and oppressive English thirties suburban mixed in with some fine examples of Art Deco, and a spectacular Chinese-style banqueting room with dragons in bas-relief curling round the walls and ceiling. Nobody knows much about Sassoon, the man who built it, except that he was a Jew, possibly from Baghdad, who came to China and made a lot of money out of the opium trade.

Drive out to see his family house, about half an hour from the centre of Shanghai. The well-trimmed lawns, the swinging garden seat and the mock-Tudor mansion with its beamed ceilings and latch doors, wrought-iron chandeliers and minstrel's gallery, are pure Sunningdale. But the grand piano is under covers and there's no one in plus-fours with a pipe standing by the fireplace nor any cucumber sandwiches to be enjoyed in the big antimacassared armchairs. It's an odd and melancholy experience to see this ghost of a past and to realise such quintessential Englishness survived the days of Mao Tse-tung intact.

Driving back into town, I sense a prosperous, confident city, with many of the manifestations of other boomtowns on the Pacific Rim. A huge amount of new construction, much of it hotels and trade centres, is under way in conjunction with foreign companies – Australians and Japanese and Americans. One sign beside a picture of towers of the future reads, 'Sister Cities Co-Operation, Shanghai – San Francisco'. It's very easy to forget that you are in a Communist country.

Lunch at the Shanghai Old Restaurant, in existence for 100 years, my first experience of traditional Shanghainese cuisine. The menu is nothing if not original: Preserved Duck Eggs, Crab Yolk and Sharks Fins, Smashed Chicken with Sea Slugs, Squirrel Yellow Fish, Minced Pork Ball and Potted Big Fish Head. Being conservative we stick to crabmeat and bean curd, and squid and eel with garlic and pepper – which is quite sensational.

An attractive and beguiling side of Shanghai exists only just off the main thoroughfares and the construction sites. There are narrow streets and squares of low buildings of some style, with louvred shutters and wrought-iron balconies, on an enjoyably human scale, lively and thriving. There are rice kitchens and small electrical shops, where, if you buy a calculator, your bill will be added on an abacus, and the elegant Tong Han Chun Tang Chinese Medicine Store (established 1783) whose speciality is the Zhang Guang Brand 101 Hair Regenerating Extract (formerly the Baldish Hair Regenerating Tincture). 'The outstanding invention of Dr Zhang has brought the masses of sufferers from alopecia happiness and good tidings.'

This is traditional medicine and the ingredients are organic and not chemical. I ask for a tonic, something to relieve travel fatigue and generally rejuvenate me. Various roots and mosses and ginseng extracts are gathered from their jars, mixed together and handed to me in brown envelopes. To achieve full potency, I must pour boiling water on these dry bits of debris twice a day for the next three days, and drink the brew.

The streets outside are meticulously swept, and appear to provide jobs for everyone. There is a car parking warden, with his white cap, and there is a bicycle warden with his red armbands. Old men and women, beyond retiring age, are employed as street attendants. They have red flags and megaphones and are deployed at busy junctions, bus queues and outside popular shops to regulate the pedestrian traffic.

As it is difficult for the average citizen to get permission to travel across China, let alone the world, the chance to speak to a foreigner is highly prized. A retired bus conductor spoke impeccable English, which he'd learnt to give him 'a better knowledge of socialism and its international application'. I keep forgetting that the theory of socialism is all of Western, not Eastern origin. For half an hour or so the bus conductor, and an engineer and a couple of younger Chinese, ask me about home, as a crowd gathers round.

This old part of the city around the sixteenth-century Ming dynasty Yu Garden, with well-preserved pavilions, gardens, ponds and rockeries, is much more amenable than the Nanjing Road, where I end up later trying to buy some protection against the sudden arrival of autumn.

It's getting dark and the crowds and the dimly lit shops remind me of Sheffield in the early 1950s. The fashions are certainly of that period, and I'm made aware of how much bigger most of us are than the exiguous Chinese. I tire very quickly of hearing 'No got' and return, empty-handed and exhausted, to the Peace Hotel.

Later, in the coffee shop, a jazz band composed entirely of elderly Chinese gentlemen is thumping out 'Alexander's Ragtime Band' and 'You Are My Sunshine'. This is a happier example of cultural miscegenation, as the Chinese seem to take to black American music with great style. They are retired players from the Shanghai Symphony Orchestra and have been resident here for years. Cities with a 'naughty past', like Shanghai and Havana, have always fascinated me, and as the band breaks into 'Tiger Rag' one can, even in the chaste surroundings of the Peace Hotel Coffee Shop, imagine a little more easily how lively things were in Shanghai in the days when Noel Coward might have slept here.

Day 48 11 November

Out early to film the Chinese at their mass, public, morning exercises. We're on the Bund at half past six, but the Tai Chi classes are already under way, and, horror of horrors, in the middle of 80 pairs of slowly circling arms is a television presenter, clutching his mike and delivering a long piece to camera. He is only one of three TV crews, not including ourselves, who are also recording this unusual and highly visual social phenomenon. I notice that they tend to concentrate their cameras on the group activities, whereas, for me, the fascination likes in the peripheral, individual behaviour. Respectable middle-aged gentlemen, looking like civil servants, can be found with legs up on a fence, foreheads bent low toward their knees, twirling swords about their heads, or literally spinning themselves around. A woman of advancing years bounces her back gently and repeatedly against a plane tree, a younger woman instructs a clumsy soldier in some balancing act, a silver-haired man who looks into his seventies is doing amazing things with an unfurled umbrella, sweeping the ground with lithe, balletic movements and ending in the splits.

All this is being done, not in any special area or with any special clothing, but on the way to work. There is none of the western paraphernalia of jogging suits and trainers and designer sweatshirts. Nor is the exercise punishing or demanding or violent. It's all controlled movement, bending, stretching; relaxing and coordinating rather than body-building. A young man comes up to me to practise his English. He's already done his Tai Chi – 30 minutes at six o'clock – and he's rather dismissive of the group everyone's filming. They are only doing 24 variations. Some people do 88.

How many does he do? '110,' he replies, without immodesty. He asks me about my business here. I start to tell him about *Around the World in Eighty Days*, and he interrupts knowledgeably: 'Ah yes, I know the book you are referring to. It is a work of science fiction.'

Despite a sore head from the beer and jazz last night, I attempt a run. The sheer weight of numbers prevents me. 12.5 million inhabitants on the move, and not an empty pavement anywhere.

Back in my room for a bath and some breakfast. It's eight o'clock and I feel I've already done a day's work. The *China Daily* bears news of the American Presidential election and a front cover photo of George Bush triumphant. Regulation grin, arms wide above his head, wife beside him, in one of those spontaneous gestures which ceased to be spontaneous years ago. The Americans seem to have voted for another four years of the same. Expected but depressing. I write postcards – dozens of them, driven perhaps by the knowledge that 60 years ago in Shanghai Noel Coward wrote *Private Lives* in four days.

Mental and physical energies recharged after a couple of hours to myself, I take a walk with Basil round the streets at the back of the Bund. My guidebook explains that 'visitors who have been to Shanghai before 1949 may find the names on the streets radically altered', and provides generous help to those who might be looking again for Bubbling Well Road (Janjing Road), Avenue Foch West (Yan'An Road), Avenue du Roi Albert (Shaanxi Road) or Robinson Road (Changshou Road).

There are a lot of comic books and magazines available on pavement stands. One has a lurid picture of a man carrying off a woman. Basil translates the title for me: *Silver Snake and the Beautiful Woman*. There are also a number of literary magazines – *Foreign Stories, Culture and Life*. Girls' faces are used to sell a lot of the mags, but I notice that the features of these alluring girls are never Chinese, always Western.

We eat dumplings and chives at a tiny table with two benches on the pavement. It's most satisfying to sit and watch the world go by. I realise, of course, that I can only do this with someone who speaks the language, and if I were in Shanghai with a tour group I wouldn't be sitting here.

Lots of food on sale at the street side. Confirms my impression that Chinese are the Small Businessmen of the World. Watercress, spring onions, fennel, red and green peppers, turnips, pickled cabbage, cauliflower and dried bean curd in chunks, like sealing wax. Live chickens and fish in small tanks, pigeons, bananas, noodles and, of course, snakes.

Along the Sichuan Zhong Lu, with its buildings in Venetian and Florentine Renaissance style, the door to an impressive office building bears the name 'Complete Sets of Equipment Corporation'.

The Opium Wars of the 1840s made drugs big business in China. Shanghai became the new centre, for only an hour up the river Huangpu was the Yangtze and a gateway to the heartland of China. This is what the reappearance of the Florentine Renaissance on the shores of the East China Sea is all about.

I'm soon to see the East China Sea for myself, for at five o'clock we're due to set sail for Yokohama. The ferry goes once a week and if there is any delay we are in trouble again. But with a deep blast of the horn it pulls out into the river, dead on time, executes a 360-degree turn opposite the Zhong Shou Road (formerly the Quai de France), which is rather like making a U-turn on the M1, and heads slowly up the crowded river to the confluence of the Yangtze.

A magnificent sunset to match this morning's spectacular sunrise. The domes and spires of the city are outlined in red and gold before sliding slowly into silhouette.

An hour or two later, after supper, I walk out on deck. I needed that coat I didn't buy. The night is clear, silent and chilly. We're free of the metropolitan sprawl of Shanghai, and the only lights I can see are coastal beacons, and small ships a long way off. We could be on the open sea, except that the water below me is muddy brown. We're on the Yangtze, and still two hours from the ocean.

Ten o'clock at night, Day 48. On the Yangtze River, heading due East, the Reform Club still over half the world away.

Day 49 12 November

Woken by the sound of inscrutable Chinese announcements on the tannoy. Knowing that, for once, we don't have an early start, I turn smugly onto my side, pull the sheets over my head and look forward to a long, late breakfast. An hour later, refreshed, bathed and relaxed I amble down to the canteen only to find that the inscrutable announcement was informing passengers that the clocks had gone forward an hour. It's now ten o'clock and breakfast has long since finished. I'm directed to the Coffee Room, where I find a bartender, a waitress and no one else. Order a coffee, orange juice and biscuits and sit by a low table spread with a Shanghai silk cloth. The room is full of fussy, abstract perspex fittings (which I come to recognise as a feature of Japanese interior design), swivel chairs and mournful piped music. The good-natured waitress brings me some carefully prepared Nescafé in a cup which bears the words 'Good Day, nice friends'. She speaks a little English and tells me that the ship, called the *Jian Zehn*, is a Sino-Japanese ferry, operated by the Chinese, built in Japan. Her capacity is 560 passengers, but there are only 165 on board today. I ask her how long she's worked on the ship, and she says eight months.

'Do you like it?'

'Only a little.'

The cassette runs out and in selecting one to replace it, she picks up a tape called 'Songs of a Stormy Night'.

'Beautifurr music,' she sighs, and slips the tape in lovingly.

The first minute or so consists entirely of the sound of rumbling thunder and heavy rain, which seems to be tempting fate a little. Eventually some strangulated synchronised chords are added to the bad weather. I smile, she smiles back, distantly. The recorded thunder rumbles. Glance out of the porthole to reassure myself it *is* a tape making these noises, and find a calm sea and the sun high in a sky of cotton-wool clouds. She smiles, I smile, the bartender smiles. It seems the only thing to do.

Later I explore the boat. Past the sign 'Gentles toilet' and endless slot machines dispensing beer, soap, coffee, noodles and sticky soft drinks.

There turns out to be another film crew aboard. Some 25 strong, from NHK, the Japanese BBC, shooting a drama about a woman of mixed Sino-Japanese parentage, born in Shanghai when the Japanese occupied it during the Second World War, who is bringing her children to China to decide what nationality they will adopt. They are shooting a scene of a waiter walking up some steps to a cabin. As these are the steps up to my cabin, and as the waiter always seems to get something wrong, I decide to go out on deck for a while.

In a forlorn games room stand two or three well-worn ping-pong tables with legs missing. A group of Japanese students are playing cards at plastic tables in the stern, set below a circular striped plastic canvas stretched across slender plastic poles to create a little plastic gazebo. I can only see two Europeans, who

I think may possibly be a honeymoon couple so deeply are they involved in each other. Shirt off and sit for a while reading Anthony Burgess's reminiscences which often make me laugh out loud.

Later Passepartout, who has enjoyed a day off, is asked to be an extra in the Japanese film. The scene is to be shot in the bar and payment is as much to drink as they want. As Nigel, Simon, Dave and Angela walk onto the set there is a spontaneous round of applause from the Japanese. On deck at 10 before turning in for an early night, I can pick out the lights of small boats and some coastal settlement to the north. Consulting my map, I deduce that we are passing through the archipelago of the Rijuku Islands, off the southern tip of Honshu. This is my first sight of Japan, as we leave the East China Sea and sail into the Pacific, the tenth sea I've entered since crossing the English Channel. I brew up some hot water in my cabin and take another dose of my Chinese medicine. The taste sensation is roughly similar to lying face downwards, mouth open in a patch of damp woodland.

Day 50 13 November

Filming around the boat. Clem decides on a 'where is everybody?' angle, only to find that the warm sunshine and calm sea has fetched everybody out, and in order to get the feeling of emptiness we have to move people out of the way.

The 'newly-weds' turn out to be a society acupuncturist from Paris who has been walking round the world for two years and a Dutch student of Arabic studies who fell in with him on the way. Having walked from Paris to Pakistan (where he had talked with General Zia less than a week before his death), into Afghanistan where he had spent six weeks with the Mujahidin, it came as a rude shock to find that China, the country that had been his goal, proposed to charged him 45,000 dollars for permission to walk across it. He came in on The Great Silk Road. I expressed my envy. 'Forget it,' he flicked his hand dismissively. 'It doesn't exist any more … it's all just the same … temples, monasteries. You've seen one temple …'

He certainly had a bad case of disillusionment. I asked if the Chinese had been welcoming.

'The minorities, yes,' said his companion … 'in Tibet especially; but in mainland China, no.'

They had been viewed with deep suspicion, followed, asked for money and forced sometimes to spend a night in a local jail. They had a fund of horror stories about the country, a lot of them, to be honest, second-hand. One concerned a student who had her camera stolen on a train. At the next stop, the train doors had been locked and the police had come on board. They found a man with a camera and asked the girl if it was hers. She nodded. Then the policeman assured her that there were no thieves in China and shot the man dead on the spot.

We talk about medicine. I ask him what he thinks about the Chinese attitude to doctors – that you pay them when you're well and stop paying them when you're ill. He seems to agree with the traditional Chinese approach, and says he no longer believes in Western medicine. He taps his head. 'So long as you eat the right food, breathe the right air …'

At three o'clock in the afternoon the east coast of Japan can be clearly seen on the port side, rising in a series of rocky cliffs. The Pacific, meanwhile, is living up to its name, and time passes slowly.

In the shop down below I buy a book of short stories by a Chinese author, Lu Wenfu. He had joined up to fight the Kuomintang rule in 1949, but later found himself, as a writer of fiction, denounced during the Cultural Revolution. 'I was forced to confess my crimes and paraded through the street with a placard round my neck.' He was luckier than some. He escaped with banishment to the countryside. Others lost their lives, many were unable to write again. The fact that Lu Wenfu is being published again in China has to be balanced against the unhappy experiences of the Walking Acupuncturist.

I also buy a sweatshirt with a glamorous picture of the ferry on it and a wonderful example of Anglo-Oriental doggerel: 'Regular weekly service with gorgeous cargo-passenger boat. A Happy, Warmed Journey with Thrilling Sealine.'

Day 51 14 November

We're due in Yokohama at 8.05 this morning, but no ship I've been on yet has arrived on time. My now dog-eared copy of *Around the World in Eighty Days* reminds me that Passepartout came alongside the wharf at Yokohama aboard *The Carnatic* on 14 November 1872 – 116 years ago to the day – but without Fogg whom he'd lost in Hong Kong. Even with the run of misfortunes they were still only 44 days out of London. I could catch up on the Pacific which Fogg took 22 days to cross, if I'm able to find a vessel able to outrun his *General Grant*, '... a large side-wheel steamer of 2,500 tons, well equipped and of great speed'.

I pull back the thin orange curtains and there is Japan. The rays of the rising sun, appropriately, fill the little cabin, spilling out from behind a dark outline of ragged hills. Elaborate announcements in Chinese and Japanese.

We move slowly towards the indistinct brown-grey skyline of Yokohama. (The brown are the buildings, the grey is a corona of polluted air above them.) Pass two of the largest vessels I've ever seen, both car transporters with the name Nissan in 20-foot-high letters on the side. They are incredible hulks which make container ships look graceful, but their size is evidence of the commercial power of Japan. Behind them equally enormous super-tankers are queueing to unload their oil. As fast as the oil comes in, the cars go out.

In this harbour full of Leviathans it's good to see the occasional grimy freighter, like the *Asian Rose* of Panama, the

Chunji of Pusan, bringing scrap metal from Korea, and one whose name can only just be made out beneath the stains and scuffed paint – *Venus*, Manila.

The tug *Yokohama Maru* gives a prolonged blast on the horn to warn off about six other vessels which seem to be heading for our spot on the jetty and begins to heave us round and into position. The Chinese students who have come to study in Japan lean expectantly over the rails. The Walking Acupuncturist shoulders an enormous pack, the back of which is adorned with the names of his twin causes: 'Enfants Réfugiés du Monde' and 'Université Européenne de Médecine Chinoise'.

Dockers in uniform yellow windcheaters stand by to catch the ropes. Customs men in immaculate navy-blue uniforms ease on white gloves in preparation for boarding. A volley of poppers and streamers crackle out from a welcoming party for the students. Next to me are a Japanese family who had taken a bus across China for a holiday in Pakistan, only to be turned back at the Pakistan border because of a cholera scare. They seem to have taken it awfully well.

A Sousa march is blaring from the terminal loudspeakers, mingling in a musical Babel with the Viennese waltzes on the ship's indefatigable Muzak system. We are processed through customs and immigration politely and briskly, and driven the short distance to Yokohama Shin-Kensan station. *Shin-Kensan* means 'New Railway', better known in the west as the Bullet Train.

The Sousa march played as we landed is a fitting foretaste of the extraordinary Americanisation of Japan, the country America bombed into submission in the war, rebuilt in its own likeness and to which it has now ceded economic primacy.

So the forecourt of the station has a restaurant called The New York Lunch Box, an advert for the Home Town Express and Tom and Jerry selling something. The remarkable part of it is that few of the Japanese speak or write English. They know a few key words, culled phonetically from American records and movies and TV shows and thrown together to create a new and batty half-language which erupts on carrier bags – 'Trad Boy, Tradition succeeded to Men', or sweatshirts 'Soul Explosion', 'Funny Crazy', 'Hey Sexy'. There's a sock brand sold at one of the numerous little station shops, called 'Naughty Boy', and I was told that someone saw an immaculate, expensively dressed woman, wearing a huge leather belt on which the word 'Bullshit' was written at regular intervals.

The station is kept obsessively clean, not just swept with a brush but scrubbed with soap and water by an army of Lady Macbeths trying to get rid of any stains that might indicate poverty or economic back-sliding.

The Japanese are very well dressed. Their shape and style reminds me of the Italians. I'm afraid we stand out like a bunch of tramps. I feel like those Chinese peasants who came wide-eyed into the lobby of the White Swan to gaze in awe at what man could make of his world. Feel a little less impressed when a dapper businessman gets onto the train wearing a smog mask.

Inside and out the train resembles an aircraft. The pointed nose, with the cabin high up, looks like the front of a 747, cut off, then stuck on to a line of wingless aircraft fuselages. The seats inside are laid out like aircraft seats, and the driver wears a pilot's peaked and braided cap. Your ticket tells you exactly where to stand on the platform. The train arrives every 10 minutes exactly on time and the doors are open for 30 seconds only. They are meant for light-travelling businessmen, not round the world film crews, and feeling like participants in some game show we only just haul our baggage aboard in time.

A 15-minute ride into Tokyo through an unbroken swath of close-packed housing. Hardly a break in the jostle of low-rise, flimsy-looking boxes which I'm told cost half a million pounds minimum in the centre of Tokyo. So little room is there that the golf-crazy Japanese have to build their courses on the tops of buildings. Well-behaved, well-heeled fellow passengers read their papers which are headlined, as I'm told they have been since late August, with news of Emperor Hirohito's illness. Nothing is spared. The big news today is that he hasn't had a bowel movement for a week. Details of his pulse and blood pressure are as meticulously recorded as the Dow-Jones Index.

At Tokyo station the magazine racks are full of George Bushes with their arms spread out. A Japanese magazine bears the English title *Heart Washing*. I bend to look more closely and rest my bag which is heavy on my shoulders. I immediately have to pick it up again as a lady on a sweeping machine bears down on me.

Parties of schoolchildren, uniformed and well-behaved, are led through the crowds by teachers holding flags above their heads. The girls are in navy blue with pleated skirts, the boys in what looks like Prussian hussars' uniforms, with black tunics, buttoned high up to the neck. (I later learn these traditional boys' school uniforms are in fact based on Prussian army jackets.)

At the entrance to the park which surrounds Hirohito's Imperial Palace stand serried ranks of silver TV vans, topped with plastic-shrouded outside broadcast cameras, waiting, like hooded vultures.

I can see trees whose leaves are turning and I'm reminded that, though Tokyo is on the same latitude as Morocco, its climate is closer to that of Manchester and I am back again in a land of four seasons. I can't postpone augmenting my wardrobe any longer and in the spirit of Fogg's instruction to Passepartout – 'we shall purchase on the way' – I sally forth to the department stores. Japanese department stores are an institution, and they take their role in national life very seriously. Apart from offering an enormous range of everything they are also travel agents, concert halls, cinemas and art galleries. Picasso's *Acrobat and Young Harlequin* has just been bought for 38 million dollars, to be displayed not in the

Japanese National Gallery but in the Mitsukoshi department store. Rivals Seibu recently bought a Monet for 10.5 million.

At twenty to seven in the evening I'm drinking a coffee at the Concorde bar on the top floor of the Hankyu department store, Tokyo. I walked in here about 35 minutes ago, found a selection of clothes I liked, mostly from Italy and England, bought a jacket, a sweater and two pairs of trousers. Both the trousers needed taking up, and the assistant apologised that this might take half an hour! As I was paying my bill they noticed my finger had a small slightly bloody scratch and, within seconds, had produced a Band-Aid and dressed it for me. As I leave the store at seven, clutching my new outfit and dying to replace my embarrassingly creased stained and travelworn shirts and parrot-pecked trousers, the staff of each department, from Soft Toys to Dental Appliances, gather at the top of their respective escalators to bow. I may look like Worzel Gummidge, but for four floors I'm the Queen.

Both Shanghai and Tokyo have populations of around 12 million, but the difference in the look of the people is enormous. Japan seems to consist of one very affluent middle class, busy and assured of their place in a sophisticated urban technopolis. Shanghai's crowds seem out of another century. Central Tokyo at night is a blaze of light, an eruption of neon, trains rumbling overhead, roads full of cars. But there are no jaywalkers and no black plastic bags. Control is the name of the game here. I take a taxi back to the hotel with my new acquisitions. Not only does the back door swing open automatically, it also closes automatically, and like the bullet train you have to move fast or you'll lose something.

Cultural magpies, the Japanese have an ability to replicate with great skill whatever attracts them. So we end up eating Tokyo Irish, in Mother Maguire's beer and steak house.

Day 52 15 November

So highly automated is my bedside console that when I stretch to put the light on in the night I find the weather forecast for Southern California flashing on to my TV screen. The curtains swing open and the kettle starts to boil before I eventually locate a light switch, and several downlighters and uplighters later before I find one which sheds some light on the place where I actually need it. First thing in the morning I phone Mr Nakajima, the shipping agent. He's not there and someone else is put on to help me. The language barrier is too high to cope with the delicacies of circumnavigation, and I resign myself to having to wait before I know the fate of my Pacific crossing.

It's a sign of the times that when Fogg arrived anywhere there was an outward-bound passenger service leaving that same day. There are now no passenger services across the Pacific, apart from cruises. I have no option but to insinuate myself aboard some cargo boat, and this requires constant pestering of those whose business is goods, not people.

Look around the side streets near the hotel. The units are small. Cafés, businesses and shops cheek by jowl, with very few high-rise blocks. (This, I'm told, is because of the ever-present earthquake threat; there is an earthquake every day in Tokyo, they say, most of them too small to be felt on the street.) The group being more important than the individual in Japanese life, it is natural for shopkeepers and businesses to band together to look after their streets and to vet further development. The result is not architecturally impressive – there are no grand and sweeping facades – but there is a lively, varied, vigorous feeling of impermanence.

I go to check out what is still a Japanese phenomenon, but which is rumoured to be spreading west – the capsule hotel. These establishments offer a city centre bed for the night for 3,600 yen, about £17 or the price of a round of coffees in a downtown café. For this extraordinary value you have to put up with a certain degree of regimentation. The hotel I try is a cross between a high-tech school dorm and an executive morgue. Shoes must be removed before you even reach the front desk (this in itself must be quite a test for the late-night inebriates). Whereas in central London cheap hotels generally mean seedy hotels, the capsule hotel is kept, like everywhere else in Tokyo, pathologically clean. Interior surveillance pictures on a bank of video screens at reception roll over like ever-changing symbols on a fruit machine. You pay as you enter, and are given a locker key, a note on how to behave ('Persons whose bodies are tattooed are requested to keep out') and a towel. In the locker on the floor on which you are to be stored you exchange your clothes for a pair of pale blue shorts and a Hawaiian shirt. Businessmen are turned momentarily into butterflies. Finally you're issued with a razor and toothbrush. You are then shown to the allotted capsule. These are nothing more than plastic boxes, six feet long by about three feet wide, stacked one above the other in long rows. A thin but comfortable mattress is provided, the temperature is controlled from a panel by the right shoulder, as is light and a tiny colour TV. The less you value individuality the easier you will overcome the feelings of claustrophobia and loss of identity. For me, waking in the middle of the night in such a place would be profoundly depressing, if not terrifying.

I lunch with David Powers, a BBC radio man in Tokyo, at an automatic sushi bar. Thirty-seven varieties of sushi (raw fish with rice) move slowly round on a constantly replenished conveyor belt, in front of which the customer sits and takes off the saucer containing the sushi of his choice. The stack of saucers is checked at the end and your bill calculated. Tea and water are dispensed automatically. It's a triumph of what the Japanese are really good at – management, distribution and control.

My stack of saucers mounts as squid, cod roe, conger eel, boiled octopus, pickled radish, raw prawns, cucumber and seaweed, chopped tuna and onion and crabsticks slip down. There is one particularly vile looking delicacy which keeps coming past which David tells me is salted squid innards and almost unpalatable to Europeans. Being a bit of an innards man this sounds like a challenge that cannot be avoided and I pop one in. Mauve in colour, slimy in texture it is, to say the least, bracing. Rather as industrial adhesive might be bracing. It will definitely join fox, dog and snake and cat soup as party conversation for many years to come.

Waiting at a public phone box to contact Mr Nakajima again I'm caught unawares by the Japanese use of the sharply exhaled exclamation *Hai* in everyday conversation. It whistles out so emphatically that it sounds like someone's just thrown a knife at you, and you duck sharply only to see it's someone talking on the phone behind.

Mr Nakajima is in his office and I have had a great stroke of luck ... *Hai!* ... a container ship of Neptune Orient Lines is scheduled to leave Tokyo tomorrow evening for a ten-day journey to Long Beach, California.

This is good news indeed and demands a celebration. Clem is set on trying a *Karaoke* bar. *Karaoke* (which means 'empty orchestra') began 20 years ago as a way of allying Japanese technology to the Japanese urge to sing in public. It's refined a little since then but basically consists of a small bar at one end of which is a performing area. The one I visit with David Powers has on laser disc the backing track to 2,000 popular songs. For the negligible sum of 100 yen a tune can be played through the club's PA system whilst the punter stands on stage with mike in hand, words relayed on a screen in front of him, singing along as best he can. But this is not all, for on two screens behind, a video adds the final touch. Respectably dressed middle-aged men, and women, can croon mournful ballads whilst young lovers on video career through corn fields in soft focus and 4-wheel drive Subarus.

The atmosphere is very jolly and everyone is encouraged

and applauded, however dire their presentation. Whilst I gulp a beer for courage, David Powers sings, in Japanese, a couple of truly heart-rending ballads which bring the house down. A tableful of nattily dressed young Japanese launch into a chant of 'T'atch-er! T'atch-er!' Not trusting my voice to linger over anything sentimental I choose from the catalogue 'You Are My Sunshine', which I've been unable to banish from my mind since hearing the Shanghai jazz band playing it. The audience is supportive, the video shows streamlined images of Muscle Beach in Los Angeles, my next destination, a bouncy Japanese girl joins me in the choruses and at the end there are shouts of 'Bee-Bee-*Cee*! Bee-Bee-*Cee*!' which will, I'm sure, bring tears to the eyes of the taxpayer.

Back at the hotel Cleese tells me on the phone from London that Japan has been the only country in the world to show no interest in *A Fish Called Wanda*. Suggest *A Squid Called Wanda* might go better.

To bed in a blaze of glory with a glass of 'Super Nikka' Japanese Scotch, which is almost as bad as my singing.

Day 53 16 November

Before I leave Japan I have one last proof of travel to collect. Robert Hewison, one of my four trustees, has asked me to bring back a menu from a place called Caffe Bongo. Fortunately the Caffe Bongo is not easy to miss. It appears that an aeroplane has just crashed into it. A wing projects out of the window and into the street. Inside the wing is lodged about 8 or 9 feet off the ground. Bent girders on tilted metal columns snake upwards into, or downwards from, the aircraft, and classical columns, broken and tilting, seem to grow through it. Michelangelo's *David* is perched against a wall. The general effect is as if a Dakota had been forced to make an emergency landing in medieval Florence.

In the middle of all this exhilarating profusion of images, designed by a British architect, Nigel Coates, a few Japanese are solemnly sitting drinking coffee at £4 a cup as if they were in Betty's tea rooms in Ilkley. I ask for a menu, and then have to try and explain to the waitress that I want to keep it. She doesn't understand. Why should she? The more I explain my mission the more preposterous it sounds. I should have just pocketed the menu card, but it's rather large and unconcealable. I approach various other customers who try not to look at me, and on my third or fourth attempt, enlist the help of a businessman who tries his hand at explaining my quest to the staff.

Not a smile is cracked throughout the explanation. Instead frowns deepen, but eventually a solution is reached: the buck will be passed. Someone with more authority is to be summoned. How long will that be? The waitress doesn't understand. I point to my watch and try to indicate that I'm expected on the Pacific in a couple of hours. She goes away. Time passes. There's a distinct chance that I shall have to choose between getting a Caffe Bongo menu or getting around the world in eighty days. Order another £4 coffee. Am about to grab the menu and make a break for it when a smart lady appears and after I give another long and time-consuming explanation, I'm met with the same bewildered response.

'Look, a British architect designed this and so surely you realise the British occasionally do very silly things ...'

'You are architect!' Her eyes lit up.

'Well, not ... er as such, but I like architecture ...'

'Ah ... yes? ... architect ... good!'

From then on it's plain sailing and I emerge £8 lighter, but with a Caffe Bongo menu *and* a Caffe Bongo cup and saucer.

A digital sign above me reads: 12 degrees centigrade, 11.20, November 16. Buy a sweatshirt with highly prized example of Anglo-Japanese: 'Sporty Life. You ought to get do some a little exercise everyday'. Well, I'll have time to think about that on the Pacific, which is where I must now head for.

My home for the next week and a half is a big, fat, well-used ship which could do with some paint on the hull. At 800 feet and 42,872 tonnes, she's 10 feet longer and 6,000 tonnes heavier than the *Neptune Diamond* and her name is the *Neptune Garnet*. A container full of containers, built to circumnavigate the world every 63 days. She has come from Singapore, by way of Hong Kong and Taipei and Pusan in South Korea. She sails tonight at 10 for Long Beach, California, then on to Charleston, New York and Halifax, Nova Scotia, from where she sails non-stop to Singapore, via Suez, in 23 days.

After 30 days ambling across Asia, and with an American crossing still to come, I need the reassurance of a tight schedule like this, and we all need a break from loading, unloading, checking in and checking out, filming daily in heat and crowds and on the move.

At the top of the ship's long accommodation ladder I'm greeted by the master of the *Neptune Garnet*, an immediately likeable Indian – Captain Suresh Amirapu.

Although the *Garnet* is a bigger and more modern ship than the *Diamond*, most of the 'improvements' have been strictly commercial. Everything has been squeezed to make more room for the containers, so the crew's quarters are narrower, showers are preferred to baths and the swimming pool's disappeared altogether. The decoration is the same – Far Eastern Functional, all artificial materials, moulded plastic, bland colours, easy to use, easy to clean, difficult to remember. There are 24 in the crew: 3 Indians, 1 Pakistani, 14 Singaporeans, 2 Malaysians, 2 Burmese cadets, 1 Filipino cadet and a Ghanaian.

I'm in the doctor's quarters again, comprising a small bedroom and a day room, six levels up from the deck. The captain has given us all a computer-printed sheet covering things we need to know, and encourages us to visit the bridge whenever we like. The captain has leave every six months, when he's flown home. He has a six-week-old baby boy he hasn't even seen yet. We cast off at 11.25 at night, an hour and a half late.

The two 45-tonne cranes have been working up to the last minute and containers are now stacked five-high from the deck. Nigel and Dave, whose quarters are unfortunately on the fifth floor, saw their view disappear about ten minutes ago.

I watch from the bows as a tug heaves us round, leaving only a few feet clearance between ourselves and the *Neptune Crystal*, which is still loading. (This was the ship which was our second option out of Singapore, and which lost a couple of containers overboard during Typhoon Tess.)

A cool wind catches us as we head off south-west, to the mouth of Tokyo Bay. Sad to see the last of Asia, but glad to be moving east again.

Over a late night Tiger beer, Roger tells me of a plan he has to pass the long hours on the Pacific. I am to produce a play with the crew. Nine days' rehearsal, one performance. What sort of play do we do with Singaporean, Ghanaian, Burmese, Filipino, Indian and Pakistani merchant seamen? Roger admits that his choice was circumscribed by the availability of English plays in Tokyo, but he *has* secured ten copies of *Macbeth*.

Day 54 17 November

Thursday morning. Bacon and egg breakfast after strange dream in which Margaret Thatcher was very nice to me. Can it be that she is now intruding into the previously exclusive domain of royalty – the British dream? Resolve to lie awake all tomorrow night in case it happens again.

It's not easy to take in that we will not see land again until we reach Conception Point, 50 miles north of Los Angeles, a week this Saturday. That's eleven days – longer than our average family holiday. Talking of holidays, Dave Passepartout will not believe that we can cross the Pacific without hitting Hawaii. After all, he says, it is bang in the middle. But of course we don't go through the middle of the Pacific. We stay as far north as is safe, taking advantage of the curvature of the earth to shorten the distance. The 'summer route' is 4,606 miles from Tokyo to Long Beach, but Captain Amirapu is taking the winter route, 360 miles longer, because, as he shows us on the charts, 'it will avoid us being clobbered by these'. He indicates several clusters of tightly packed isobars hovering to the north and east of us.

'We just missed a big gale. If we'd left a day earlier ...' More gnashing of teeth from director. More converts to astrology.

The clear skies, which last night gave such a fine parting panorama of Tokyo, have been replaced this morning by thickening grey clouds. A fresh north-east wind sighs round the plastic passageways.

After breakfast I have to go to bed again so they can film me getting up. After that I walk out on deck again so I can be filmed walking on deck and in this way a morning passes briskly, if derivatively. In the late afternoon I explore a running circuit around the ship. There is a narrow gangway between the deck rail with containers stacked above and to the side. A tight squeeze across the bows, but it's possible, weather permitting, to run the circumference of the deck which is a neat half-kilometre.

Evening: Almost all the crew apart from a couple on the bridge are watching *Stakeout* in the narrow room that serves as bar, games room, reading room and library, but which nearly always has the curtains drawn and a video on. It doesn't seem the time to get them out for a *Macbeth* rehearsal so the idea is indefinitely postponed. On the floor below there's a table-tennis table and Roger and I resume our rivalry.

We lose an hour tonight, one of eight time changes on this Pacific crossing. The 12 hours that we've progressively lost since leaving London, together with another 12 that we shall lose between the Pacific, America and London, will be refunded in full at the International Date Line in the shape of one extra 24-hour period. Though only ten days on my schedule, the crossing will be eleven in reality.

Day 55   18 November

The only waves troubling me this morning are waves of delayed fatigue. The supply of adrenaline which pushed me through Hong Kong and China and Japan has dried up and as I lie in bed this morning, having lost an hour's sleep to the clock, my body feels as immovable as the 6-foot-high anchor on the bow deck. Rain beats against the window. I look out on the first unequivocally wet day of the journey.

Eggs and bacon have run out already and breakfast is a Singapore dumpling that nestles, white, round and naked on my plate like a miniature early warning system. The intrepid eater is rewarded with a smudge of red bean curd at the centre. A mug of coffee, then a sorting out of clothes and a visit to the laundry room. There are two machines, above one of which is written 'Dirty Overalls Only'. This looks to be stating the obvious until I see one of the engine crew looking with satisfaction at a filthy, blackened, grease- and oil-stained boiler suit – which he has just taken *out* of the machine.

Up on the bridge at 11.45. 250 miles out of Tokyo and on a course East North East up to latitude 38 and longitude 165 at which point we shall head due East for the rest of the journey. Our speed is steady at 20 knots. I ask the captain why we are 3 knots slower than the more aged *Neptune Diamond*. He says it's all a matter of economics. At 20 knots his engine is using 10 tonnes of fuel a day. At 23 knots it would use 20 tonnes.

I manage a run later in the day, but only up and down the sheltered starboard side. The weather is worsening – rain pelting down and the wind's sighs becoming shrill screams. Roger looks cheerful. Apparently he's just encountered the captain who greeted him with:

'Bad news for me, good news for you.'

A fast developing frontal depression is advancing on us from the south west. Force 7 or 8, it should hit us this evening.

Up on the bridge the barograph has plunged and the captain is carefully marking the path of the storm from his own observations and from information he receives from Ocean Routes, a subscription weather information service run by the Americans, who supply a daily faxed weather chart and regular telex update of conditions.

The evening's video is *Live and Let Die*. The gathering storm makes for an interesting game of table tennis. Scrabble is brought out later in the Doctor's Day Room which Roger has christened 'Mike's Bar'.

Eleven o'clock: Mike's Bar has just closed and I'm in bed with Oscar Wilde – Richard Ellman's biography that is. The wind is moaning and the ship is shuddering as if reliving some awful childhood trauma. The containers creak and clang mournfully below my window. I haven't taken any anti-sickness precautions. I want to see if I need to.

Difficult to write now. In the bathroom poltergeists are at work. My shower curtain draws itself and undraws itself. First a toothbrush, then the toothpaste, then the tooth mug topple into the basin. Put them all to rights, but as I turn over to try and sleep, I hear the Scrabble slide the length of the table and spill onto the floor. It's an uncomfortable night. Impossible to lie in one position for more than a few seconds. As the ship rolls the body tenses waiting to counteract the roll. Instead the ship decides to quiver and pitch forward. It's like having your cradle rocked by a giant with a twitch.

Day 56 19 November

The worst of the gale is over, but on the faxed chart there is another approaching from the west. Our speed has dropped and America is still 4,000 miles away. We have just passed off my admirable Kummerly and Frey map of Asia on which I've been able to chart progress since we left Crete 50 days ago. Now

I have nothing but my inflatable globe to show me the vast distance I still have to travel.

Passepartout is scattered in various accommodations. Ann is in the pilot's room, Roger in the 2nd officer's, Nigel and Dave are cadets 'A' and 'B' and Simon is spare officer. At breakfast there is much one-upmanship over how badly we slept last night...

'An *hour*! You were lucky!'

'Nothing woke me up, nothing. I never went to sleep.'

After breakfast we assemble to discuss the day's work in the 'Meeting Room', seven floors above the deck, and just below the bridge. The wall is covered with certificates and mementos of the *Garnet*'s maiden voyage in January 1986: a silver and black model lifebuoy inscribed 'Bon Voyage' from the port of Osaka, a miniature ship's wheel from the stevedores of Terminal 18 at Port Seattle, and a pink, glass-eyed geisha doll presented by the Hyundai Shipyard, South Korea, on completion of the vessel.

Talk at lunch to the Pakistani chief engineer. He is anxious about the new Sulzer fuel-efficient engine, which is giving him 'many sleepless nights'. This sounds ominous.

Tonight, to celebrate the Indian festival of Deepavalli, a special buffet supper and party is to be held. We have managed to steer the Singaporean chef away from attempts at European food and he comes up with an Indo-Chinese spread which scores highly. Curried prawns, red snapper, chicken with mangoes and rice, followed by Tiger beers in the bar followed by introductions and speeches, emceed admirably by a Singaporean officer whose name I think is Hang On.

There is much laughter that I should be making such a meal of going round the world in eighty days when they do it in sixty-three. Six times a year.

Then the party begins. Such oriental specialities as Pass the Parcel and Charades are entered into with an enthusiasm that would delight the United Nations. The games are well organised and forfeits are very popular. The captain has to mime someone without money trying to grab an illegal ride on the Hong Kong subway, Simon has to sing 'Yesterday', Nigel has to give George Bush's first Presidential address and Roger to imitate his favourite animal. He gets down on all fours then lifts his leg on the captain's shoe, to great applause.

Charades are more problematical as none of our team knows any of the films the crew have given us. They're the video favourites and usually involve killing and retribution, and despite our energetic efforts with *The Evil that Men Do*, *Street Killer* and *He Knows You're Alone* the result is only bafflement.

We're more successful in the Tug of War. This takes place in the passageway outside, and as it's a hot sticky night, both deck doors are open, so there's always the danger that the team that loses its balance might disappear for ever into the North Pacific. But the contest is close and myself and Passepartout hold the young, fit, though well-Tigered, *Garnet* crew to a draw over three contests.

Pouring sweat, retire triumphantly to bed. Twelve thousand miles away in London my second son will be waking up on his eighteenth birthday. The fact that I'm missing this and an important university entrance exam he has to take in two days makes me momentarily regret being so far away and so helpless.

Day 57   20 November

Wake, very hot. Something is wrong. The air-conditioning seems to be sucking in moist, humid air, and the engine note has changed. Pull the flimsy curtain back from the porthole. The long causeway of containers – six high and thirteen across – stretches ahead, but there is no sign of the surging white wake from the bows. In fact, we've almost stopped. The chief engineer, raised at dawn from another sleepless night, is not a happy man. Captain Amirapu tries to keep cheerful. Precious time drifts away.

Mid-morning. The engines are up to power again. A feeder pipe had sheared off and we've lost three or four hours.

Run early today as the weather service has forecast another storm, marked this time on the fax with an S.W. (Storm Warning), a notch up on yesterday's G.W. (Gale Warning). Once again it's from the south-west, and once again it's expected about the time Mike's Bar opens for the evening session.

At five o'clock, I take a walk on deck and can see the edge of the approaching storm, spread diagonally across the southern sky like a huge grey wing, sheltering beneath it a mass of mist and rain which will soon overhaul us.

Even in this solid great ship it's easy to feel vulnerable, as the wind brings in the storm, and the pots and pans are battened down in the galley. At a somewhat shaky dinner I talk to the chief engineer about Benazir Bhutto's election – news of which I picked up on my shortwave radio earlier. He is not happy. She is an untried politician, voted in on a wave of sympathy for her father's death. Sounds as though people supported Zia in Pakistan for the same reason many support Thatcher in Britain. He may not have been personally popular but he was tough, forever standing up to people. Not those with money however. Zia was a good businessman and the chief engineer fears that Bhutto, elected by a popular rather than establishment vote, will squander a carefully built up international reputation.

Day 58 21 November

On the bridge early this morning. Remains of the storm still blowing, but it moved across us fast, says the captain, and the worst is long gone. Bulky low cloud and drizzle, a sluggish sea and not a strand of sunshine can be seen through the long, wide windows. In short, inauspicious conditions for an auspicious day – the return to the Western Hemisphere, the halfway point of my journey, the crossing of the International Date Line. Since nature has refused to play up and no international corporation has yet considered the advantages of sponsoring a line of Date Line marker buoys, we are reduced to marking this great occasion by watching the line appear on the satellite navigation screen, which is a bit like seeing the New Year in with Radio 3. There are no trumpets sounding, not even an extra electronic bleep to mark our passage into another hemisphere, just the split-second changes of little white numbers. 38.02 is our latitude (about the same as Benidorm), and at 8.20 precisely, longitude 180.00.E flashes for a second, then remorselessly moves on to 179.59.W.

As we have moved east with the sun we have gained a day over the rest of the world and must now mark time and let the others catch up. So we have an extra day. This was the coup for Jules Verne at the end of *Around the World in Eighty Days* when Fogg thought all was lost for he had seen eighty sunrises. His colleagues, stationary in London, had only seen seventy-nine. So the bet was won and Mrs Aouda became Mrs Fogg. But all this is jumping ahead. It's taken me 58 days to travel halfway round the globe, and I've 22 days to do the rest.

My fate depends ultimately on one propeller and the ability of the engine to turn it non-stop, 24 hours a day, in all weathers, for at least the next six days. The propeller weighs 55 tons, is cast in bronze and has four blades with a diameter of about 27 feet. The engine room area occupies five floors below decks, and the cylinders are three floors high. If noise were enough to drive the ship along I would have no worries. We are given ear-protectors, but I slip them off to feel the sound of so much power. It is just below the limit of aural pain. The chief engineer with his permanently worried look (either because of Benazir Bhutto or the problems with the Sulzer engine) is testing electrical circuits. With his white coat, neat black beard and moustache, obsessive enthusiasm and small frame dwarfed by pumping hissing machinery he reminds me of Willy Wonka in Roald Dahl's *Charlie and the Chocolate Factory*.

From the caves of heavy metal below decks I walk out before lunch to my favourite spot above decks. This is a gallery at the stern, open on three sides, low to the sea, on which are winches and capstans and stanchions of powerful appearance standing like sculptures at some futuristic art gallery. At the stern rail I am only a few feet above the churning propeller and I can happily stand for ages watching it send the water flicking up and flinging back to mark our progress across the Pacific with a green and white gash two or three hundred yards long, above which wheel half a dozen sea-birds, who have followed us for days. Along the sides run swelling waves, massive and unbroken after crossing thousands of miles of open sea, rising sometimes high above my head. With the noise of the engine and the wind, it's a sobering but exhilarating glimpse of power. So easy would it be just to slip through the rail. If I did what would be my chances? There's no one with me. The noise would drown any shouts. How long would it be before my absence was noted? Another half-hour at least. The ship would be 15 miles away by then and a full turn would take another half-hour. Decide to go to the quieter end of the ship. Today, because of a following wind the bows are almost eerily silent. Like cloisters.

The Table Tennis Competition is hotting up. Nigel Passepartout is now known as Hurricane because of his mercurial style. Sometimes unplayably deadly, other times unable to hit the table. The ball flicks and spins off radiator pipes, shelves, air-conditioning vents and opponents' heads. But win or lose, his approach is pure Welsh passion. Roger, on the other hand, is becoming a cool, calculating opponent, poker-faced and consistent, and now known as the Professor. The man to beat.

There is a bizarre announcement halfway through the evening meal: 'You are reminded that it will be Monday again tomorrow.'

Day 58 21 November

What one always wants. A chance to have the day again, and get it right this time. Long lie-in. The Professor has decreed that this shall be a no-filming day, and the signs are that it could become a non-day altogether. It's as if no one has any confidence in a day we've had already. I see nothing of Passepartout until late morning.

The sea is calm on the surface but a big swell is running at us from the south-east, and the captain is worried that this is somehow affecting our speed. We are over halfway across the Pacific now, the weather warm and humid and cloudy. A ship is sighted on the starboard side, heading west, the first we've seen for four days. The captain makes radio contact:

'Hello westbound ship ... This is eastbound ship *Neptune Garnet*, do you read me?'

'Hello eastbound ship, we read you.'

'What is your name?'

'*Manila Prosperity.*'

'Where are you coming from?'

'Great Lakes and Montreal to Nagoya and Bangkok.'

'We are on liner service, Tokyo to Long Beach.'

'How is weather?'

'Two lows, quite developed, have passed up to the Aleutians. We hope we are in high pressure now.'

'You're lucky.'

'Not so lucky after all, we have swell on port side. Rolling and pitching badly. We've lost time.'

The Filipino ship doesn't sound convinced. She is a much smaller ship heading into a steady succession of depressions. Our captain signs off breezily: 'Have a safe voyage, avoid the lows.'

Investigate the library. It's that sort of day. Nearly all the books are in English, though there isn't an Englishman in the crew. A selection of sea classics – *Requiem for a Wren, A Night to*

Remember, Moby-Dick, The Iliad. Can't imagine container ships spawning any literature of their own – *In Which We Load, Voyage of the Canned.*

There are fat Micheners and Urises and Clavells. Long, thick and international. The container ships of literature. There are games – chess, draughts and Mah Jong – but videos are more popular. This afternoon they're watching *Silent Night.* Far from being a nice little tale of carol singers it's another load of screams and terror. These gentle people's capacity for watching other people's violence seems almost unlimited.

On the notice board outside there is information about stress and how to combat it, the danger of Aids and an invitation to participate in Vernons Football Pools.

Day 59 22 November

The swell shows no let-up and makes sleep uncomfortable. Wake to find my world rolling around on the floor. Sitting at a solitary late breakfast of coffee, toast and marmalade, I see only sky through the porthole, a moment later only sea.

It's the Professor's birthday, and I give him J.L. Carr's *A Season in Sinji,* as it's about cricket, which he is fond of, and is an excellent and absorbing tale. A clutch of letters from his family, all assembled unbeknownst to him at Tokyo, make his morning.

On deck the containers are groaning and wailing more spectacularly than ever. They sound like Stockhausen and the Professor thinks a symphony for containers should be commissioned. Simon, on the other hand, thinks they might be communicating something to the whales.

By mid-afternoon the flat, muggy, moist, overcast conditions which have prevailed since the weekend give way to sharper, clearer, cooler weather. Ideal, it is judged, for an initiation ceremony to mark the crossing of the Date Line.

Such is the nature of my relationship with Passepartout that when something potentially as unpleasant as this has to be faced, it is faced by me alone. The gulf between presenter and crew, normally the width of a fordable stream, becomes a Pacific Ocean. So it is I alone who represent the supernumeraries and gather down in the Radio Room at half past four to be prepared for this time-honoured and humiliating ritual. Fortunately there are members of the crew who have not been initiated – Francis, a 25-year-old Ghanaian, who served in his own country's merchant fleet until Jerry Rawlings reduced it to only four vessels, George, a tall, languid, 22-year-old Burmese cadet and a small slim Malaysian who we know as Saatchi – his full name being Sachithanathan and a bit of a mouthful.

The four of us are lined up and the crew members, dressed in an odd mixture of handmade ceremonial robes, with cardboard hats and in one case a Korean flag worn like a toga, start to make us ready. Parek, the mild-mannered chief officer, has become a monster for the occasion. He has the role of Neptune's High Priest, so he can shout louder and more abusively than anyone apart from the King. We are ordered to strip down to underpants, and are given only a thin strip of sacking to act as a loin cloth. Then our wrists are bound together with adhesive tape and a rope is looped round all our necks. Yoked thus, like the burghers of Calais, and preceded by a pounding gong, we are half-led, half-shoved onto the deck and up two flights of steps to the Captain's Bridge Deck.

Here is enthroned King Neptune, a cardboard crown and cotton wool beard barely disguising the dark Singaporean features of the chief electrician. He holds a trident and next to him sits the Queen – his wife Lily. Their little boy Rajiv, who is travelling with them, is not one of the participants but looks on in total amazement. We are ordered to kneel. Just time to notice there's a handsome sunset behind us before being shouted at to keep my head bowed. A scroll is then unwound and charges read to the effect that we transgressors have strayed over the Date Line without asking King Neptune's permission.

The King is then asked what punishments are required before he will be appeased. Already Passepartout, safe behind his camera and tape recorder, looks a little embarrassed at our predicament, but when the first punishment turns out to be that we must 'shit and urinate', I just have time to see four mouths drop open before being flung forward, and a small glass bowl (of the sort we have puddings in) placed beneath my groin. This is then rapidly filled with syrup from a tin of fruit salad, into which a frankfurter is then dropped. The next order, somewhat predictably perhaps, is that we should 'eat shit and urine!' This done we are dragged to our feet and daubed with tomato ketchup. 'Hands above your heads!' Despite the cold and the smell and general discomfort I keep my spirits high by thinking of Alan Whicker doing this. I think Clive James might have drawn the line at eating his own shit and urine. The tomato ketchup having been liberally applied, particularly to the armpits, we are then sprinkled all over with soy sauce, thrust to our knees again and flour rubbed into our hair, after which there is a momentary breather before an egg is broken over each of our heads. I feel the yolk, gratifyingly warm, as it slides down my back. Between all this there is much banter between the King and High Priest on the lines of 'Have they done enough, O King, to atone for their crime?' The King, of course, decides we haven't done enough and orders us to drink something very nasty. This turns out to be a half pint of some bilious brown concoction which contains coffee, Tabasco, curry powder, chocolate, raw eggs, soy sauce and mustard – to name but a few; we have to drink it in one go.

I think of Alec Guinness and tip the glass. George the Burmese gags halfway through and keels over, coughing violently. Saatchi, without an ounce of fat to protect him, is shivering visibly, and it's still not over. More shouting, and we're dragged up again to be stencilled on the forehead with a potato in which the red sign of a trident has been roughly carved. Something warm and red trickles down my face, but it's only the dye from the potato. This is worse than appearing in a Terry Gilliam film. And still it goes on. Hoses are prepared to sluice us with cold seawater. But a power behind the throne decides that it's gone far enough. We are ordered to shuffle up in front of the electrician (sorry, King Neptune), who after one last impassioned harangue, dubs each of us with his trident and hands us a scroll which confirms that, in my case:

'On the 20th November 1988, A.D. at 20.20 hours GMT I, Michael Palin, crossed the International Date Line on ye goode ship *Neptune Garnet*, and was humbled before the King Neptune, Great Ruler Of The Seven Seas, and thus accepted into The Brotherhood of Mariners.'

Except that I'm not accepted yet. Signatures have to be secured from both the King and the High Priest before the certificate is valid – these can be obtained at a separate ceremony this evening.

The evening ceremony turns out to be also a party for the Professor. Forfeits abound, and in order to get my signatures I have to impersonate a sexy model, a pregnant woman, a housewife *and* give a display of break dancing.

It's a very good party, attended by all except the two crew members on watch, and many games are played, a tug of war is pulled, which I'm sorry to say the BBC loses this time. The Professor reveals there is no end to his talents by singing a song in Russian to his own guitar accompaniment, and Saatchi having endured the afternoon with great dignity produces his guitar, and plays a long and rather mournful rendition of 'Hotel California'.

A day to remember, however much one might want to forget it.

Day 60 23 November

Eighth day on the Pacific. Woken at six by what I take at first to be a hangover. My cabin reeks of diesel fuel. Surely I hadn't drunk that as well. Somehow after the tomato ketchup and the Tabasco and mustard cocktail anything was possible. But it turns out to be another of the eccentricities of the *Garnet*, that when the wind is in a certain direction, it blows the engine fumes into the air conditioning.

Still suffering from ship lag. Last night was the 14th time I'd put my watch forward since crossing into France, 60 days ago.

Up to the bridge. 3,562 miles from Tokyo. Our speed is 20.9 knots with a Force 6 to 7 wind from the West pushing us along, but the rolling keeps our speed lower than it should be. The captain is still mystified as to why, and reiterates his preference for Japanese over Korean shipyards. The chief officer and ex-High Priest is more concerned about yesterday's ceremony. Was it too violent? I assured him that it was a great performance and will make television history. I didn't like to tell him that the language was so foul that the BBC will probably have to keep their bleep on throughout. He in turn assured me that it was usually much worse than that. He had had his testicles painted different colours and knows of someone on *Neptune Amber* who was given a Mohican haircut, and another who had his head shaved completely and was made to stand at the bottom of the accommodation ladder at Long Beach and escort customs and immigration aboard, dressed as Gandhi. Run eight laps of the ship this afternoon – four kilometres. There's hardly ever anyone on deck, except for a couple of people checking the container fixings, or the temperatures on the refrigerated containers, so I have the Pacific to myself.

Read further into Ellman's Oscar Wilde, watch a video of *Salvador*, iron some shirts and prepare for another evening at the table-tennis table and the Scrabble board. The rolling of the boat seems to be getting worse. Simon pours a Scotch twice and each time it falls off the table. Resign myself to another night on the move. Wedge everything that might roll and put pillows on either side of the bed to prevent me hitting the wall. It's close and muggy again and just when the air conditioning is needed it's impossible to have it on because of the diesel fumes. On all the ships I've been on there seems to be a psychological Sargasso Sea round about two-thirds of the way into the voyage. A period of lethargy and dissatisfaction between the excitement and novelty of setting out and the anticipation of arrival at the other end.

As I'm lying in bed, rolling gently, I reflect on the fact that India, more than any other country, has dominated this journey so far. Indians took me from Dubai to Bombay to Madras, now an Indian is taking me from Tokyo to Long Beach. A third of the journey altogether. Captain Amirapu couldn't be bettered. A polite and considerate host, a highly competent and inspiring captain and a nice, friendly and straightforward man. I was surprised to hear him today expressing interest in leaving the sea and taking a shore job. Sensible for a family man I suppose, but a great loss to the sea.

Day 61 24 November

Sleep in half-hour bursts. The ship feels like a tormented soul tonight, shuddering, quaking, tossing and turning, teeth chattering, as the rolls become steeper and longer. Up the hill one minute and down again the next. I nod off only to be woken moments later by a swingeing change to my centre of gravity, or the sticky heat of the airless cabin, or backache from the semi-foetal position into which I've concertinaed my body. When I do sleep I fall into a vivid dream of home. Clear details of collecting my mail from the Python office (which has added to its staff a lot of young men in red braces), hailing a taxi and at last turning into the street where I live. A hundred yards from my front door I wake in the middle of the Pacific. A warm glow of anticipation and happiness vanishes instantly to be replaced by frustration, then resignation, then backache.

There is a crash and the sound of breaking glass from the Dayroom. I totter through expecting to find a carpet awash with Johnny Walker Black Label, but fortunately it's only a couple of glasses that have broken free of their moorings. Later, on the bridge, the captain is apologetic about the boat's behaviour.

Saatchi shows me our position on the charts and I tell him we are going to have to re-shoot the initiation ceremony. He looks so utterly terrified that I have trouble persuading him it was a joke. We talk about football. Saatchi the Malay, like Captain Abbas the Egyptian, is a Liverpool supporter. He says people all over the world watch English football. For some reason it's more exportable than French or Italian or Dutch. Everyone he knew made sure they were near a television set to watch live coverage of the European Cup Final at the Heysel stadium. It's easy to forget the international repercussions of the disaster. The millions of Liverpool well-wishers let down, embarrassed and shamed by the events.

Still, he says, it's past and there has been a sympathetic backlash over the continued exclusion of English clubs from international football. 'You're not so bad,' he says, and, as if to cheer me up, 'Everyone knows Mrs Thatcher ...'

The captain has asked us to his cabin for a drink before supper. It's comfortable up there with soft sofas and plants and Mozart coming through elegantly on the hi-fi. The chief engineer (Mr Wonka) is there. They talk of cricket, the Japanese (admired but not liked), reduced manning levels on container ships (neither admired nor liked) and the experiences of Neptune Orient Lines in the Gulf war. Two company ships were hit. One was completely destroyed. The other, a tanker, was hit fifteen times, but only one crew member was killed.

After supper there's bingo in the games room. The captain joins in as usual, and takes it very seriously. He's hoping to win at least 50 dollars.

Day 62 25 November

Breakfast at 9.30. The Singaporean food on the *Garnet* has been good but I miss fresh-baked bread, freshly ground coffee and milk. I've been existing on instant coffee and Coffee-Mate, 'America's Favorite Non-Dairy Creamer', which I see is full of non-dairy goodies like: 'Corn Syrup solids, Partially Hydrogenated Vegetable Oil and any one of the following oils – Coconut, Cottonseed, Palm, Palm kernel, Safflower or Soybean. Sodium Caseinate, Mono and Di-Glycerides, Dipotassium Phosphate, Artificial Flavor and Annatto (a vegetable derived artificial color).' The outlook for fresh food doesn't look hopeful as I approach a new continent.

At ten o'clock our satellite fix is 36.35 North, 129.21 West, 4,380 miles from Tokyo and making 20.6 knots. Seven hours behind schedule.

Nothing much to do but wait. At lunchtime the sun comes out, and, for the first time since we left Japan, I feel its warmth on my face. Inspired to try and make 10 kilometres round the deck, and do so. Shower, read and bask in general feeling of achievement.

Rajiv, the three-year-old son of King Neptune, is going to be a world-class footballer. I confidently predict this after seeing him dribble my inflatable world up and down the passageway, and strike penalties with either foot through the cabin door. After saving the world from further punishment, I learn that his father was a footballer and his mother Lily (Mrs Neptune) trained as a parachutist until a particularly horrific accident in which her harness caught as she leapt from the aircraft and slammed her against the fuselage. She fell most of the way unconscious. They're a nice family, but I feel for Rajiv sustaining such a long journey with no friends of his own age.

Despite all the modern technology many traditional nautical terms remain and the deck crew is still organised by the bosun, who on this ship is Mr Ong. I find him taking measurements for an insurance claim for the 40-foot-long accommodation ladder which was torn off the ship by Typhoon Tess. He's sad to hear we're leaving at Long Beach.

'Why do you not come to Panama? Where else could you see a ship climb a mountain?'

I'm sorely tempted. After all I've seen the Corinth and the Suez canals, and the Panama where ships are raised up through a series of locks, must be the most spectacular of them all. I explain to him my targets and dates and deadlines, which he quite rightly doesn't regard as at all important compared with the splendours of Panama. 'Weather down there very nice ... sunbathe,' he suggests hopefully. I think my sunbathing days are over on this journey.

Day 63 26 November

We are to land in America today. The long Pacific crossing is abruptly over. I wish I could hope, like Fogg, that 'the most difficult part was done ... they had left the fantastic countries of China and Japan ... they were returning to civilised countries'. But I have 17 days to cross America on an infrequent and neglected railway system, and then I have to find some way of crossing the Atlantic at the onset of winter, when as Captain Amirapu assured me, 'You can almost be certain of running into something nasty.' In short, I don't altogether share Fogg's confidence in 'civilised countries'.

But for now, at eight o'clock in the morning in the Santa Barbara Channel it's a day for optimists. A peerless morning, the best on the Pacific. The sun shines from a clear blue sky, the swell has dropped, and there's a crisp, fresh breeze high up on the bridge deck.

It was in these waters, 46 years ago, that a Japanese submarine surfaced and fired seventeen rounds in the direction of Ellwood oilfield – the only direct enemy attack on continental USA this century. There are now a lot more offshore oil rigs for them to aim at and a steady stream of tankers heading north for the Alaskan oil. The chart indicates that we are in a Traffic Separation Zone, one lane for north and one lane, further out, for south. Such zones are in operation in all the maritime traffic black spots – the English Channel, the Gulf of Suez, the Malacca Strait.

Plenty of signs now of approaching landfall. A profusion of pelicans, cormorants and terns. Fat seagulls perch proprietorially on the containers. A school of dolphins, small jets of water signalling their progress, arc lazily through the water to the east. I feel concerned about their safety as deep-sea fishing boats bob about in these waters, bristling with rods. The sea begins to smell salty, as it never does out on the ocean. The inevitable plastic and polystyrene detritus accumulates, there's a sudden profusion of radio stations and the sound of airliners again. There's also the sobering sight of a low cloud stained brown with pollution, extending about half a mile out into the clear air of the Pacific. It's frightening to see so clearly the mess we live in. It's like stepping from a rock pool into dirty bathwater.

By lunchtime we're down to 12.5 knots and passing Malibu beach. The stars and stripes flies from the masthead, alongside the flags of Singapore and Neptune Orient Lines. We may be an ugly duckling, stacked with boxes, scuffed and yellowing in the hull, but we're 40,000 tonnes and eleven storeys high. A sailboat flutters perilously close to us, like a moth drawn to a light. Our deep and sonorous horn blasts out and Captain Amirapu shakes his head, 'This is the land of the free, you see. Any rich American can take his boat out right into the lane, without knowing *anything*.'

Now experiencing, yet again, AES – Arrival Euphoria Syndrome. The adrenaline begins to flow, clicking my system into receptive mode, responsive to a whole new set of sensations. I feel as I did coming into Bombay after a week on the dhow – a quickening of the pulse, a need to be there. Sure signs of a landlubber.

At five past two the pilot comes aboard. Unlike any other I've encountered he is in a civilian suit, an elderly man surely near retiring age, with crinkly grey hair. The smooth efficient American accent goes into action. It's odd to hear the real thing after so many international imitations. It makes me aware that I'm a foreigner – along with Captain Amirapu and Chief Engineer Durrani and Lily and Rajiv and Bosun Ong and Saatchi, Hang On, and all of us aboard.

There are small boats all around us now, but the difference between here and anywhere else I've been is that they're not working boats. These boats are for play. All modern, well equipped, fibreglass-hulled. None of them looks more than six months old. One sweeps by close to us and its occupants wave. A classic American quartet of rugged men and huge honey-haired women. We're in the land of giants.

Escorted by our tug, the *Sea Robin* from San Francisco, we pick our way carefully to the container terminal, where the American stevedores wait beside their cars (no bikes here), shouting, joking, swaggering, flexing muscles – every one of them from Central Casting. Captain Amirapu gives his last instructions to the engine room: ''ard a port ... 'ard a starboard', an Indian bringing me to the New World. The temperature is in the upper 60s, a light wind blows from the desert.

The customs men come aboard. Passepartout and I are officially signed off the ship's register. 'OhhhhhhhKay,' pronounces the senior officer, a grey-haired black. 'You're clear for customs. Enjoy your time in the U.S. Don't drink the water or eat the food.'

Transfer to another ship, my tenth so far. It's also the biggest, the most comfortable and by far the fastest. But it's moored in concrete and hasn't moved an inch in 22 years. It's the R.M.S. *Queen Mary*, striving to maintain some dignity despite being stuck in a pond and clamped to the shore by a modern steel and glass umbilical cord of elevators and service towers, on one of which is attached an illuminated sign confirming her new status as 'Hotel Queen Mary'. An arrow, pointing inland, invites me to 'Cross the Parking Lot to London Towne'. I suppose I should feel at home, but it isn't easy.

The first words addressed to me on American soil come from a thin, epicene registration clerk, with a spiky peroxide blond haircut. He punches a keyboard and looks up only briefly, just to ascertain I'm not a gorilla or armed with an axe. 'Hi, I'm Randy.' With a flick of the fingers Randy summons someone of a different ethnic group to carry my bags to Stateroom 306 on 'B' deck. We pass groups of partying Americans. They are twice as big and twice as loud as anyone else in the world. It's not just the grunts and laughs and whoops but also the sheer volume of the voices which ring out as if they are trying to communicate over vast distances. I feel like a mouse amongst bull elephants. In no time AES (Arrival Euphoria Syndrome) gives way to PAP (Post-Arrival Pathos), which in turn gives way to TT (Transition Trauma).

Once on land everything accelerates. No sooner have I arrived in a place than I have to make plans for getting out. The only boat across the Atlantic leaves from New York. I have now to cross to the East Coast as soon as possible, which is easier said than done in the land where any alternative to flying is not really taken seriously. There is an express to Chicago, called the Desert Wind, but it doesn't blow until Monday afternoon.

Whether I like it or not I have a day and a half to cool off in Los Angeles.

Day 64   27 November

My face, with dreadful permed hair, stares out at me from the top of the television on a card advertising *A Fish Called Wanda* as one of the four in-house movie hits. As it's currently taken 55 million dollars in the States I resolve to shut up about the Americans and their taste. At least they saved the *Queen Mary* and enabled me now to relax in a heavy enamel bath the length of a sentry box with a choice of four fillings: 'Freshwater Hot', 'Freshwater Cold', 'Sea Water Hot' and 'Sea Water Cold', and a shower control which marks Tepid.

A short walk up on deck. The Art-Deco fittings of the interior, the inlaid wood and cut glass, the classical bas-relief figures in bronze and the murals of England in the thirties are superb. On deck, I find I've been pursued from Shanghai by Noel Coward, whose life-size photographic likeness graces the wide teak floor that he himself once graced, along with other swingers of the thirties and forties such as Fred Astaire, Spencer Tracy, Winston Churchill and Marlene Dietrich.

A display shows the *Queen Mary* up-ended, alongside the Eiffel Tower and the Empire State Building. She's taller than the first and only a touch shorter (at 1,018 feet) than the second. Fifty-one years ago she sailed between New York and Cornwall in 3 days and 20 hours at an average speed of 31.69 knots. If she still did I'd be home and dry. The very newest and most powerful container ships can make 26 or 27 knots.

To breakfast at the Sidewalk Café on Venice Beach. At the turn of the century a rich man decided, as rich men do in Los Angeles, to spend an awful lot of money to re-create something that already existed elsewhere, in this case Venice. Unfortunately Abbot Kinney's Venice wasn't as sturdy as the original and only lasted about twenty-four years. There isn't much left (a columned arcade scrawled on by street artists or just people leaving messages) but the name persists and suits the neighbourhood, which is light and sparkles in the reflected waters of the Pacific Ocean, a hundred yards away. Venice Beach is America at its least self-conscious. Loud, informal, brash, individualistic, ostentatious, tolerant and unapologetic. A perfect reintroduction to Western culture.

The Sidewalk Café is attached to a bookshop and you can buy a first edition Sinclair Lewis and read it over a generous plate of bacon, eggs, links (sausages) and hash brown potatoes with a slice of orange. I bought the *L.A. Times*, a bundle of newsprint that looks like a week's supply of any English newspaper, but when whittled down to what is actually readable is equivalent to Monday's *Independent*. Though Venice, Los Angeles, looks the only place to be on this heavenly, healthy Sunday morning, it's Florence, Los Angeles, that's in the headlines. 'Another weekend in L.A. Gang Violence and Death.' No country I've passed through is without its violence, and you get to hear about it pretty quickly. On another page under 'Saturday's Air Quality' is an analysis of air pollution in the city, monitoring daily ozone, carbon monoxide and nitrogen dioxide levels. Which newspaper will be brave enough to do the same for Britain? Sidney Sheldon's *The Seeds of Time* is top of the fiction chart and Stephen Hawking's *A Brief History of Time* top of the non-fiction. There's nothing about England except the football results.

Walk along Ocean Front Walk. Against a Hockneyed backdrop of palm trees sharp against blue sky, a man juggles with two balls and a rotating chainsaw. Whilst performing this extraordinary and terrifying feat he warns the crowd who've gathered to watch: 'The last time I did this the chain broke off and went into the audience.' At the end he passes around a hat, examining contributions with disgust: 'Ten dollars! Hey! This is what I do for a job, shithead!'

Another man does a robot act, so good that only when he breaks sweat are you actually sure it's not a machine.

At Muscle Beach the bodybuilders work out, pulling 225 lbs on a single cable without apparent effort. Like everything else here this is a spectator sport. There are tiered benches beside the weights enclosure that could accommodate a couple of hundred people. The crowds wander by, barely commenting on our filming. In India they stare straight in the lens, in America they ask: 'Is this a movie, commercial or local news?'

Though there's a crowd, there's never a rush. This is Sunday, in California. The sun's shining and no one's going anywhere.

Except of course the circumnavigators, who feel twitchy if they stay still for too long. So a couple of hours later I find myself in a quiet canyon off Sunset where Michael Shamberg, the American producer of *Wanda*, *The Big Chill* and other movies, gives a most un-Hollywood Thanksgiving lunch for me. No noise, no cameras (except ours), no one being paged to the phone, no live appearance of the Count Basie Band, not even a celebrity punch-up. A low-key get-together of sympathetic folk, who can't really comprehend what I'm doing and why I'm doing it. Jamie Lee Curtis comes by later and saves the afternoon for Passepartout, who had long since decided I knew nobody famous in this town.

By five o'clock I'm exhausted. Is it ship-lag or the hectic pace on land after the monastic days on the Pacific?

Buy the *New York Times* and *Bonfire of the Vanities* and retire to my 'stateroom' for an early night. The *Times* has a romantic piece in the travel section about Christmas in London. No mention of traffic jams and black plastic bags, but it does provoke a sharper than usual twinge of homesickness.

Day 65 28 November

Up at 7.30. Call my mother in Suffolk. There's been thick fog there for days. Today the fog's gone but the rain's begun. Outside in Los Angeles the sun shines once again on the walls of London Towne, and the TV weatherperson forecasts 75 degrees in downtown Los Angeles, but heavy snowfalls in the

Rockies, with 40 inches at Alta Lake. It's the latter part of the forecast that gives me pause, for our train will be crossing the Rockies this time tomorrow morning. Switch channels to a discussion of why families quarrel more at Thanksgiving than any other time of the year. Switch off. Farewell to the shackled *Queen Mary*. Leave with mixed feelings, as if having visited a good friend in prison.

Drive downtown to another great relic of the thirties. Completed three years after the *Queen Mary*, in 1939, Los Angeles Union Station had an even shorter life in the style for which she was intended. The last of the great American railway terminals, her moment of glory was cut short by the Second World War and pre-empted by the rise of air travel immediately afterwards. But at least she's not completely retired, and trains still run from beneath the slender and graceful tower of the Spanish-style building. A belittling sticker, 'Shoes and Shirts Required', is pasted on the grubby glass of the door, beyond which is a magnificent interior of marbled floors and colourfully tiled walls, soaring 52 feet, to a timbered roof, intricately beamed, from which hang massive wrought-iron chandeliers. The atmosphere of the interior is dark and comforting like the wood of which so much of it is composed. Shafts of sunlight pierce the gloom from windows high up. The seats in the waiting room area are big and comfortable with thick wooden arms. Outside there are two cloistered gardens full of bougainvillea and frangipani – the only self-contained gardens I've ever seen at a station.

Sadly, the nearer you get to the trains the tattier the station becomes. The platforms are so desolate and uncared-for that on first sight I thought the railway might have closed without anyone telling us. There is not a single sign bearing the name of the city. The platforms, along which run narrow, rusting metal canopies, are empty of all the usual railway paraphernalia, except for the occasional seat and a rank of pay-trolleys.

The Desert Wind is made up of Amtrak Superliners, two-tiered coaches in silver, red and blue livery. Its interior, like the bullet train in Japan, but unlike the trains in China and India, owes much to aircraft design. A lightweight shell, moulded seats in open coach formation, inadequate but neatly designed individual lights, fold-down tables. There are also sleeping cabins, utilising the space quite skilfully but failing to disguise the fact that there isn't much of it. An attendant welcomes us aboard.

'No hurry, we got problems with the engine.'

Most of the passengers look to be holidaymakers or train buffs, so no one seems to care very much. I have the feeling that I'm the only one chasing time. Two big diesels pull us out almost an hour late.

'Thank you for travelling Amtrak train Number 36, The Desert Wind.' The announcements come thick and fast, and we are all issued with useful information on the country we're passing through. All of it rather tame compared to the days when Fogg crossed America and Passepartout had asked him 'if it would not be prudent, before starting on the Pacific Railroad, to buy a few dozen Enfield rifles or Colt revolvers'.

'We're now crossing the Los Angeles River, dry 350 days of the year.'

Well-stocked railway sidings indicate that though passenger traffic, run by federally financed Amtrak, is still struggling, freight traffic, still in the hands of private companies, is healthy. If I'd jumped a freight train I could have been in Chicago in 36 hours. The fastest passenger express takes 42.

Once out of industrial L.A. we pass a string of good-looking, well-maintained stations in the Spanish Mission style like Fullerton and San Bernadino, complete with domes, balconies, wide-eaved tiled roofs, wrought-iron fences and twirly stucco, built by the Southern Pacific railway, one of three working this line, the other two being the Santa Fe and the Union Pacific. 'Here at San Bernadino the very first McDonald's hamburger stand opened 50 years ago.'

The engine horn wails as we pull out of the station into countryside which seems to have turned suddenly lighter. The earth is now a rich golden brown. Is it an illusion? Is there really more light outside at four o'clock than there was at three? A knowledgeable couple in front of me, forest rangers from Colorado, assure me it wasn't an illusion, we're just out of the smog.

'On the left of the train, the birthplace of Richard Nixon.'

No one rushes to the windows. Perhaps they should, for it was under Nixon in 1971 that Amtrak was created. By unburdening private companies of the need to run passenger lines, his administration expected passenger travel to wither and die. But it has, against all the odds, survived, is popular and will not be cut again. Indeed Dukakis, until weeks ago a Presidential contender, had promised to double Amtrak's spending. Bush hadn't.

Dusk falls as we climb up into the Sierras. A red and dusty light catches the boulders strewn along dried up river beds. We pass a point where we can see the San Andreas Fault, a blue line of rock in the hills.

I scan through Amtrak's blurb: '... come to where the sun rules the earth ... where canyon walls give up the secrets of rivers long dead ... where desert winds carve steeples to the sky.'

The PA adds a more realistic note: 'We do advise all passengers not to place Kleenex tissues in the toilet bowls.'

As the last light of a good-looking day fades we move slowly up and over the Cajon Pass, and down into the Mojave Desert. After a couple more hours we're in Nevada. I know it's Nevada because the only signs of life are casinos, explosions of neon which dot the darkness like tribal fires.

At mealtime we move along to the restaurant car which is run with the same benign air as a prison canteen. Food here is strictly to be delivered and consumed. Enjoyment is not an issue. The menu is printed on an order form, which must be signed and the number of the car in which you're accommodated filled in. If all this is not done, frosty looks all round.

Midway through the meal, and six hours out of Los Angeles, Las Vegas appears, materialising from nothing, like a magician preceded by a flash of light. 'Stardust', 'Circus Circus', 'Caesar's Palace' ... familiar names blaze out of the night sky. Las Vegas station is a cursory affair, like the rest of the city, not quite believable. Almost immediately we're in pitch darkness and emptiness again. Clocks on an hour between here and Salt Lake City. Not enough beds for Passepartout and myself so recline in the seat in coach class. A sociable atmosphere. Meet a man who uses the train for business. He's an accountant out of Chicago, with work spread out in front of him, even at midnight. 'It confuses some clients, impresses others.'

'This is the way I like to do it. If people don't understand that then I don't want them as clients.'

A lady called Beth, insubstantially slim and soft spoken, has set up a business of her own in upstate New York, making and selling her own dresses.

'Can you make a living out of that?'

'Not really,' she smiles almost apologetically. 'I deal in real estate as well.'

Onwards into the darkness of the land of opportunity.

Day 66   29 November

At seven o'clock I pull aside the curtains and look out on a silvery-grey morning. A light covering of snow lies between the tracks as we ease into Salt Lake City.

Fogg came here to 'the curious Mormon country' on the 6th December, his 65th day out of London. I'm only a day behind now, after the *Garnet* crossed the Pacific ten days faster than the *General Grant*. On my 66th day I find myself in Passepartout's footsteps, climbing down onto the platform 'to take the air'. The 6th December 1872 and 29th November 1988 sound much the same. 'The weather was cold, the sky grey, but it had stopped snowing. The disc of the sun, enlarged by the mist, looked like an enormous piece of gold, and Passepartout was busy calculating its value in pounds sterling ...'

Plenty of time at Salt Lake City this morning to calculate the value of the hazy sun as we are waiting for a connecting train from Seattle which is reported stuck in a snowdrift high in the mountains. The Seattle train, known as the Pioneer, combines here with the California Zephyr from San Francisco and the Desert Wind to form the California Zephyr service to Chicago. We are thirteen cars long when we eventually pull out of Salt Lake City, with three diesel locomotives to haul us up and over the Rockies.

One thing I do miss from Fogg's days are the bison. 'About three o'clock in the afternoon a herd of ten or twelve thousand blocked the railroad. The engine ... tried to plunge its spur into the flank of the immense column, but it had to stop before the impenetrable mass.'

The landscape we're travelling through has long been rid of bison and Sioux and Pawnees too, but it's a spectacular backdrop for a bacon and egg breakfast, with snow-sprinkled fields in deep shadow and sun-capped mountains in sharp contrast behind. The train snakes its way into the Rockies following half-frozen streams up curving valleys that are narrowing and steepening all the time. The rocks have been folded and faulted and weathered into tortured, crumbling shapes. Pinnacles and boulders rest on tiny stems, there are precarious overhangs and knobbly stacks.

Into the small town of Helper, Utah, about mid-morning. Helper is one of those functional names that abound in this literal, pioneering part of America. Towns with names like Parachute, Rifle, Gypsum, Carbondale and Basalt, Colorado. Helper was where additional locomotives required to help trains on the final assault of the Rockies were housed. The town, built for the railway crews, is now a coal-mining centre and has upgraded itself to Helper City.

Early lunch as we pull into Grand Junction, Colorado. Elevation 4,906 feet. Confluence of the Colorado and Gunnison Rivers. The chief steward, improbably called Abdul Mahmoud, exhorts his team of waiters in the fine art of service: 'Come on. Get 'em in here.'

Today's lunch menu features the forbidden delights of 'The Hot Open Face Sandwich. Your attendant will describe this to you.'

The sun spills into the train as we set off again alongside the Colorado River. It's about 25 yards wide here, and on its flat banks, protected from the winds, grow orchards of apple, pear and peach. Halfway down the train is an observation car. It's filling up fast on this clear and sunny afternoon.

There's a lady of late middle-age calling herself Mar-Mer, who became a clown two years ago. She sparkles with the delight of it all and bursts into song and jokes with the zeal of a new convert. How does her husband cope with her new profession, I ask. 'Oh … he's kind of an introvert,' she reveals, as if describing an incurable illness. There's a man travelling with his son simply because he prefers trains: 'Sure knocks heck outta driving.' His wife is a cellist with the gloriously named Mile High Orchestra in Denver. But I get the feeling these are not average Americans. They're people who care about their environment, who despise and fear what big business is doing to it and who are immensely knowledgeable about where they live and determined to protect it from unnecessary development.

Back to my seat and doze a little. The mother of the Colorado couple sings to her daughter, in a soft and lilting voice. 'Freight Train', 'When Johnny Comes Marching Home', and others. The combination of this gentle voice and the wide empty country by the winding river is enchanting.

The PA system has become a staff intercom as well as a passenger information service this afternoon. 'Get your cameras ready for some truly great photos' is followed abruptly by a breathless shout of 'Earl, come to the dining car. We need you bad!'

At a quarter to four we reach Glenwood Springs. Elevation 5,600 feet. I must take a decision. However short of time I am, I cannot go through the Rockies without a pause to look around. To travel and see nothing is my complaint about aeroplanes, and I can feel myself falling into the same trap. I alight here for a detour which I hope I can afford.

Whilst there's some light left I take a dip in the Glenwood Hot Springs – geothermal waters that soothed the Ute Indians a hundred years ago and beyond. Today they're part of a busy health spa peppered with notices – rules and signs and health warnings in thorough but bewildering American style. The waters, at 104 degrees Fahrenheit, are in the open air, which is currently 35 degrees Fahrenheit. My body quite enjoys this schizophrenic experience. Passepartout sets up on the side of the pool to witness my immersion, but the cloud of steam is so dense that the camera can't find me.

Then drive up to Aspen, about an hour away and two and a half thousand feet up into the Rockies. It's a sort of Christmassy Beverly Hills, but though it may be Californian in income it's East Coast in taste. To the Hotel Jerome whose placid 1889 brick exterior masks an exuberance of Victorian excess inside.

My room is wide and well-furnished in impeccable re-creation of the Naughty Nineties. I take a long, slow bath in a room floored in Carrara marble. Then in one of those cultural cross-connections that have characterised the journey I end up picking my way through the snow to a Mexican restaurant, walking through the neat streets of Aspen, treading carefully along icy sidewalks. The unfamiliar feel of ice-cold air on my face is very refreshing. Nothing brash or strident intrudes on the rows of carefully maintained houses. No sodium or neon lights allowed here. The town feels like a village, intimate and enclosed.

A last look out of the curtains at midnight. On the ski slopes behind the town, huge machines hurl white plumes of artificial snow onto the mountain.

Day 67 30 November

It's the last day of November and the outside temperature is minus 8. Checking through my notebook, I find that I passed the *first* day of November in a floating Yugoslav hospital on the Malacca Strait. The balmy heat of that wet tropical day could not be further from the bracing freshness of this morning, nor could my activity be more different.

I am to try a new form of earthbound transport, to add to trains and buses and ships and fiacres and taxis and camels and rickshaws and Rolls-Royces. Not to be outdone by Fogg who took a snow-yacht across Nebraska, I'm to cross a bit of America by dog-sled. At Krabloonik kennels in Snowmass village, Dan Maceachen and his colleagues have 250 huskies, some of whom are being trained for a 5,000-mile trans-Antarctic expedition next year, some of whom will pull sleds in the Iditarod – the annual race across Alaska, in which the dogs are expected to cover more than 100 miles a day for 17 days. The dogs spend the winter season pulling 'guests' as the visitors are called, on handcrafted sleds around beautiful mountain trails.

No one can sneak into Krabloonik kennels unannounced. As soon as the dogs hear a suspicion of a footfall they spring to their feet, tugging at their leads and barking and baying in an ever-swelling chorus that resounds through the woods. A young man with a mass of blond curls, padded out like a Polar explorer, is to be my musher – the human element in the dog-team. His name's Marion, and he's from Mississippi, where they give men names like that, and he left law school after a year to come up here. He's married to another Mississippian, who runs the library in Aspen, and they live in a log cabin up in the mountains, 'all by ourselves'.

He works hard for his idyllic life. Dog sledding, as Dan Maceachen says, is 10 per cent glamour and 90 per cent hard work. These are dedicated men. The composition of the 13-strong dog team is vitally important, and before anything else, Dan and Marion work out a team sheet, rather like the ones posted on the school notice board. There is a lead dog. His or her qualities are 'instinctively born', says Maceachen. 'It is not a trait I can breed or train.' This was the team chosen for me:

Dishaan (lead), Atangee, Tuliaan ('gentle one'), Liseen, Nunapik, Naken, Nutek, Twintoo, Akarta ('red fox'), Kuna ('great warrior'), Donawoo, Uquila and Takkuk ('moon spirit'). The names are Inuit, for these are Eskimo dogs.

The harnessing-up is a traumatic process for all concerned. So eager are the dogs for an outing, that they intensify their cries, fling themselves to the ends of their leash, straining and howling with all their might to catch the musher's attention. Dan and Marion have the assistance of one other musher, an ex-harbourmaster, steamboat captain and film school student whose card reads 'Pilot Lord Frieherr B'Wana Joe Edmonds, Adventurer For Sale'. He has the aspect of a true eccentric, unconventional even by mushing standards. An old sweater, straggly and very worn, sags off him. 'Put it this way, it's lasted longer than the girl who made it for me.'

The control over the dogs is based on cooperation rather than coercion. No whip or rein is used and the instructions are communicated verbally. At the moment there's a lot of 'Siddown!' and not much else as the dogs are forced, much against their instinct, to wait for Passepartout to find a camera position.

Marion asks me how I'm coping with the altitude. 'There's usually some nausea or headaches.'

Funnily enough, until he said that I felt fine.

Then suddenly we're away. Any feelings of guilt at sitting like Queen Victoria in the back of the sled, covered in rugs and furs, whilst small dogs pull me along, are dispelled by the obvious delight the dogs take in being on the move. Marion leaps on and off the sled, running, sliding, leaning out over corners like a cycle speedway rider, and keeping up a running stream of imprecations and exhortations to the dogs.

The dogs, sadly, have to be constantly stopped, while Passepartout scuttles off to another position. Marion's hardest task is to keep them down. To this end he employs a length of rolled-up paper ('it's just an old dog food packet') with which he slaps them cautionarily. He is embarrassed about doing it. 'The whapping doesn't usually go on, I want you to know that.' He claims that it's the noise of the impact rather than any pain that calms them. And the embarrassment: 'They just don't want to be the one that gets told off like that.'

The less experienced dogs are showing increasing reluctance to sit and wait, and the moment one of the older ones rises, the others follow, and whilst Marion's back is turned they're off, hauling me helplessly over a mound of cleared snow. A branch flicks down taking out my hat instead of my eye, but only just. Marion screams them to a halt and quite a bit of paper is applied. Much surly whining. The phrase 'mutinous dogs' comes to mind.

On the occasions when they are allowed a run the sensation is wonderful. The sled moves silently over the snow, and the air smells good and clean (apart from the more than occasional pungent odours from the dogs themselves who have to learn to defecate on the move). As we toil back up the last hill, Marion becomes softer with the dogs. 'I'm going to barbecue you.' The dog gazes happily up at him. 'You're a real knucklehead today,' he tells another. I ask him if he knows every dog in the kennel by name.

'Yep! And I know their mother and their father and their grandfather and their grandmother.' Because of the exigencies of filming we've travelled maybe 4 or 5 miles, and it's frustrating when you think these dogs think nothing of 100 miles a day. A bit more snow and they could have taken me to Chicago.

Day 68 1 December

December arrives in Aspen, Colorado, which seems suitable. The air is very dry and I wake far too early with a thick, abrasive sore throat.

With another fine day dawning there seems little point in moving from this agreeable spot. But I have cut things very fine. I must not miss the California Zephyr this afternoon, nor its connection with the Lake Shore Limited in Chicago, for if I'm anything more than a few hours late in New York at the weekend I shall lose the last vital link in the chain.

But I've one adventure more before leaving the Rockies. It begins, prosaically enough, in the municipal car park at six o'clock in the morning. Two enormous vehicles are being assembled here. One is called The Rat, the other The Unicorn. There isn't much passenger space in either of them, they have no means of independent propulsion and once started they may end up anywhere. They are the one form of transport everyone connects with *Around the World in Eighty Days*, and yet Jules Verne never mentions them. I'm about to board a hot-air balloon.

Passepartout and myself and Jake the pilot – burly, moustachioed and, like everyone else in Aspen, aged between 22 and 35 – are squeezed into the 4-foot-square wicker and leather-padded basket of The Unicorn. Clem and the BBC New York film crew are in The Rat.

We have to ascend at this ungodly hour before the land warms up and starts giving off thermals which disturb the air current. Hot-air balloons do not, it appears, like hot air.

I feel rather silly standing in this little basket on the ground, like a piece of forgotten shopping, whilst each flame of propane swells the shroud above my head.

Then, quite suddenly, without a lot of fuss and bother, we're rising majestically above the car park, above the hotel, above the neat, clean-as-a-new-pin streets, above the substantial Victorian bulk of Wheeler Opera House, above the Aspen Fresh Fish Co. and The Great Divide Music Store and the eye-catching old bandstand in Paepcke Park. Over Highway 82 and Hyman Avenue and Pepi's Hideaway and suddenly the town is in miniature and there are shouts from the occupants of the other balloon for me to stand up and be photographed and I'm not sure if my knees will support me.

I can feel the blood draining from my face, God knows where to. If only Jake were wearing some sort of harness instead of just balancing casually on the edge of the basket as if he's going for a picnic up the Thames. There is nothing to stop me jumping out. I'm not attached to a damn thing. I stand up, feeling queasy as I've never felt since that night on the dhow. Think back to the astrologer's words of reassurance. Everything smooth ... back in plenty of time ... no problems. But I'd told him I was taking surface transport only. I've cheated, I've left the ground and now I'm paying the price.

'Where are we going?' I manage to ask in a voice as thin as the air.

'Aw ... I dunno for sure.'

Oh, great.

Jake looks around. He looks around without getting off the edge of the basket! He just twists his unharnessed body on the thin leather rim 300 feet above Aspen!

'You see, it just depends on the way the air behaves.'

'You mean you don't know that?'

'Not until we get up here.' He consults one of the distressingly few instruments, which shows wind speed. Below me now Main Street has become Highway 82. A long line of

Dinky Toys thread their way slowly into the town. What's a traffic jam doing in a beautiful place like this? Remember to ask Jake this when my voice has broken.

'Y'see, the cold air flows down this valley like water in a river. It's not till you're in it you know where or how fast those currents are flowing.'

I know where. Aspen International Airport, that's where. A light plane is actually flying in beneath us.

'Er … Jake … Do …er … do … airport control … er … *know*. About us?'

'Oh, I guess so.'

So on a swell of currents and hope we drift slowly towards the mountains. And quite suddenly I've lost that fear of the unlikely and I'm leaning over the side with the rest of them. We can watch silently from up here without disturbing the wildlife, and I catch sight of a pair of elk in amongst the trees. The view is wide and majestic, from Aspen round to Snowmass as well as the snowcapped Mount Daly, a peak of classic Paramount Films proportions. I may be cheating, but by the time we drift down, making an endearingly clumsy descent into some prickly scrub, I calculate I've moved a mile nearer the Reform Club.

Back into Aspen for a late and hearty breakfast, such as the condemned man might enjoy after his reprieve. My *Rocky Mountain News* tells me that it's Woody Allen's 53rd birthday and that Michael Dukakis' waxwork has been removed from Madame Tussaud's after the shortest display on record.

Walk a last time around Aspen. Gaze enviously at the skiers, who, at this early stage of the season, have wide slopes to themselves. Feel glad that I kitted myself out with some new clothes in Tokyo. Everyone here looks as if they're straight out of the windows of the local boutiques, which proliferate under names like The Freudian Slip, The Hedgehog and Shirtique.

Christmas carols sound from somewhere, and I realise that I want to be back home. As if to acknowledge the wish, I find a bar serving Sam Smith's beer from my home county. A pint, a bowl of clam chowder, and a last lungful of the cold, dry, reviving air before heading back down to the real world.

Glenwood Springs station could be out of the Scottish Highlands. Rough-hewn stone, overhanging eaves and a feeling of having been nearly glamorous. The same could be said of The California Zephyr. 'A soft gentle breeze' as it's defined in the dictionary, and certainly it's no hurricane today. An hour passes and still no sign. A massive goods train goes by, quite possibly the longest train I've ever seen. Seven diesels of the Rio Grande and Southern Pacific Railroads hauling one and a quarter miles of trucks. The Zephyr arrives one and a half hours late and it's getting dark as we wind into the canyon, the tips of whose walls are caught by the last rays of a golden sunset and glow like the points of a crown.

All that's needed to enjoy it is sight and silence. But the train manager has other plans.

'I've collected all the Trivia sheets. Mrs Dorothy Connelly, you got all your questions wrong. I'd like to meet you. You're the person who got *all their questions wrong!*'

Pause.

'On our left Interstate Highway 70. In construction for fifteen years. The most expensive highway ever built in this country.'

And there it is, in the gathering gloom. Squashed in between sheer rock walls and the much-abused Colorado River – squeezed dry in its later stages to service the lawn sprinklers of L.A. and here in the canyon half-filled with the rubble and concrete of America's most expensive highway.

'Margaritas goin' for a dollar fifty cents in the lounge car. Why don't you come and join us?'

At five past eight we enter Moffat Tunnel, the third longest in the world. It runs beneath the watershed of the Rocky Mountains, the Continental Divide, reducing what was a five-hour journey for Phileas Fogg to ten minutes today.

Have a cabin to myself and Chuck, the attendant, warns me that tonight's ride could be a little rough, as we shall be moving

onto The Burlington and Northern Railroad and we'll be switched
to their secondary track to leave the fastest free for freight.

Dinner taken as we descend into Denver. Four thousand feet
in thirty minutes. It looks as if we're coming in by plane.

Chuck has some bedtime stories for me. Mostly gruesome
and to do with the dangers of modern travel for an elderly
clientele. The more modern the appliances, the more neat and
clever and labour-saving the designers try to be, the greater the
scope for disasters. They can range from a simple dousing for
those who mistake the shower button for the lavatory flush, to
the Rabelaisian experience of a very fat lady whose fleshy
bottom was sucked into the stainless steel toilet bowls by the
electric flushing system. Chuck had the delicate task of trying
to prise her free, but without success. The train had to be halted
and the entire electrical system switched off before she could be
removed. The stop was described over the PA as a 'routine
electrical check'.

His most feared passengers are the Boy Scouts. Maybe the
strain of hours tying knots and trying to light fires with two
sticks provokes a vehement counter-reaction but their
behaviour makes Attila the Hun sound like Beatrix Potter. They
are in the habit of leaving sachets of tomato ketchup
underneath the lavatory seat. At the first heavy pressure the
sachets break squirting their sticky red contents down the next
customer's leg.

Boy Scouts or no Boy Scouts, I lifted the seat carefully before
turning in. Rocked to sleep on the Burlington and Northern
somewhere between Denver and Omaha.

Day 69 2 December

7.45: Rosy-fingered dawn over the Midwest. The topmost
points of leafless trees see the sun first and burn a light red.
Fifteen minutes later at Omaha, Nebraska. Big railway centre.
At one time supported nine railroads. The Union Stockyards, a

huge cattle-shipping centre established in 1884. This is all culled from my excellent Amtrak Route Guide, something which British Rail could well introduce. It has a lot more practical value than any 'Inter-City' magazine.

I *like* small-town America. I'm not entirely sure why, because I've little practical experience of it beyond films and writers like Garrison Keillor and Nabokov and Updike. I fear it may be the curse of nostalgia. Nostalgia for a 1950s world culled from the pages of the *National Geographic*.

Today as we cross into Iowa, 'the land beyond', it's all there in the hard bright sun and it doesn't seem to have changed. Small, clean, white-painted clapboard settlements, bordered by woods and barns and ponds, focused around a steepled church. Modest and tidy, set in an easy rural landscape of low hills and tree-fringed streams. Only the ubiquitous presence of satellite dishes distinguishes them from the dreams that filled my schoolboy years in Sheffield.

'Are you meatless?' a waiter screams at me at breakfast. 'I've been called many things in my time,' I'm about to reply when he jabs his pen toward the bacon and sausage section of my order which I've omitted to fill in.

Copies of *USA Today* are on every seat in the train. News from the present day. Benazir Bhutto is soon to be sworn in as the world's first Muslim woman leader. I think of the *Garnet*'s chief engineer. Not happy news for him. He's probably down near Panama. Mike's Bar empty now, I suppose.

Eddie Murphy has bought Cher's house in L.A. for 6.5 million dollars, and Spielberg's latest hit features 'a bunch of lovable dinosaurs'. Could well have been filmed aboard the California Zephyr.

There is a new man on the PA this morning and mercifully he is very good to listen to. This is because he gets everything slightly wrong. So, in a piece of historical information, Lucy Kilpatrick comes out as 'Lucky' Kilpatrick, and a film as *Who's Afraid of the Virgin Wolf?*

At 2.20 in the afternoon we're at the good-looking town of Burlington on the Illinois border. Spires pierce the skyline and bonfire smoke drifts across a graveyard in a wispy autumn breeze. We're about to cross the Mississippi and all seems well with the world, except that we are running ever later. Due in to Chicago at 4.30, with what seemed an easy 6.25 connection to New York, we're now looking at an arrival time nearer 6. Chuck isn't worried. He's going to call ahead and have redcaps and trolleys standing by for us.

Rumble over a three-quarter-mile-long Mississippi bridge. After crossing a world of largely empty rivers it's good to see such an unequivocal expanse of water. No rocks and sandbanks. Water stretching from side to side, a river of noble size.

'Our next stop is Princeton. The big capital of the world ... I'm sorry, the *pig* capital.'

Four o'clock, and the sun is losing its intensity. Red and browns dilute the gold. It has been a magnificent day and it's a pity that it has now to be coloured, as have so many days on this journey, by a faint but nagging feeling of anxiety. Perhaps the Rocky Mountain detour had been an indulgence. I don't want to go home having seen nothing, and I've already sacrificed Muscat and Singapore to the pressures of the schedule, but having come so far and so close, it would be ignominious to end up on a deserted New York quayside.

4.45: America silhouetted against the dark blue horizon, the outlines of bare trees, trucks on the highway, sheds and factories rise and fall sharp and geometrical. Dear God, don't let the train stop, please. Into my mind comes a statistic from the *Queen Mary*. She never suffered a mechanical breakdown at sea, never had to use a single lifeboat, and never transmitted a distress signal on her own behalf. Reliability like this, plus a few extra miles an hour, is all I can hope for from Amtrak.

5.15: Christmas trees in the streets of Aurora, Illinois, in the Chicago suburbs. Six-lane tailbacks on the freeways, two-tier trains roll past, full to bursting with Friday night commuters.

At last the towering downtown skyscrapers come into view. The Hancock Tower and the Sears Tower, once the world's tallest building, now for sale at 2 billion dollars.

The only good thing about Union Station is that we are there with 35 minutes to spare. There are none of the promised redcaps to meet us, and we are at the far end of a bleak and grubby ice-covered track, without even a platform. We have much more than my bag to move and by the time we have a trolley, it's only 15 minutes before the Lake Shore leaves. By the time we've reached the departure platform, 10 minutes are left. Then Simon hears my name called on the station tannoy. 'Mr Palin, arriving from Los Angeles, please go to Station Information.'

This is a time for strong heads. Station Information is back the way we've already come. To go is to run the risk of missing the train, not to go is to run the risk of missing what could be a vital message. Go straight to Halifax? Ship leaving tonight from Montreal? About turn and race through the station. Find the information desk. A queue. Push my way through. Yes, there is a message. Lady disappears to collect it, scowls from others in line.

'Here we are, Mr Palin ....' With the exquisite timing of a B-thriller, she unwraps the note. 'A Mr Seth Mason says if you have any time in Chicago he'd love to see you. Please give him a call at home.'

6.35: Never been so happy to be on a train, and a comfortable one at that. The Lake Shore Limited left on time, seconds after we boarded, and it's racing out of Chicago most purposefully, like a train that has business to do, rather than the pleasantly peripatetic California Zephyr.

Through South Bend, Indiana, another good functional name. In England we so seldom have to make up new names. Apart from a few Skelmersdales and Telfords our cities, towns and villages have had their names for centuries. America has no such inheritance, and yet a much greater demand. No wonder they run out of inspiration and have to pinch other people's names. Most of the cities I've passed through in the last sixty-nine days have been replicated somewhere in the U.S. There's Bombay, New York; Madras, Oregon; Tokio, Texas; as well as four Venices, seven Cairos, and no fewer than seventeen Cantons.

Clocks go on an hour, my seventh lost since the Date Line, as we enter Eastern Standard Time. Hard to get to sleep for the sound of loud, grating voices from a very busy next-door compartment.

'We have been in court for custody, in ten years, a total of *seventy-four* days!' Rumbles of reaction from deeper voices over which a harridan cry rises once more: 'Seventy-*four* times, in and out of court in ten years!'

Do these people know there's anyone else in the world?

If all goes well this could be my final night on land before we reach Britain. And lying here looking out into the dark as we pull up at some unnamed Ohio station on the shores of Lake Erie, I'm having a last concentrated dose of America.

Forty-five-foot trailers are being humped noisily into a siding, the bare anonymous station is lit by a pair of cold overhead lights like an Edward Hopper painting and the soap opera continues next door ... 'I'm thirty years old and my life is goin' nowhere ...'

I take recourse to my headphones. Blank out the noise with Leonard Cohen.

Day 70 3 December

Sometime in the night we must have passed through Cleveland and Buffalo and Rochester on the southern shore of Lake Ontario. We're in New York State, heading due east along the gap in the Appalachian Mountains formed by the Mohawk River. The map is studded with classical names – Ithaca, Utica, Seneca Falls, Rome and Syracuse, the city we're drawing into as

Nigel and I, the non-meatless, dig into eggs and bacon and that strange burnt and watery substance that passes in America for coffee. Sitting across from us is a distinguished elderly man. He turns out to be 90 years old, an ex-air force commander called Skeel, who has traced back his Danish ancestors to the year A.D. 800 when they left Denmark and settled in East Anglia. He told us that this part of New York State, from Lake Ontario down to the Pennsylvania border, was given in gratitude to soldiers who had fought in the War of Independence. Most of the soldiers, wanting only to return to where they'd lived before, sold their share of the land, but a high-minded group of officers formed a co-operative to run the area, on the republican ideals of ancient Rome and Greece. According to Mr Skeel, naming the cities after the homes of these ideals 'was just about the only thing they ever did'.

Despite it being a Sunday this courteous gentleman was on his way to Albany for a board meeting of some industrial company of which he had remained a director. Albany, at the confluence of the Mohawk and Hudson rivers, presents a proud city skyline, as confident and serious as befits the capital of one of the most prosperous states of America. Here the 'Lake Shore Limited' splits, half continuing east to Massachusetts and Boston and half turning due south to New York along the Hudson Valley.

As a valedictory dose of American landscape the ride down the Hudson could hardly be bettered. Though the intense autumn colours have faded from the woods that climb the cliffs on either side, the wide valley and its steep rocky banks offer a long and impressive stretch of grand and unspoilt river scenery, brilliant today in the unflinching sunlight.

Enjoying it too are a group of jolly ladies in their forties from Albany, who are leaving their husbands for a girls' night out in New York. A little shy to start with, but once it's established they're not going to spend the evening at the opera but at a male strip club, and that all of us think they're quite right, they loosen up and more Molson's beer is called for. It's a little early in the day to start, but as the Professor puts it we're all feeling a little demob happy. High on the opposite bank is a long sprawling pile that looks like a Russian jail. On enquiring I'm told it's West Point Military Academy.

There's an air of heightened excitement as we approach New York, so different from the easy-going almost sleepy atmosphere on the train as we pulled out of L.A.

Across the Harlem River and into Manhattan rolling slowly above the derelict urban landscape described so enthusiastically by Tom Wolfe in the book I have by my side at the moment, *Bonfire of the Vanities*. Around 132nd Street the city looks more like Cairo. Rubbish is strewn everywhere, smashed cars and discarded beds are scattered over plots of land empty save for sheets of corrugated iron and people living beneath them. As if this might have been just a momentary waking nightmare, an aberration not to be confused with the real thing, we are swept away into the darkness of Park Avenue Tunnel.

Passengers begin to move to the doors. The garrulous openness of the Hudson River ride has been replaced by an edgy silence, as if everyone is mentally preparing themselves for the demands of this ruthless and impatient city. As in Chicago and Los Angeles, the railway approach to New York is not one to lift the spirits. We disembark in subterranean gloom and trudge along the platform sustained only by an act of faith that New York really is up there above us, and that we haven't all died.

The shabby tunnels lead to what could quite easily be Heaven and Hell combined – the great concourse of Grand Central Terminal. The massive celestial ceiling, pinpricked with gold-leaved constellations, shelters two sorts of people – those who are going somewhere and those who are not. In the latter, more interesting category, are flute players, those fighting off imaginary aerial assailants, those conducting urgent conversations with themselves, and those sitting with vacant eyes, staring down at the ground, unable to take life in New York any other way.

I'm neck and neck with Fogg now, for the first time since I left. He arrived on the seventieth day at 'thirty-five minutes after nine at night' at Jersey City 'near the very pier of the Cunard line of steamers, otherwise called the British and North American Royal Mail Steam Packet Company. The *China*, bound for Liverpool, had left thirty-five minutes before!'

Fogg of course had not panicked, and taken himself off to the St Nicholas Hotel on Broadway to sleep on the problem.

At least he had the choice of a dozen other transatlantic passenger carriers, none of them in business nowadays. My eggs are all in one basket – a 53,000-ton container ship, hopefully loading now at Newark Docks en route for Felixstowe. I must get over there fast, but cannot, at the vital moment, find Passepartout. They'd been filming on the concourse, but were no longer to be seen.

Search for them unsuccessfully. New York, for all its virtues, is not a safe place to hang around. The man who stands still in New York is either buying or selling. For what other reason would you want to stand still? Eyes turn toward me, eyeing me, sizing me up suspiciously.

At last Passepartout appears from a side entrance looking ruffled and in the company of one of New York's finest. Demands to know what we're doing, who gave us permission and so on. Clem strides over to deal with it, but the whole episode loses an unsettling amount of time.

Fight gracelessly for a taxi which is driven by a Haitian.

'I shouldn't think you get many passengers asking for the container terminal?' I venture.

He says nothing.

I have chosen the only New York cabbie with nothing to say.

4.30: at the Port of Newark. The penultimate connection has been made. We have berths on the *Leda Maersk*, a Danish container ship, leaving tonight and reaching Britain in eight days, given fair weather. Though this is by no means guaranteed on the Atlantic in winter (as Captains Tuddenham and Amirapu warned us), my chances of success have never looked so good.

The first surprise on climbing aboard was not how spick and span the ship was – after all, you expect that from the Danes – but that the first officer who greeted me was a slim blonde girl. She shrugs off our disconcertment. Apparently it's quite common to have women officers now, especially in the American merchant fleet, which has women captains. Still, she is the first lady merchant seaperson I've encountered.

10.45: Grubby, after two and a half days on the train, and looking forward to a shower before turning in. I've just walked the 880-foot deck and am looking towards the New York City skyline, crowned by the winking lights of the World Trade Center. Between me and Manhattan is Jersey City, and nearer still, a huge transportation complex. The docks themselves lie beside ten-lane turnpikes on the other side of which is Newark airport. The night is full of lights and activity. But by the time I sink into the twenty-eighth bed since leaving London, the ship has still not sailed.

Day 71 4 December

Wake up to feel us moving, but only just. Certainly not out on the high seas where we should be. It's now seven o'clock and we are moving gingerly out along a maze of wharves and into Newark Bay. Dress quickly and go straight up onto the bridge to catch a last look at New York on this brilliant morning. It's cold but clear and there is a magnificent panoramic view from New Jersey to Manhattan and Long Island beyond. The captain says that when he arrived from Charleston yesterday he could see the New York skyline from 50 miles away. The Statue of Liberty slides by, looking greener and sexier since her restoration, and so spellbinding is the view that no one goes down for breakfast until we have passed beneath the Verrazano Narrows Bridge, the East Coast's Golden Gate, and the pilot has been dropped at the Ambrose lighthouse. From here there are three traffic separation zones funnelling ships out of the crowded New York area. On the chart they point off like the arms of a country signpost. We turn north and east for Nantucket. The journey repeats itself neatly when I hear the captain's instructions.

'Frem ... Fuld.'

The sound of the words on the controls of *The Saudi Moon II* (crossed out and *I* written in). Captain Rodebaek looks like the archetypal sea-captain. He's round, ruddy-faced and smiles readily. He even has a slightly wandering 'Long John Silver' eye. He's not worried about the late start. The Maersk line is renowned for its timekeeping. He'll easily make up any backlog, and we should be alongside in Le Havre next Sunday at 4.30 a.m. It's a bit earlier than he'd like but he doesn't trust the French stevedores after Sunday lunch.

The only jarring note in all of this is the mention of Le Havre. Both Passepartout and myself were under the impression that next Sunday the *Leda Maersk* would be at Felixstowe. Ah, no ... that's the next day.

Over a breakfast of yogurt, coffee, eggs, bacon, and thick rich white bread baked on board by a German chef, we discuss the implications of the Le Havre delay, and various alternatives are proposed, ranging from catching the Le Havre–Southampton ferry, to a more tele-worthy ship-to-ship transfer at the mouth of the Thames and a launch up to Westminster Pier. No one feels we should waste time on the French coast.

There is an almost palpable sense of company pride about the *Leda Maersk* which did not exist on any of the other ships. A. P. Moller, the founder of the owning company, is a controversial figure in Denmark. The richest man in the country and an unapologetic advocate of private enterprise, his views rarely coincide with those of a liberal, progressive government. But his business, 'run with a rod of iron' I'm told, is the biggest employer in the country, including shipyards, oil exploration equipment, trucks and aeroplanes. This ship was built in Denmark in 1982 and registered there, despite worldwide trends to register in the cheaper free ports like Monrovia, Singapore, Panama and Limassol. The captain has been with the ship for its whole life, unlike the Neptune Orient captains who may do only six months before being transferred. The crew, with the exception of the chef and an Indian radio officer, is Danish, and the whole atmosphere seems to reflect confidence and top-dogginess rather than the retrenchment of Neptune's Singapore-based operation. Mind you, this impression could be the result of having a company man on board. This is Jesper, thin and sardonic, and with him two other 'civilians', Erik and Thorval, both office workers gaining travel experience. Erik is an accountant and Thorval isn't.

Pass the day in mundane activities with the rather traumatic exception of a haircut. The Professor has discovered that Lillian, one of the stewardesses, cuts all the crew's hair, and she and the gloating Passepartout assemble in my cabin after lunch for the ritual depilation. Lillian, armed only with a cigarette and a pair of scissors, has a strong lived-in face and a wearily enigmatic manner. Does she not feel that it's a lonely life at sea?

She pulls in a mouthful of smoke and exhales unhurriedly before answering: 'It suits me. I prefer to be alone … I would like to be an able-seaman. Then I could be always at sea.'

She seems to be spending a long time at the back of my head and hair is falling in divots. Is she not perhaps taking off a little too much?

'You are an actor. They will see only the front of your head,' she grins malevolently.

A marvellous Sunday dinner. Roast beef (though no Danish equivalent of Yorkshire pudding) and good red wine, a rarity on the journey, as Queen Margrethe and her French consort look down from the wall.

Day 72 5 December

A cold, presaged by a sore throat and a thick head since leaving Aspen, has finally come out of the closet and I wake feeling dull and drained of energy. The switchback course of the weather hasn't helped, and after our chilly, dry and dazzling days across the States, we are now in the warm fug of the Gulf Stream. So warm is the current that the sea this morning steams like a Turkish bath. Wraith-like wisps of vapour drift around the boat, blotting out the horizon. Instead of being on the wide ocean we are suddenly enclosed in caves of white cloud, through which a ghostly sunlight filters, and from which you half-expect to see a ship of lost souls emerge.

9.30: I'm halfway through a late breakfast when the alarm sounds for lifeboat drill. This is obligatory on all ships, but has been observed with varying degrees of thoroughness throughout my journey. It's typical of Maersk lines that they are the most conscientious of the lot, and there's clearly little chance of my resuming my breakfast. We are all given a lifeboat rendezvous position, which is not difficult to find once you've reached the boat deck. The real problem is finding the boat deck.

There are six floors of accommodation and all around us bells are ringing and doors swinging shut automatically. I find myself up in the crew's laundry with the second stewardess. Bente, the blonde first officer, clutching a two-way radio, eventually rallies us all, and we have to don chunky orange lifejackets and wait for the lifeboat engine to be started. The engine won't start today, so we're stood, out on deck, looking like Flowerpot Men, for some considerable time. Fall into conversation with the chef (or chief steward as he is officially known) whose blue and white check trousers poke out incongruously from beneath his life preserver. He's from Schleswig-Holstein, and has a sad face but humorous eyes. Like Lillian he smokes assiduously, and enjoys a drink too.

'Last night,' he confides, 'I was quite intoxicated, you know. I go to the door three times before I can go out of it.'

At this point Dave Passepartout appears, looking a little grey and rather hurt that no one had woken him up. 'I could have died,' he mutters, before being told he's at the wrong lifeboat.

Given the occasional unresponsive gurgle from the lifeboat's engine I imagine all of us on this deck might have died as well, if this were a real emergency. Eventually it spurts into action and is promptly turned off. Divesting ourselves of the lifejackets we are about to head back to breakfast when the alarm bells start jangling again, lights flash, and the doors start to shut themselves. Over the din voices are raised:

'Fire! … Fire! … Assemble on main deck … Fire!!'

Momentary panic that this *could* be real. Especially as I've gone one way and everyone else has gone another. Again, I'm rescued by Bente, and led down five flights to a demonstration of fire-fighting equipment.

Chris, the young solid chief officer, gets to let off an entire foam extinguisher over the side, which awakens schoolboyish envy in all of us. Chris has a rather pedantic delivery and a way of leavening all he says with figures, which soon completely befuddle the listener. A case of confusing with too much precision. So when he tells us of the tensile strength of the container connecting rods or the awesome foam emission pressure of the extinguishers, one knows one is in the presence of greatness, but is not particularly reassured.

However, he's a mine of information on the *Leda Maersk*. In 1986 she was extended by 80 feet. A Japanese shipyard sliced the bows off, inserted a new section, welded, made good and had the ship ready for work again in forty days. A year later the superstructure was heightened one tier to accommodate more containers. There is hardly a ship in the Maersk fleet which hasn't been enlarged. The next class to be built will narrow the accommodation, widen the hull and provide spaces for 700 more containers, making a carrying total of more than 4,000.

At present the fastest service they offer is Hamburg to Singapore in 17 days, which means among other things that a whole new range of tropical foods will be available in Europe in bulk, rather than for the lucky few who can afford the costs of air freighting. Refrigerated containers are the coming thing. They require constant supervision and a separate and self-contained power supply for each one, but pay good money. The *Leda Maersk* has 300 containing anything from prunes to helium. Chris can remember once carrying a load of 20 million grapefruit. Punch-drunk with figures I retire to lunch, which is the main meal of the working day and this morning is oxtail in a thick and juicy gravy.

After lunch Passepartout and I assemble in the Captain's Day Room, which has been generously loaned to us for the crossing, for the first read-through of *Under Milk Wood*, which has been organised by Nigel as a way of passing the time. Seven of my ten roles are women, I notice.

Day 73 6 December

Lie low for most of the day as my cold flourishes. At dinner the conversation turns to boat people again. Captain Rodebaek picked up 55 in one trip and 63 in another, 'many of whom are now working for the company'. In a side-discussion on world ports, Singapore comes out fastest, with five cranes per vessel capable of 125 moves an hour. Felixstowe, free-enterprise jewel of British container ports, can offer a maximum of 40 moves an hour. Still no decision on what to do at Le Havre. At the moment we opt for safety and an extra day on the *Leda Maersk*, especially as the weather has been kind and we are on time.

Day 74 7 December

Feeling no better. Headache persists. No appetite for breakfast but climb up to bridge in the hope that Atlantic breezes will clear my head. More than breezes. A Force 8 wind blowing East North East is covering the sea with spray, and the prunes and helium are rearing and plunging over the waves. We're lying 1,453 nautical miles from New York, a little more than halfway to Europe, Newfoundland is 580 miles North West and the Azores archipelago 600 miles South East. It's a warm 61 degrees but very wet. Looking out at the Atlantic from the rain-lashed windows of the bridge, ten storeys above the hard-running waves I can hardly conceive of the courage, or foolhardiness that would make anyone want to cross all that alone.

At lunch today there is a big discussion about the elegant damask tablecloth on the captain's table. Jesper, the A. P. Moller company representative, says that in future, because of a ruthless cost-cutting exercise, the new tablecloths will not have the white Maersk line star woven in to them. We all take the captain's side on this one and urge the company to reconsider!

It'll be the tureens next.

Talk to Christian, the second officer, up on the bridge this afternoon, alone amongst computers and VDU screens. It occurs to me that apart from the dhow, in all this journey I have hardly ever seen a ship steered by a human being, except when going into port.

Christian shrugs and looks gloomy. Even on a successful and expanding line like this one, the future is not good for seamen. He is from the Faroe Islands, of which I know nothing apart from their frequent starring roles in weather forecasts. I certainly didn't know that they have their own Parliament, flag and language, and have never been members of NATO or the EEC. They're remote but not cold, lying in the path of the Gulf Stream. Shotguns are allowed on the island, pistols and rifles are not.

Tonight, Danish cold table with beer and Aquavit. Try two or three of the latter for my cold. No obvious relief but recurring dream of my grown-up boys as five-year-olds riding Shetland ponies. Faroes ... Shetland?

Day 75 8 December

Wake feeling much better. Head clearer and though there is a coffee cup-sliding swell out there, the ship copes with it much better than did the *Neptune Garnet*.

Christian, the Faroean, is alone on the bridge. He is one of the most lugubrious people I've ever met, but seems quite happy about it. He calculates our position for me.

For the first time in 75 days the chart shows Britain, and on a nautical map our favoured position is very clear. The fish-rich Continental shelf extends right around the British Isles and in places a hundred miles beyond, whereas it is only a thin strip along the coasts of France, Spain and Portugal. And the North Sea is covered in a black rash of oil rigs. We're making a respectable 22.1 knots and are 1,929 miles from New York.

There is, on the aft deck, lashed into a space which would have accommodated 50 containers, a very interesting piece of cargo. It's the shell of a slim, elegant sailing boat. It has no name, no superstructure, and the planks of its all-wood hull are wet and rotting, but someone must value it enough to pay the substantial amount to transport it at the cost of so much container space. Today Jesper solves a little of the mystery for me. The yacht dates from 1932, her destination is Felixstowe and she's being transported by the Sea Containers Group, whose chairman, James Sherwood, was responsible for the re-creation of the Orient Express.

Abandon my afternoon exercise as a wind strong enough to prevent walking, let alone running on deck, has appeared from nowhere. The Professor is concerned that there might be supernatural forces at work on the ship. He had lost his faithful tobacco tin, his navy sweater and now it seems that his whisky bottle is suffering from the Widow's Curse syndrome. No matter how much he drinks it seems to maintain the same level. It has been a long journey and I suppose one of us was bound to crack up.

Day 76 9 December

The sea is calming. Quite the opposite of what's supposed to happen on the Atlantic at this time of year. I lie in bed this morning and seriously consider what it will be like to be back home. Up till now I've not allowed my thoughts to take such a morale-threatening direction for very long, but now it seems increasingly likely that the Bombay astrologer's prognostications will be accurate. I realise for the first time that I shall miss this journey, which many times I couldn't wait to end. At sea the pace of life slows to a very agreeable level, and the thought of a return to city life is not, this morning, as tempting as I expected it to be. In fact I could easily go round again.

The Danes seem private people, not given to drawing attention to themselves, and despite having been six days on the *Leda Maersk* we keep meeting members of the crew we've never seen before – today a thickly bearded Captain Haddock of a man appears in the engine-room lift. He, like one or two others of the crew, seemed determinedly uncommunicative. Not so the captain who is becoming quite mischievous at the expense of the company, whose representative, Jesper, supervises every aspect of our filming.

We're talking at lunch about lucky and unlucky ships. It took three attempts before the champagne bottle broke at *Leda Maersk*'s launch, which the captain says is not a good omen. I asked him if there were any likelihood of a ghost on board.

'Not on an A. P. Moller ship,' was his brisk reply. 'He doesn't allow them!'

Much laughter from the crew, less from Jesper.

The company will have the last laugh though. The captain admits that in future a ship of this size will only need five officers to man it, and Noel, the Indian radio operator, knows he will be one of the first to go. Plans are to do away with radio operators entirely within the next two or three years. Supervision of a largely automated radio-room will be added to the duties of one of the other officers. Noel is dubious about how they will cope without an independent operator, especially at times of emergency when the others may all be occupied elsewhere.

Even as we're talking to Noel, as if to underline the volatility and unpredictability which can upset the most rational man-made system, the news comes through of a massive earthquake in Armenia, with rumours of 100,000 killed.

Running on deck today for the last time, squeezing along the heavy-metal tunnels, with wind buffeting me gently and tugging at the tops of the waves, I realise I shall be very sad to leave the sea. I stop in the bows and look around me. Through 360 degrees nothing is to be seen. As far as the horizon, 15 to 20 miles away, there is only sea and sky. No noise except for the throb of the engines, the soft swish of the bow-wave and the flapping of the wind.

At supper Roger announces that he thinks his whisky bottle may be being replenished by a less than supernatural force.

Day 77 10 December

Today we should have our first sight of England. Make a big effort to fight ship-lag and get up for breakfast. At 7.30 it's pitch dark outside, and the temperature indicator on the refrigerated container outside my windows glows red '−0006F'. By 9 o'clock it's still dark, with a faint yellowing of the Eastern sky over a flat featureless sea. The terrors of December on the Atlantic have not materialised yet. Roger says he's now absolutely convinced someone is augmenting his whisky.

The captain doesn't come down for lunch today as he's promised his wife he'll lose a pound or two. Equally concerned crew members, including Lillian, gather in the engine room for a weekly weight-watcher's meeting, whilst outside we can see porpoises unconcerned with weight problems rise gracefully out of the sea, marking, along with wheeling sea-birds, our arrival in shallower waters. We're now on the Celtic Sea, in the evocatively named Western Approaches, familiar territory for all brought up on Nicholas Monsarrat's *The Cruel Sea*. On the bridge Bente takes out Admiralty Chart 2649 on which is the tip of Cornwall.

The richest detail on the chart is reserved not for land but for the sea, whose bed is annotated and named as thoroughly and richly as any corner of the countryside. We are sliding in over King Arthur Canyon, whose sides drop 3,430 fathoms and rise to 840. There's Haddock bank and Melville Knoll and Porcupine Sea Bight and Nymphe Bank and Shamrock Knoll. Inviting places one hopes never to see.

The charts have to be continually updated. A correction manual is issued each week. It's not that Newfoundland may have moved two inches to the right, but that things like oil rigs, traffic separation lanes, militarily restricted areas are changing all the time. Bente says that the big tankers will carry up to 3,000 charts on board at one time, because they rarely have fixed routes, being sent off to wherever the oil is available and most needed.

Also open on the bridge's wide map table is the next Admiralty chart – Lizard Point to Berry Head, a smaller-scale map of the English Channel, Central Part, a book of port operations and pilot services – open at Le Havre – and a Mariner's Routeing Guide Chart, incorporating passage planning charts. There is a book with full details of local currents. 'In the English Channel the streams separate on a line running Hastings–Dieppe.' As an old sentimentalist, I'm rather glad to see all this written material laid out beside the radar scanners and the computer screens.

After lunch we record for posterity our rendition of *Under Milk Wood* with Nigel bringing a fine Burtonian gravitas to the part of Eli Jenkins, the Professor giving the definitive Captain Cat and Dave scuttling between Willy Nilly, Third Drowned and the tape recorder. Angela, Ann and Simon all deserve Oscar nominations.

Considering only Nigel lays claim to Welsh blood it comes out well, and the final lines are still resounding as the pin-point of Bishop Rock lighthouse mounts the northern horizon. The Scilly Isles, then Lizard Point and the lights of the Cornish coast follow. Home base is tantalisingly close. If they could loan me a lifeboat I could be ashore in half an hour, and home three days early. As it is the English coast recedes as we turn away to the south for Le Havre and the estuary of the Seine, and soon the only lights I can see are those of other ships, and above me, of a magnificent night sky.

Day 78 11 December

Forty-eight hours to go before the deadline. Fogg at this same stage was literally burning his boat in an attempt to get the *Henrietta* to Liverpool. He's already got rid of the cabins, the bunks and the poop-deck. 'The next day … they burned the masts, the rafts and the spars … Passepartout, hewing, cutting, sawing, did the work of ten men. It was a perfect fury of demolition.' At least he was on the move. I have the uneasy feeling of being marooned.

In grey, characterless weather much like that when, eleven weeks ago today, I first caught sight of the French coast at

Boulogne, we are coming alongside the almost deserted container port of Le Havre. It's all rather anticlimactic. I remember the captain's concern to get his ship unloaded before the dockers had their Sunday lunch. Well, it's turned 10 o'clock and we're not even tied up yet. The Southampton ferry has sailed and all Passepartout and I can do is sit and wait. Remembering the dockers and their Sunday lunch gives us an idea, and as the trucks begin to roll past the gantry cranes and the unloading begins at a decent, if not manic pace, Passpartout and I leave the *Leda Maersk* and set off in search of a French Sunday Lunch.

We pass the smartest ship in Le Havre docks, a white-hulled multi-decked cruise liner, not from Monte Carlo or Bermuda, but from Russia. She's the only thing that is smart in what is essentially an industrial complex, and the French, cultivators of the comfortable lifestyle, builders of handsome cities and attractive villages, are quite unsentimental when it comes to industry, so there's not much attempt to conceal the grime as we walk up beside a railway track with silos and warehouses on one side and the sad and derelict remains of the transatlantic passenger terminal on the other. That the glamour of the place where the great liners docked should be thus reduced is quite a shock and reminds me how long ago it was that I fell in love with Jane Russell in *The French Line*.

An hour's walk brings us at last into the town itself. The centre, destroyed by bombs in the Second World War, has been rebuilt without flair. Long low terraces are dull in scale and finish and present a dour background to the waterfront area. Quick look in the cathedral, from which people in their Sunday best are emerging after mass. A slightly mad-looking man is trying to get the priest's attention. The priest eventually throws him out.

In these unpromising surroundings we come across a restaurant which serves us a superb five-course lunch and which is by extraordinary and suitable coincidence designed like a railway train. It is family-run and cramped in the French style, and we wonder if it's to save space that the patron employs his tiny son as a waiter. Nigel asks the boy his age. He looks about eleven but turns out to be even younger.

'He's seven,' translates Nigel after a brief conversation.

'No … no!' the boy protests vigorously. 'Seven*teen*!'

We don't stint the wine, and drinking the likes of Sancerre and Gigondas after all we've been through is like finding a waterfall in the desert. The walk back to the *Leda Maersk* seems much shorter and more convivial, and though none of us is admitting it, this unscheduled lunch in Le Havre had a definite celebratory air.

We leave France at seven in the evening. The weather is settled. The Channel is millpond calm. There's a chill in the air as we move slowly out toward the harbour wall of the fishing port which Francis I christened Le Havre de Grace in 1516. Past the euphoniously named Bassin Théophile Du Crocq and a last illuminated Christmas tree and onto the high seas again.

As soon as we're clear of the sodium glare of the city lights another wonderful night sky is revealed. It reminds me of nights on the Bay of Bengal, but as Captain Rodebaek points out, it's better. There's more to see in the northern sky.

The day ends with a party, of which I dimly remember a tug of war in which a BBC team, sapped by over-confidence and French Sunday lunch, were pulled to defeat, and a 16-person doubles table tennis tournament in which the Professor and myself triumphed by a whisker over Jesper and Erik the accountant.

At one point we listened to our recording of *Under Milk Wood*. Noel, the radio operator, was so taken with it he asked for a copy to take back to his wife. Listening to it with him was particularly appropriate, for Noel has maintained the Indian presence that has been such a feature of my journey. If I were superstitious I'd say that this presence has brought us luck, and as I stand with a buzzing head at the deck rail at two in the morning, watching us turn North through the Straits of Dover on seas of almost freakish tranquillity, I think back to the twenty-eighth day when Jagjit Uppal told my fortune and wonder whether this whole journey wasn't made in Bombay. A last few deep breaths of sea air and back to my cabin to pack my bag and deflate my world for the last time.

Day 79 12 December

Four hours' sleep and up to catch the dawn over the Suffolk coast. A golden sun is rising slowly into a clear sky as we approach the low-lying, neat green shoreline, with Harwich's old church and surrounding houses sitting on their low headland and Felixstowe opposite. I didn't expect such a caricature of England. Felixstowe seems tiny compared to the ports I've visited round the world – a container terminal John Betjeman might have approved of. Not hugely out of scale with the undemonstrative coastline and giving way quite quickly to green fields beyond. There is hardly a ripple enough on the surface of the North Sea to ring the mournful bell on the big green buoy that stands at the entrance to the port. We are home on a morning of glassy calm.

The pilot is already on the bridge, supervising our approach. On this journey pilots have been like heralds, embodying the first sight and sounds of new places.

So I know exactly where I am as I hear, 'We're going to swing her in, we'll need two tugs,' spoken in the dry matter-of-fact English professional monotone. I'm back in police stations and Crown courts and customs sheds and airline cockpits and doctors' waiting rooms. 'Dead Slow,' he orders, and jokes to Captain Rodebaek about a friend who's just come back from a holiday in Spain: 'He got a whole year's rain in three days!'

The captain smiles but only out of habit. Maybe there is always this feeling of strain between captains and pilots.

With the tug *Brightwell* at our stern and *Victoria* of Liverpool at the bow, we wend our way between the marker buoys into the mouth of the Orwell. A seaman (and I realise that, unlike the *Garnet*, I know hardly any of the names of this crew) selects a Union Jack from the wooden pigeonholes full of national flags and goes outside to run it up the mast. The pilot talks to one of the tugs:

'Give her a helping hand, *Victoria*, starboard bow.'

We are aiming for a mooring beside *Canadian Explorer* of Hong Kong, and a Russian ship. Bente stands in the bow with her walkie-talkie, Danish flag fluttering above her, and blonde hair streaming from beneath her 'Maersk Line' baseball cap. A strange wild Nordic figure in her light blue deck overalls.

For me this is the end of an epic and unusual journey. I'm almost home. For Captain Rodebaek and his crew it's the first of a gruelling series of North Sea stop-overs. From Felixstowe they must cross to Antwerp, from Antwerp to Bremerhaven and Bremerhaven to Hamburg, before turning and heading down the Channel again to Singapore. This is where the crews earn their money, and while TV presenters drool at sunrises, they have only a week of sleepless nights to look forward to.

I unfold a small piece of paper given to me by the jolly German chef as I said goodbye to him this morning. He said it summed up the sailor's lot: 'We the Willing, led by the Unknowing, are doing the impossible for the ungrateful. We have done so much for so long with so little, we are now qualified to do anything with nothing.' As we disembark, Passepartout admits to having supplemented the Professor's whisky bottle each night of the journey – four before he even noticed.

Have to keep reminding myself that it's not over yet, and will not be until I'm inside the Reform Club again. A *Leda Maersk* truck gives me a lift through the tidy, well-kept streets of Felixstowe to the railway station. There is no train for an hour, so we repair to the Moat House Hotel across the road. Ironically the hotel bar has a colonial feel. The only other customers apart from ourselves are elderly ladies ordering scotch and sodas. I fantasise that they are widows of men who travelled, maintaining the tradition of the quick snifter before tiffin. A young barmaid with strident lipstick plays listlessly with a beer mat. Though I've been hurtling round the world, against the clock, my progress has been marked by moments like these, still pools at the side of the stream, where for a while, nothing at all moves.

At half-past twelve, well into my last twenty-four hours, I pick up the local two-car diesel and we rumble off towards Ipswich. England looks greener than anywhere else in the world. And much neater than I remember. On the Inter-City train from Ipswich to London I decide to treat myself to a Great British Lunch and receive instead a Great British Apology.

'I'm very sorry, sir, there's no chef and no food, but I can offer you afternoon tea.' So I have afternoon tea at five past one, and very good it is too.

Liverpool Street station is a building site and has been for two years, but we're in on time.

There then occurs something which could have put Passepartout, me and the astrologer out of business in a big way. Our Central Line train from Liverpool Street to Oxford Circus pulls into Tottenham Court Road station. No sooner have the doors slid open than a disembodied warning voice rings round the platform, which I notice with a shock is completely empty.

'Stay on the train! Stay on the train! There is a suspect package at the station. Stay on the train! Do *not* alight here.'

It's the first time that I've seen the Professor, a veteran traveller and hard man to scare, lose his colour. It drains from his face as I imagine it must be draining from mine. For a frozen moment we are stuck beside an empty platform far below the ground with a 'suspect package'.

We look at each other, the same thought crossing all our minds. After all we've been through. There is a moment's complete silence. Breaths are held. Then, not a moment too soon, the doors swish closed.

After that London never recovers. It is like being back in the very pit of hell. At Oxford Circus the Christmas lights stretch away into the distance, and the Christmas spirit is similarly stretched. We attempt to film me buying a newspaper, to confirm my date of arrival, and are subjected to a volley of abuse from the vendor such as we've experienced nowhere else on the journey. When we do buy a paper, the front page is full of grim pictures of the Clapham rail disaster, which had happened as we were docking at Felixstowe. (All of us were sobered by the thought that if we had taken the Le Havre–Southampton ferry we could quite possibly have been on one of those trains.)

We hurry through the crowds down Regent Street, and at five minutes to five, shabby, tired, rushed and ruffled I stand before the steps of the Reform Club, seventy-nine days and seven hours since I had walked down them to go round the world. Would love to have bought Passepartout a drink, but we weren't allowed inside.

Afterword

Reflecting on the journey from a safe distance of five and a half months back home I cannot imagine quite how I did it. After all, I was exhausted at the end of Day 1. My body must have produced a Niagara of adrenaline to keep me on the road for the next 79. There was only time to keep going.

Of course I would do it again, but I know it would never be quite the same. Despite the best laid plans of the BBC we ended up bustling, hurrying, rushing, improvising to get ourselves home only by the skin of our teeth. And that's what made it worth doing. The smoother the journey, the duller it would have been.

The generosity with which people we met along the way gave us their time and their help increased my optimism for the future. Travel of this kind, travel when the hands get dirty, when contact is made, brought home to me how much we all see of the world on television and in the newspapers, and how little we know of it. Journeys like this can only be good for us. Perhaps it's time for 80-Day Circumnavigating to become a recognised pastime, then a sport and who knows, eventually an Olympic event.

Another Afterword

A bit of sad news. Nigel, Ron and Julian Passepartout have faced prison for their pains. Together with Angela and Clem they were arrested for a train-spotting offence while filming extra shots for the series in Egypt. They were released after a few hours after giving the police some story about going round the world in 80 days.

Around the World in 80 Days

Revisited

Dubai 8 October 2008

TWENTY YEARS AGO, following in the steps of Phileas Fogg, the journey from London to Dubai had taken Passepartout and me fifteen days. Today an Emirates Airbus brought us here in seven hours. Twenty years ago, Dubai was a desert town with a population of 350,000. Today it numbers one and a half million and more are arriving as fast as they can build homes for them. And that doesn't include the six million visitors who stop off here every year.

In October 1988 we put up at one of a tiny handful of hotels. Now there are over five hundred to choose from, including the Burj Al Arab which calls ifself a seven-star hotel and serves a cocktail costing £3,800 a shot. The minarets and mosques which defined the skyline have been overshadowed by secular constructions, including the Burj Dubai ('burj' meaning a tower), currently the world's tallest building, in which you can live and work 2,500 feet above the ground. There are plans to top even this, with a tower that will be more than a kilometre high. The *International Herald Tribune* describes the city as 'Las Vegas on steroids'.

At the Dubai Off-Shore Sailing Club, I meet up with Bill Nelson. As Head of Ports and Customs Bill had been our first point of contact twenty years ago. Now eighty-six, in poor health and having to leave Dubai as his house is to be bulldozed to make way for the new airport, he was in remarkably good humour. He gives me the number of his one-time deputy, Khamis Ghamil, who actually found us the *Al Shama*, and who is now himself Head of Ports and Customs.

Captain Khamis agrees to meet us the next day, which gives me a chance to sample some of the delights of the new Dubai. As we head out to the Jumeirah quarter, one new tower after another rises on either side of us and progress on the twelve-lane Sheikh Zayed Highway is sluggish. Alongside runs an almost-completed monorail system which is due to open next year, though few believe that it will make much difference to the traffic. This is a shopping culture, and with the aid of modern technology the crowded souks and bazaars of the old Arab world have evolved into the colossal shopping malls of today. The New Emirates Mall, in which we find ourselves this morning, boasts one of the world's largest indoor ski slopes. The fact that the outside temperature is 37° C and that it hasn't snowed here for centuries is exactly the sort of reason why the developers created it. It seems that the only requirement for building schemes in Dubai is that they start with the impossible.

The brazen confidence of the city is personified in the face of Sheikh Mohammed, one of the Al Maktoum family which has run Dubai for 175 years. His likeness is everywhere, reminding the foreigners who comprise over 70 per cent of the population that the Arabs are still masters here. This morning I feel his craggy features and gimlet eyes on my back as I walk past a billboard on my way to take an *abra*, a water-taxi, to the Customs House. *Abras* are a rare example in this city of cheap and cheerful public transport. Little more than floating benches with a thin roof providing cover from the fiercest of the heat, they provide a continuous ferry service across the Creek at its most attractive point, close to the old Bastakia quarter whose narrow alleyways and shining domes remind me more of Venice than Vegas.

Captain Khamis greets me with a broad smile. His face has filled out and though he's now Head of Customs, and a husband and father, he wears his responsibilities with the same unhurried ease which I found both comforting and a little worrying twenty years earlier. He takes me to Al Hamriya, the same small cargo dock from which I sailed with *Al Shama*. Khamis tells me *Al Shama* would have been tiny by today's standards, with new dhows of two thousand tonnes being built, and horror of horrors, some of them made of fibreglass. But as I stand watching a chain of Indian labourers unloading apples, and the gentle rise and fall of wooden hulls two or three deep at the dockside, I can easily recapture that combination of fear and fascination with which I stepped aboard the boat that was to carry us across to Bombay all those years ago.

Khamis can't give us much help, as he hasn't seen *Al Shama* since the day we left, but he does offer to find me a similar-sized dhow leaving Dubai, so at least I can relive the past for an hour or two. He wangles me aboard a boat heading for Bandar-e Bushehr in Iran. As on *Al Shama* the conditions are still basic. The crew live, literally, on top of their cargo, and the only real change I notice is that they have an on-board, rather than outboard, lavatory. At the dockside the crew seems nervous and suspicious, but once away from the authorities they relax, asking me all sorts of questions in severely fractured English. I show them the DVD of the original dhow journey, which they watch with amazement. Though we don't have much time away from Dubai, it's long enough for me to feel strangely at home, whilst at the same time asking myself, as I try to get comfortable on covers of greasy tarpaulin, how I ever survived a week on a boat like this.

Mumbai 14 October 2008

Superficially it seems that Dubai reeks of opulence and Mumbai reeks of poverty. In fact both are illusions. There are armies of Asian construction workers living in Dubai on less than two hundred dollars a month, and, as well as the street beggars and the huge slums of Mumbai there are more millionaires here than in any other Indian city. Dubai is an indoor, air-conditioned world. In Mumbai life is out on the streets: noisy, demanding, relentless and inescapable. We've not been long in a traffic jam from the airport when I hear a persistent tap-tapping on the side of our minibus and a moment later the stumps of two arms appear at the window and a face, teeth bared and eyes wide, peers up beseechingly. Then the traffic moves on. Near the hotel women with babes in arms hold out cupped hands. Nothing seems to be very different from when I walked in through the Gate of India twenty years ago, except of course for the name of the place. Since 1995, at the instigation of the Shiv Sena political party, strong Maharashtrian nationalists, Bombay has become Mumbai and Victoria Station, from which I left for Madras, the Chhatrapati Shivaji Terminus. Not everyone approves of these changes, just as not everyone approves of the hard-line policies of Shiv Sena, whose leaders have whipped up sectarian hatred against anyone they see as outsiders, including fellow Indians, if they happen to be Muslim or born outside Maharashtra state.

The Taj Hotel is still here and thriving, and their welcome is friendly and congenial. Garlanded with marigolds, I'm for a moment tempted into thinking I'm to be given the Rajput Suite, the most luxurious accommodation in an already luxurious hotel, but it turns out they're just showing me where John Lennon, Yoko Ono and, later, George Harrison stayed. I'm in Room 276.

From the BBC files, we know the name of the ship brokers who chartered *Al Shama*, Dewkaran Moorjee and Sons. At first we draw a blank. The phone numbers have all had extra digits added to cope with Mumbai's growing population, which has increased from around 10 to around 18 million since we were last here. The new number puts us through to a company called Damodar Dharamshi and Co, which inherited Dewkaran Moorjee's business. Its run by a man called Digant Joshi, who sounds busy but agrees to look in his files for us.

I spend next day reacquainting myself with Mumbai in the company of a knowledgeable lady called Jyoti Namaste. We meet up at Churchgate Station. With only four platforms, two in and two out, this unprepossessing terminus performs minor miracles, managing to process six or seven million passengers every day. At rush-hour the trains come in and out every one minute, thirty-eight seconds. Two of them are reserved for ladies only. Jyoti says it only works because punctuality is near-perfect and the rolling stock, ancient and battle-scarred, completely dependable. Mind you, they don't have any doors on the coaches, which must help speed things up.

We alight from the train at Mahalaxmi station, beside which is the largest of the city's open-air, soap and stone laundries. Built in British times, it is worked by five hundred dhobis – laundrymen – all from the same 'fourth caste', the working class. They collect laundry, wash it in pens of water, then beat the dirt out on a stumpy granite stone.

I road-test their service with a pair of chinos, terminally oil-stained from my brief sojourn on the Iranian dhow. I was on the point of giving up on them, but after a good thrashing my dhobi hands them back to me without a stain to be seen. I'm raving about this new, natural, chemical-free approach to laundry when Roger brings me down to earth. 'So you'll be buying Helen a stone for Christmas, then?'

The offices of Damodar Dharamshi and Co, formerly Dewkaran Moorjee and Sons, are in an infernally busy street in the Dockyard area of Mumbai. A constant stream of men and goods passes by; handcarts piled high with plastic piping, enormous cardboard boxes balanced on tiny heads. Digant Joshi is a shortish, well-built man, mid-forties I'd guess, with thick black hair and neatly trimmed moustache. From him I learn the sad news that *Al Shama* is no more. She sank to the bottom of the Arabian Sea, quite peacefully and with no loss of life, whilst being towed by her new owners along the coast of Gujarat. Digant has better news of the crew, some of whom, including the captain, are, he thinks, living up in the town of Mandvi in Kutch, the northernmost part of Gujarat. He has information that the captain lives in the Sulaiya district of the town.

'Everyone will know him,' he says confidently.

Which is why we find ourselves at Bandra Terminus to catch the overnight Kutch Express. It sounds romantic but sadly isn't. The windows are tiny and dirty and the heavy metal light covers and roof fans give the odd impression of being in a submarine. Obligingly, they leave the doors at the end of each coach open and I fight off incipient claustrophobia by standing at the doorway as we rumble northwards. An hour out of Mumbai the countryside looks timeless and serene, bathed in the dusty pink glow of the setting sun. Only thirteen more hours to go.

We eventually reach the town of Bhuj, the capital of Kutch and the end of the line, some fifteen hours after leaving Mumbai. On Republic Day, 26 January 2001, a terrible tragedy befell this place. Bhuj was close to the epicentre of an earthquake with a strength of 8.9, and at least 80,000 were killed. Aid and reconstruction came quickly and the central area of town is apparently much improved, with wider streets and better-built, low-rise accommodation. But there are some buildings which still stand as witnesses to the power of the earthquake, including the Jubilee Hospital, once a fine example of the graceful Anglo-Indian style, her strong stone walls now cracked and tottering.

As we drive to Mandvi, forty miles due south, the surroundings become less industrial and the countryside greener. Fields of cows and narrow lanes with their arches of overhanging trees remind me of East Anglia. Mandvi is approached by a bridge over a very dry tidal creek. There has always been a shipbuilding industry here. Its heyday was the 18th century when four hundred ships were moored up in the estuary, including one that went all the way to England. Now, with the pile-up of sediment, it's a shadow of its former self.

We're staying just outside the town, in a 'beach resort' comprising ten colourfully striped tents and a dog that howls like a maniac in the night. The tented camp, beside a long, fine, virtually empty beach, is the property of the Maharao of Kutch. The Maharao, or to give him his full title, HH Maharao Shri Pragmalji Madansinhji III, 19th Maharao of Kutch, apparently owns not just the coast but the sea as well. When I meet him later he clarifies this. He only owns the sea at high tide, when it comes up over *his* beach. He has a very fine palace next door, open to the public, with polite signs everywhere ranging from 'No Firearms' to 'Kindly Remove Footwear And Maintain Decorum'.

Mandvi, Kutch 20 October 2008

This morning we prepare for the climax of our trip, the reunion with Captain Suleyman. Digant Joshi mentioned Salaiya, which turns out to be the district across the river from the main town. So clogged is the estuary that the sea channel at low tide can be waded across, as some do, walking beside, and almost as fast as, the leisurely punted ferry. As I disembark I notice the green flag of Islam fluttering above a cemetery, reminding me that the captain and his crew were all Indian Muslims.

Digant was right. Everyone I speak to knows Hassan Suleyman. Indeed most of them seem to be related to him. But when I find his house its location is almost too good to be true. Outside the front door, between the house and the sea, looms a huge, half-constructed dhow.

This is the moment of truth. The captain knows I'm in town but doesn't know exactly when I'm coming to see him, and the moment when we meet can only be filmed once. Even at this late stage I have misgivings. What if it's the wrong Captain Suleyman? It's a common enough name. And if it isn't, how much will he really want to see me again?

A cat lies stretched across one of the three front-door steps, oblivious to the moment. I'm suddenly aware of how very hot it is. Then Nigel runs the camera and I step up to a pair of white wooden doors, decorated with an abstract shell-like pattern, and knock.

I hear his voice before I see him and I know I've got the right man. The door is pulled open and there he is. The man who welcomed me on *Al Shama* at Dubai now welcomes me, with open arms, to his house in Mandvi. He's put on weight, his face is fuller and his beard well-trimmed and distinguished. As he clasps me in a powerful embrace I sense that this man, a little jumpy on the dhow journey, has matured into someone of substance, a Godfather of the dhow world.

He ushers me into a long thin courtyard, and suddenly from the darkened interior of the house come other faces I recognise. Anwar, the cabin boy with the shock of black curls, is now thirty-six, married to Suleyman's daughter and a captain of a ship in his own right. Ibrahim the Chief Engineer grasps my hand as does Kishore the 2nd Engineer and, long before I'd intended to, I bring out my portable DVD player and put on the episode in which we all starred and everyone squeezes round for a look.

Captain Suleyman keeps up a running commentary as each member of the crew appears on the film. Kasim, the old man who listened to Bruce Springsteen and walked on my back, is dead, so is the cook and Deyji Ramji, the studious-looking navigator. Mahomet, Anwar's father, who had talked on film about his preference for working on dhows for no money, rather than supertankers for a lot of money, is not so well now, the captain says. A couple of minutes later the front door opens behind us and there he is, his skin drawn tight across his face, his figure brittle and thin, but his face wide in a smile.

It's all happened so fast, but I can think of no better way for it to have happened. Mandvi may be over four thousand miles from London, but here beside the dhows of the future with my friends of the past it is a home from home. Twenty years ago I said it was 'almost impossible to accept that I shall never see them again'. Today, here in Mandvi, we celebrate the art of the possible.

Acknowledgements

It's impossible to list all the individuals, companies, organisations and governments who helped me round the world. Most are in the book. Among those who aren't, I would especially like to thank: Romany Helmy, Don Bannerman, Captain Bill Nelson, Shernaz Italia, Bruno Burigana, Ian Markham-Smith, Mark Tozer, Sandy Gall, Alan Whicker, Huw Young-Jones, Dave Thomas, Howard Billingham, Brian Hall, Kitty Anderson, Anne James, Alison Davies and, at BBC Books, Linda Blakemore, Sarah Hoggett and Suzanne Webber.

Acknowledgements for new chapter

Thanks to all those who made our return journey possible. Many are already named in the text, but I should like to add my debt of gratitude to our crew: Roger Mills, director, and Nigel Meakin on camera (companions on the road for over twenty years now), John Pritchard, for sound and photographs, Vanessa Courtney for immaculate planning and organisation – and photographs. To Steve Abbott, Sue Grant, Paul Bird, Lyn Dougherty and Mimi Robinson at Prominent and Richard Klein at the BBC.

And to Clem Vallance, who dreamt up the *Eighty Days* idea all those years ago.

To view all the photos from
Around the World in 80 Days

visit

www.themichaelpalin.com

Go around the world with

Michael Palin

Out now in paperback and ebook

Find out more at www.themichaelpalin.com